Inspirational stories arranged according to the weekly Torah reading

by Rabbi Shimon Finkelman

Published by

Mesorah Publications, ltd

More Shabbos Stories

FIRST EDITION
First Impression . . . October 1997

Published and Distributed by
MESORAH PUBLICATIONS, Ltd.
4401 Second Avenue
Brooklyn, New York 11232

Distributed in Europe by
J. LEHMANN HEBREW BOOKSELLERS
20 Cambridge Terrace
Gateshead, Tyne and Wear
England NE8 1RP

Distributed in Israel by
SIFRIATI / A. GITLER — BOOKS
10 Hashomer Street
Bnei Brak 51361

Distributed in Australia & New Zealand by
GOLDS BOOK & GIFT CO.
36 William Street
Balaclava 3183, Vic., Australia

Distributed in South Africa by
KOLLEL BOOKSHOP
22 Muller Street
Yeoville 2198, Johannesburg, South Africa

THE ARTSCROLL SERIES ®
MORE SHABBOS STORIES
© Copyright 1997, by MESORAH PUBLICATIONS, Ltd.
4401 Second Avenue / Brooklyn, N.Y. 11232 / (718) 921-9000

ISBN
1-57819-177-7 (hard cover)
1-57819-177-5 (paperback)

Typography by Compuscribe at ArtScroll Studios, Ltd.

Printed in the United States of America by Noble Book Press
Bound by Sefercraft, Quality Bookbinders, Ltd. Brooklyn, N.Y.

ఆ§ Table of Contents

Vayikra

Bamidbar

Devarim

Preface

The very last words of Moshe *Rabbeinu* (our Teacher) to the Jewish people were: וְאַתָּה עַל בָּמוֹתֵימוֹ תִדְרֹךְ, *You [Israel] will tread upon their [their foes'] high places (Devarim* 33:29). Rabbi Shimon Schwab interpreted this as symbolizing the exalted moral and ethical levels expected of our nation. When a Jew sets standards for himself, he should use the moral and ethical standards of the nations as his *starting* point; where their striving *ends*, ours should *begin*.

In his old age, the Chofetz Chaim was a man of slight, frail build. Yet his presence evoked the awe and reverence of anyone who was privileged to see him. A correspondent covering the First *Knessiah Gedolah* (World Conference) of Agudath Israel in Vienna, in 1923, reported:

> When you first see this little ninety-year-old man, he makes a strange impression on you — you feel a shudder of awe and love, an enormous respect and regard which is boundless. When you look more closely, you see the face of an angel, of a servant of G-d. The Divine Presence rests on that face and you must close your eyes because of the brilliance that shines from the small, gray, wise eyes . . . His voice is weak, but clear. He calls Jews to unity, to peace, to goodness, to piety, to love and to action . . .
>
> Everyone wants to see the Chofetz Chaim, to touch the hem of his poor, long coat. Gentiles remove their hats out of respect. It is chaotic . . . the police are powerless. They can't bring order. They, too, push and look captivated and respectfully at the small old man

with the satin cap on his white head ... the Chofetz Chaim.[1]

The Chofetz Chaim's radiance reflected the awesome levels which he had attained in all areas of Divine service, both between himself and Hashem, and with his fellow man.

In our generation, we are not privileged to have a Chofetz Chaim in our midst, though we are blessed with Torah leaders from whom we have much to learn. And there are others, as well, from whom we can learn. The *Mishnah* states, "Who is a wise person? One who learns from everyone" (*Avos* 4:1). Every Jew has qualities and every Jew has his special moments, when the beauty of his personality or the strength of his faith is brought out for all to see.

The stories collected in *Shabbos Stories*, and now, בעזה״ית, in *More Shabbos Stories*, illustrate the collective greatness of our people. There are stories of faith, kindness, love of Torah, and sensitivity. There are stories about renowned Torah personalities, *baalei teshuvah*, simple laborers and businessmen. It is my sincere hope that these stories will inspire us all to strive for greater heights in our service of Hashem.

❈ ❈ ❈

I am deeply grateful to the many distinguished individuals who shared their stories with me. I would be remiss not to take this opportunity to thank three of these individuals — Rabbi Shmuel Dishon, Rabbi Myer Schwab and Rabbi Yitzchak Sekula — for the Torah and inspiration which I absorbed from them during my years in yeshivah.

My appreciation to Rabbi Yaakov Reisman, who took time from his busy schedule to read some of the stories and offer constructive comments.

My appreciation to Rabbi Hillel David, for his advice and assistance in this endeavor, as well as other areas.

---

1. From an article in the New York *Forward*, September 23, 1923. Translated from Yiddish by Rabbi Nosson Scherman.

A number of the themes in this volume were drawn from the Dial-a-Shiur talks of Rabbi Yitzchok Isbee, ל״ז, whose tapes on the weekly *parashah* and *Sefer Chovos HaLevavos* are treasuries of wisdom and inspiration. יהי זכרו ברוך.

❀　❀　❀

I do not take for granted Rabbi Nosson Scherman's guidance, insight and friendship, and I appreciate how he makes himself available to me, despite his very hectic schedule. Rabbi Meir Zlotowitz has always done his best for me whenever I have called upon him, and this, too, is something I deeply appreciate. Reb Sheah Brander has given added meaning to *k'vod haTorah* by producing books of striking beauty. I am grateful to these friends for having granted me the opportunity to participate in their monumental *harbatzas Torah* efforts, and I pray that their work continue with great success עד ביאת גואל צדק.

My thanks to all the very dedicated people at ArtScroll/ Mesorah. Avrohom Biderman has been an excellent project coordinator and is a good friend. My thanks to Eli Kroen for his work on the beautiful cover; and to Mrs. Toby Goldzweig and Miss Toby Heilbrun for their skillful typing and graphics work.

I would like to take this opportunity to express my appreciation to Rabbi Yaakov Bender, under whom I am privileged to teach at Yeshivah Darchei Torah; to Rabbi Boruch B. Borchardt, Executive Director and Secretary of Agudath Israel of America; to Meir Frischman, Director of Camp Agudah and to Rabbi Simcha Kaufman, Head Counselor at Camp Agudah, where I am privileged to teach and spend my summers. May Hashem grant them all good health and *siyata DiShmaya* to continue their dedicated efforts for the sake of Hashem and His Torah for many years to come.

❀　❀　❀

I take this opportunity to express my gratitude to Rabbi Moshe Wolfson, *Mashgiach Ruchni* of Mesivta Torah Vodaath and *Rav* of *Beis Medrash Emunas Yisrael*. May I offer a *bircas hedyot* that he be granted good health to teach and inspire for many years to come.

My father and mother, שיחיו, teach and inspire through word and example, and in a real sense are an embodiment of this work's contents. I pray that Hashem grant them both good health and many more years together.

I am grateful to my father-in-law and mother-in-law, שיחיו, for all that they have done for my family and myself. No task is ever too difficult for them. May Hashem grant them long, healthy years together.

The final weeks of this project were difficult and stressful. I could not have accomplished it without the support and encouragement of my wife Tova, תחי׳. May Hashem grant her all her heart's desires.

I thank the *Ribono shel Olam* for permitting me to carry out this project. May the new year bring joy and salvation to all of *Klal Yisrael*, both collectively and individually, and may we witness the fulfillment of the *Yamim Noraim* prayer: שמחה לארצך וששון לעירך וצמיחת קרן לדוד עבדך, speedily and in our time.

Shimon Finkelman
Tishrei 5758

פרשת בראשית
Parashas Bereishis

A Different Perspective

זֶה סֵפֶר תּוֹלְדֹת אָדָם
בְּיוֹם בְּרֹא אֱלֹקִים אָדָם בִּדְמוּת אֱלֹקִים עָשָׂה אֹתוֹ.

This is the account of the descendants of Adam — on the day that G-d created man, He made him in the likeness of G-d (Bereishis 5:1).

Rabbi Akiva said: " 'Love your fellow as yourself'[1] *— this is a great rule in the Torah." Ben Azzai said: " 'This is the account of the descendants of Adam' " is a greater rule" (Toras Kohanim).*

The Talmud (*Shabbos* 31a) tells of a gentile who came before Hillel the Elder, asking that he be "taught the Torah while standing on one foot." Hillel told him, "What is hateful to you, do not do to your fellow. This is the entire Torah; the rest is commentary — go and study it." Hillel was, in fact, teaching the gentile the Torah's "great rule" — Love your neighbor as your very own self. Ben Azzai, however, taught that there is a yet greater rule: One should seek to benefit others

---

1. *Vayikra* 19:18.

even in ways that one does *not* wish for himself. For example, though one has no need for personal honor, he should seek to honor others to the best of his ability. This, says *Daas Zekeinim,* is derived from the end of our verse: ". . . on the day that G-d created man, He made him in the likeness of G-d." In our dealings with others, we should see their *tzelem Elokim,* Divine image, before us, and act according to *their* needs, not our own.

❧ ❧ ❧

Yitzchak Stern[1] worked in New York's Forty-seventh Street diamond district during the 1970s. He was respected as a man with good business sense and a good-hearted nature. It was not surprising, therefore, that he was approached one day with a request.

A girl had become engaged and was soon to be married. Her story was most poignant, as it was laced with tragedy. She had been orphaned at a young age and had spent her childhood years being transferred from one foster home to another. Now, she was looking forward to her wedding, but her monetary resources were almost non-existent. There was no money to cover the cost of the wedding, or to pay for the clothing and other items a bride needs.

Yitzchak was asked to undertake to raise money for this worthy cause, and he could not refuse such a request. He went about his sacred mission without delay and with great dedication. He approached friends and business acquaintances and explained the urgency of the matter. The responses he received were usually modest but heartwarming nonetheless.

One day, someone handed Yitzchak a donation and then added, "Listen, I'm very happy to contribute to so worthy a cause, but I think that you're making a mistake. You know what it costs to make even the plainest of weddings — you need to raise thousands of dollars! Thirty-six and fifty-dollar donations are not going to amount to anywhere near what you need.

"Have you ever heard of the Sadovner *Rav?* He's a *gaon* and

---

1. Not his real name.

a *tzaddik,* and he raises thousands of dollars for such causes. I'm sure he would help you."

R' Yisrael Sekula, the late Sadovner *Rav,* [1] was a man who was outstanding in his knowledge of Torah and perhaps equally outstanding in his efforts at raising *tzedakah* on behalf of the needy. Though a leader of a *kehillah* (congregation), he could often be seen in the early morning hours trekking from *shul* to *shul* as he collected monies for poor brides and other worthy causes.

On his next visit to Boro Park, Yitzchak knocked on the Sadovner *Rav's* door. The *Rav* welcomed him in graciously and listened to his story with rapt attention. The *Rav* then excused himself, went to another room and returned with eight hundred dollars. "Had I known you were coming," he said, "I would have prepared a larger sum. Please be in touch with me so that I can give you more."

However, a few days later, Yitzchak's collections came to an abrupt halt. In the course of conversation, someone had mentioned to him that the bride for whom he had been raising funds with such dedication was to be wed in an elegant catering hall. Yitzchak was shocked. That day, he met with the bride and got straight to the point. How, he asked her, could she expect anyone to collect *tzedakah* for her wedding in good conscience when thousands of dollars were to be wasted on unnecessary extravagance? Yitzchak added that he personally would never spend money on such a wedding hall for his own children even if he could afford it. Such expenditures were totally wasteful and unnecessary.

By the time he finished, the girl's eyes were brimming with tears. She was sorry to have upset him and she understood why he was upset. Nevertheless, she said, she still wanted her wedding held at that particular hall, and she was not going to change her mind.

Disappointed, Yitzchak reached into his pocket and withdrew a large sum of money. "Here," he said with more than a touch

---

1. See *Shabbos Stories,* vol. I, p. 196.

of sadness, "is the money that I have raised thus far. It's yours. But I will not be raising any more. It's just not right."

The Sadovner *Rav* would spend most of his day studying Torah in his *shul,* which was downstairs from his modest apartment. As he did not want to use the congregation's money unnecessarily, the *Rav* would leave the lights closed and study by a window. One day, something caused him to glance out the window and he noticed none other than Yitzchak Stern walking by. The *Rav* tapped on the windowpane to get Yitzchak's attention and motioned for him to come inside.

"Where have you been?" he demanded. "When you were here, I said that I wanted to give a larger sum toward your cause. Why haven't you returned?"

Yitzchak explained the situation, certain that the *Rav* would be shocked by the revelation and grateful that he had not contributed more. Strangely, though, the *Rav* appeared agitated by the man's explanation. When Yitzchak finished speaking, the Sadovner *Rav,* obviously very upset, grabbed him by his lapel and said, "You don't understand that brokenhearted girl? You don't understand why she can't see things your way, when you would never waste money on an expensive hall?

"How can you expect her to see your point of view? Don't you realize where she is coming from? This child has not had a good day in her life, as you yourself told me! She was orphaned of both parents, went drifting from home to home . . . her life was one of endless misery. Now, finally, she is engaged and is beginning to know a bit of joy for the first time in her life. And you cannot understand why she might feel that she is entitled to a somewhat extravagant wedding? Do we have a right to pass judgment on her? Can we understand the pain she has suffered? Dare we abandon her? "

The *Rav* then went upstairs to his apartment and returned with two thousand dollars. "Here is some more money towards her wedding," he said. "I hope that you will resume your collections without delay."

The *Rav* paused for a moment and then said with emotion, "Do you think that collecting *tzedakah* is a simple matter? To succeed at this *mitzvah,* one must see himself in the position of those for whom he is collecting, to understand their situation, to feel their pain."

When Yitzchak related this story after the Sadovner *Rav's* passing, he reflected, "What amazed me most is that by that time, the Sadovner *Rav* had raised countless sums of money for hundreds, perhaps thousands, of needy individuals. Yet he was still sensitive to the particular needs of each individual and felt that person's pain."

פרשת נח
Parashas Noach

Achieving the Impossible

עֲשֵׂה לְךָ תֵּבַת עֲצֵי גֹפֶר . . .
Make for yourself an Ark of gopher wood . . . (Bereishis 6:14).

There were many huge beasts and so many species of all sizes that even ten such arks could not have held them all, along with one year's provisions. It was a miracle that the

Ark contained them. Even though the miracle could have taken place in a smaller ark, thus sparing Noach the hard, physical labor of building such a huge one, Hashem decreed that such a large one be built in order to minimize the miracle. For in any given situation, one must do whatever is humanly possible before a miracle will occur (*Ramban*).

There are open miracles and there are hidden miracles. Through the course of its history, the Jewish people, both collectively and individually, have merited countless hidden miracles. Sometimes, even one man can accomplish the seemingly impossible, by working tirelessly for the sake of Heaven and placing his trust in Hashem to turn his dream into a reality.

❦ ❦ ❦

R' Yosef Shlomo Kahaneman arrived in *Eretz Yisrael* in 1940, having escaped from war-torn Lithuania where he had served as *Rav* of Ponovezh and head of the city's yeshivah of higher learning. The inspiration to reestablish his yeshivah upon the holy soil of *Eretz Yisrael* came to the Ponovezher *Rav* at the height of the war as he lay stricken with a serious throat ailment. Doctors had given him strict orders not to speak, but news of Nazi atrocities did not allow him to remain silent. Forcing himself into a sitting position, in a barely audible voice, he declared:

"Lithuanian farmers are lazy by nature. It is amazing, though, to see how invigorated those farmers become during harvest season. And if, during harvest season, storm clouds appear overhead which threaten to destroy their crops, the farmers immediately become infused with a sudden burst of energy that surges through their bones. One can hardly recognize the lazy farmer of yesterday!"

The Ponovezher *Rav* paused for a moment. Then, in a voice charged with emotion, he declared:

"I will begin immediately to reestablish the Ponovezh Yeshivah here in the Holy Land. In Bnei Brak! There is no time to lose — there are storm clouds overhead — the time is now!"

Soon after, the *Rav* paid a visit to R' Avraham Yeshayahu Karelitz, the Chazon Ish. The Chazon Ish was recovering from a heart attack and was staying at the home of his disciple, R' Shlomo Kohen. Also present was R' Yaakov Halpern, a wealthy, scholarly Jew who played a major role in the development of Bnei Brak as a city of Torah. At the conclusion of the Ponovezher *Rav's* visit, the Chazon Ish escorted him outside. Directly opposite them was a beautiful hill.

"What a magnificent site upon which to build a yeshivah!" the Ponovezher *Rav* exclaimed.

That hill was the property of R' Yaakov Halpern, who immediately offered it to the *Rav* for a modest sum — with one condition: A yeshivah had to be built and functioning within the year. The Ponovezher *Rav* accepted the offer.

Shortly thereafter, the *Rav* brought some visitors to the top of the hill and described his plans. "Here we will build a huge *beis midrash,* adjacent to it we will have a number of classrooms, here will be the dormitory . . ." His visitors smiled politely, but were actually quite skeptical. The world was at war, funds were scarce. Could such grand plans ever be realized?

Someone remarked, "I hope the *Rav* will forgive me, but I think he is dreaming."

The Ponovezher *Rav* replied, "Yes, I am dreaming — but I am not sleeping!"

Within a year, a building had been erected and a *Rosh Yeshivah,* the *gaon* R' Shmuel Rozovsky, had been appointed to teach a small group of *talmidim.* With time, the Ponovezher Yeshivah developed into one of the world's great citadels of Torah. Today, its student body numbers in the thousands.

The Ponovezher *Rav* was not content with this accomplishment alone. From the time he arrived in *Eretz Yisrael* until his passing some thirty years later, he founded a total of eighteen yeshivos in the Land. His accomplishments seemed almost superhuman. They were the products of a man who possessed greatness in Torah, far-reaching vision, boundless energy, love of every Jew and — perhaps most important — pure faith in the One Above. It was through such faith that he merited incredible *siyata DiShmaya* (Divine assistance) so that his dreams became realities.

In his eulogy of the Ponovezher *Rav,* the Ponovezher *Rosh Yeshivah* R' Eliezer Menachem Shach said:

> His faith burned within him. When he acquired the *aron kodesh* (ark) for the yeshivah, he prepared two chairs to be placed alongside it, saying, "One will be for *Mashiach,* the other for Eliyahu *HaNavi* (the Prophet)." When he dedicated the [Ponovezh] yeshivah for younger students, he said, "I am certain that *Mashiach* and Eliyahu *HaNavi* will pass through these doors."
>
> If there was one person among us regarding whom we can apply the words, "My father, my father . . .!", which were said by the prophet Elisha when his teacher Eliyahu departed this world,[1] it was the Ponovezher *Rav.* It was he who founded the *Battei Avos* institutions for children who survived the Holocaust, so that these children would have a warm home in which to eat and sleep. These institutions were as their name implied — *Battei Avos* (lit. Homes of Fathers), a fatherly home for each and every child. With the love of a father for a son — literally — the Ponovezher *Rav* hugged and kissed each child, showering him with love. He was a "father" in a most literal sense.
>
> And he was a father and teacher to the entire Jewish nation. He brought back the time-honored tradition of *Yarchei Kallah* [where laymen spend their vacation time studying together within the confines of the *beis midrash*] . . . He was never content with what he had already accomplished, never did he relax or rest. He constantly strove to accomplish more, and yet more, to do for the community without limit, and one *mitzvah* led to another.

---

1. *II Melachim* 2:12.

We are all his children and can cry out in a most literal sense, "My father, my father!"[1]

Salvation Through Kindness

וַיִּשָּׁאֶר אַךְ נֹחַ וַאֲשֶׁר אִתּוֹ בַּתֵּבָה.
*Only Noach survived,
and those with him in the Ark (Bereishis 7:23).*

*"Only Noach" — The Midrash interprets this to mean
that Noach . . . was injured because he delayed giving
food to the lion and the lion attacked him[2] (Rashi from
Midrash Tanchuma 9).*

T he fate of the generation of the Flood was sealed on account of robbery.[3] The rampant robbery of that time meant that the world had become filled with "takers," people who had become concerned only with satisfying their own needs. To merit survival at such a time, it was necessary that Noach and his family engage in non-stop benevolence, selflessness instead of selfishness. For the entire year of the Flood, the eight people inside the Ark engaged in round-the-clock *chesed,* caring for the scores of creatures which Hashem had placed under their care. Noach's one lapse in feeding the

---

1. From *Michtavim U'Maamarim* (Collected Letters of Rabbi Eliezer Menachem Shach), vol. III.
2. The word אַךְ, *only,* connotes exclusion or minimizing. Here it implies that Noach himself was "minimized"; that is, he was injured (*Leket Bahir*).
3. See *Rashi* to *Bereishis* 6:13.

lion deprived him of some of the spiritual sustenance through which he merited to live. Therefore, he was injured (*Michtav MeEliyahu*).

The imperative of *chesed* at such a time can be understood in more simple terms. Death and destruction had been decreed upon that generation; it was a time of strict judgment. When the Attribute of Judgment reigns, one must engage in acts of *chesed* so that the Attribute of Mercy will be awakened in Heaven. This, writes the Chofetz Chaim, is why according to the Midrash (*Tana D'vei Eliyahu* 23), the Jews in Egypt made a pact to do kindness with one another. Their *chesed* was one of the primary factors in their meriting redemption. So, too, the kindness which the family of Noach practiced earned them the Divine compassion needed for them to survive.

❈ ❈ ❈

R' Moshe Neuschloss, who served as *Rav* of New Square from the founding of that community in 1958 until his passing in Adar 5757 (1997), was renowned as an outstanding *posek* (one who renders halachic decisions) of our day. He was also recognized as a *tzaddik,* whose kindness and compassion was boundless.

As we know, the *Aseres Yemei Teshuvah* (Ten Days of Repentance), beginning with Rosh Hashanah and concluding with Yom Kippur, are days when every Jew seeks to tip the Heavenly scales of judgment in his favor through added effort in his service of Hashem. In many communities, the Monday or Thursday closest to Yom Kippur is one when special *Selichos* prayers[1] are recited and efforts at *teshuvah* are intensified.

For decades, R' Neuschloss would begin that day by arising before dawn to recite the book of *Tehillim* prior to *Selichos*. The entire day was devoted to Torah study and prayer. R' Neuschloss would fast throughout the day, and in the afternoon he would visit a body of water to recite the *Tashlich* service.

---

1. Most notably, a piece which opens with the Thirteen Attributes of Mercy.

One year, when he was well into his seventies, R' Neuschloss arrived at home after his fast, tired and drawn. The table was already set; at his place was a slice of bread, a simple portion of food and a steaming cup of coffee. R' Neuschloss walked toward the sink to wash his hands, but then abruptly turned around, took some bread, filled a bowl with water and headed toward the stairs. His family did not understand, but he could not explain himself. It was his custom that on that day of repentance and prayer, he would utter only words of Torah and *tefillah.* Only after he had broken his fast would he engage in conversation.

With his nephew, R' Shulem Neuschloss, following behind him, the *Rav* descended the stairs to the basement below, where a few live chickens had been delivered that day, to be used the following morning for the *kaparos* ritual.[1] R' Neuschloss crumbled the bread at the feet of the birds and divided the water among them. Satisfied that they had been properly cared for, he then ascended the stairs to partake of his meal.

After he had eaten a bit, he explained, "The chickens were shipped from far away and had not been fed since they arrived. They were surely hungry and thirsty. Besides, they are now mine and one is not permitted to eat before feeding the creatures which he owns and for whose well-being he is responsible."[2]

❦ ❦ ❦

No doubt, R' Neuschloss' placing the needs of his birds before his own was a great source of merit as the day of Yom Kippur approached. The Manchester Rosh Yeshivah, R' Yehudah Zev Segal, related how, on *Erev* Yom Kippur, great *tzaddikim* would busy themselves with acts of *chesed.* R' Yisrael Salanter pulled out nails which were protruding from the benches in the

---

1. An ancient custom performed between Rosh Hashanah and Yom Kippur in which a rooster (for a male) or hen (for a female) is held above one's head while prayers are recited. The ceremony symbolizes that our sins cry out for atonement, and that our good deeds and repentance can save us from the punishment we deserve (see *Mishnah Berurah* 605:2).
2. *Shulchan Aruch, Orach Chaim* 167:6. *Mishnah Berurah* (citing *Magen*

women's section of the synagogue, so that the women would not tear their clothing as they sat praying on Yom Kippur.

As the time for *Kol Nidrei* approached, the Chasam Sofer arranged a *shidduch* (marriage match) between an orphaned boy and an orphaned girl. His daughter, who was to serve as his emissary in contacting both parties, had one question: "It will soon be time to leave for *shul* to begin *Kol Nidrei*. Could this not wait one more day?" Replied the *Chasam Sofer*, "My daughter, I must take this *mitzvah* along with me to *shul*. It cannot wait."

We, who in these troubled times seek to awaken Divine compassion for ourselves and for the entire Jewish people, should focus our attention on the needs of others and seek to help them to the best of our ability.

Avraham who quotes *Sefer Chassidim*) writes that it *is* proper for one to drink before giving his creatures to drink. Apparently, R' Neuschloss felt that the situation demanded that he not even drink before caring for his chickens.

פרשת לך לך
Parashas Lech Lecha

Faith Amid the Darkness

וְהֶאֱמִן בַּה׳ וַיַּחְשְׁבֶהָ לּוֹ צְדָקָה.

And he [Avram] trusted in Hashem,
and He reckoned it to him as righteousness (Bereishis 15:6).

The Holy One, Blessed is He, reckoned it for Avram
as a source of merit and as righteousness regarding the
trust that [Avram] trusted in Him (Rashi).

In a world steeped in idol worship, our forefather Avraham came to recognize the existence of the One and Only G-d Who created heaven and earth and guides all that occurs. Hashem subjected Avraham to ten difficult tests, climaxing with the test of the *Akeidah,* the Binding of Yitzchak.

In our morning prayers, we make mention of Avraham's pure, unshakable faith: "It is You, Hashem, the G-d, Who selected Avram . . . made his name Avraham. You found his heart faithful before You." Avraham's faith is part of the spiritual inheritance of every Jew; it is the spark within our souls that can never be extinguished. And it is this faith which has given Jews the strength to face the darkest of times with composure and courage.

❧ ❧ ❧

R' Shimon Schwab's passing in the spring of 5755 (1995) marked the end of his glorious career as a distinguished *Rav* and Torah leader, spanning more than half a century. For almost forty years, he had led Khal Adath Jeshurun in Washington Heights, which faithfully observes the traditions of the Frankfurt *kehillah* of pre-War Germany. R' Schwab was appointed to his first position as *Rav* in 1933, when he became District Rabbi of Ichenhausen, Bavaria. He was twenty-five years old.

It was during that same year that the Nazi party swept to power and Hitler was appointed Chancellor of the German Republic. As the months passed, the situation for German Jewry deteriorated rapidly and rabbis were prime targets of Nazi harassment.

On Shabbos *Parashas Ki Sisa,* R' Schwab ascended the pulpit and discussed the Sin of the Golden Calf. He quoted the commentary of R' Samson Raphael Hirsch, that in making the Golden Calf, the Jews had not sought, Heaven forfend, a substitute for their Creator. Rather, they wanted a substitute for their teacher Moshe, for they erroneously believed that they could not possibly have a relationship with G-d without an intermediary. R' Schwab quoted R' Hirsch's words that, in fact, a Jew can achieve a connection to Hashem even without such a *"mittler"* (German for "middleman").

An informer in the audience went to the Gestapo and reported that the *Rabbiner* had declared before his congregants that the Jews did not need a *"Hitler."* Soon, a member of the Gestapo appeared at R' Schwab's door, informing him that he had been blacklisted for his treacherous statement against the Fuhrer. He was ordered to appear at Gestapo headquarters.

Fully composed, R' Schwab entered the headquarters carrying with him a copy of R' Hirsch's commentary on the Torah, written in German. After the charges against him were read, R' Schwab explained how they were based on a gross misunderstanding of his words. To prove his point, he opened the volume which he held and pointed to the passage where the word *"mittler"* appeared.

Though the officer seemed satisfied with this explanation, he said that it was not easy for one's name to be removed from a Nazi blacklist. He instructed R' Schwab to phone him the following week to see what had been decided.

For the next two months, R' Schwab placed a weekly call to the officer, only to be told each time that nothing had been decided and that he should call again the following week. When he placed what would be his final phone call in this episode, the Gestapo officer exploded. "How dare you call me each week, pestering me like this? What Jewish insolence!" R' Schwab listened as the officer continued to insult him. But in between his diatribes, he also shouted, *"Es is shein arleidegt!* It [the matter of the blacklist] has already been taken care of!"

R' Schwab understood. The officer had already seen to it that R' Schwab's name be removed from the blacklist, but he did not want his cohorts to know what he had done. Therefore, he sandwiched this crucial message in between a barrage of insults.

R' Schwab knew, however, that it would only be a matter of time before he would be arrested. He therefore sought a rabbinic position overseas. He was appointed *Rav* of the Shearith Israel Congregation in Baltimore and arrived in New York on 10 Teves, 5696 (1936).

Years later, when recounting the above episode, R' Schwab revealed that throughout those harrowing two months, he never once went to sleep in his nightclothes. An acquaintance of his who had spoken out against the regime had been taken away in the middle of the night and was found hanged the next morning. R' Schwab knew that he might meet the same fate and he felt that it would be a degradation to the Torah for the *Rav* to be found hanging in his nightclothes. He was prepared to sacrifice his life if need be, but he was not prepared to sacrifice the honor of Torah.

פרשת וירא
Parashas Vayeira

A Most Welcome Guest

וַיֹּאמַר אֲ־דֹנָי אִם נָא מָצָאתִי חֵן בְּעֵינֶיךָ אַל נָא תַעֲבֹר מֵעַל עַבְדֶּךָ

And he [Avraham] said: "My L-rd, if I find favor in Your eyes,
please pass not away from Your servant" (Bereishis 18:3).

Bringing guests [into one's home] is greater than
receiving the Divine Presence[1] (Shavuos 35b).

In 1976, R' Nosson Einfeld[2] traveled to America to raise funds on behalf of Yeshivas Beer Sheva, which he then headed. R' Einfeld has always made a point of utilizing every opportunity to meet with Torah luminaries, in fulfillment of the commandment, "To Him shall you cleave" (*Devarim* 10:20), which one achieves, say our Sages, by cleaving to Torah scholars.[3] Thus, upon arriving in the Flatbush section of Brooklyn, R' Einfeld wasted no time in calling R' Yitzchak Hutner, late *Rosh Yeshivah* of Mesivta Rabbi Chaim Berlin.

---

1. For although the Divine Presence had appeared to Avraham, he took leave of Hashem in order to be hospitable to his guests.
2. Author of *Minchas Nosson* and *Sichos Chaim,* from which this episode is drawn.
3. *Rashi* from *Sifre.*

He introduced himself as "a Jew from Yeshivas Beer Sheva who would like to visit *Maran* (Our Guide), the *Rosh Yeshivah.*" The person who answered the call responded that it was unnecessary for the caller to make such a visit. R' Einfeld replied that he would not be soliciting for money, he merely wanted to meet the *Rosh Yeshivah.* This, too, received a negative response.

The next few days were hectic for R' Einfeld. As he prepared to leave New York for Toronto, he received a message that R' Hutner had called a number of times to speak with him, but there was no time to return the calls. Later, as R' Einfeld prepared to leave Toronto for his return trip to New York, his host received a call from R' Hutner which, again, could not be immediately returned.

R' Einfeld flew to New York and arrived at his lodging in Brooklyn. His host was waiting with a message: "R' Hutner called for you. He asked that you visit him at your earliest opportunity — you cannot imagine how anxious he is to see you!"

R' Einfeld put down his luggage and immediately phoned R' Hutner. When he introduced himself, the person who answered the phone cried out excitedly, *"Rosh Yeshivah!* It's R' Einfeld!" R' Hutner picked up the phone to happily greet his caller and invited him to come over immediately, adding, "It is more than a week that I am waiting for you."

A short while later, R' Hutner came to the door to welcome R' Einfeld into his home. With tears in his eyes, he embraced R' Einfeld and said with emotion, *"Baruch Haba* (Welcome), HaRav Einfeld, *Rosh Yeshivah* of Yeshivas Beer Sheva. *Baruch Hashem,* you have finally come.

"You have no idea how much pain and distress I have endured since your call more than a week ago. I was not the one who answered your call. An elderly Jew who was here at the time spoke to you. When I found out how he had responded to you, I said to him, "A *talmid chacham* from Beer Sheva wants to visit — why did you say that he should not come?"

R' Einfeld apologized for not having returned R' Hutner's previous phone calls, explaining that this had been impossible. He then asked, "When I called, I did not mention my name. How did the *Rosh Yeshivah* know my name, and how did he locate all the lodgings where I had been staying during this time?"

R' Hutner responded that he had phoned some acquaintances in *Eretz Yisrael,* and asked them to call Yeshivas Beer Sheva, find out the name of their representative visiting America and learn where he could be reached. After receiving the information, R' Hunter called R' Einfeld's place of lodging in Boro Park, then a house in Willamsburg where he was said to be visiting, and then his lodgings in Toronto. "I have not slept peacefully — literally — since your phone call."

R' Einfeld could not conceal his amazement. "To such an extent . . .? But why?"

"I am amazed at your question!" R' Hutner responded. "A Jew wants to visit and he is told "No!" — that itself is frightening! When my contacts in *Eretz Yisrael* informed me that my caller is a *Rosh Yeshivah* in Beer Sheva, my pain was yet greater, for I know how important it is that there be a yeshivah in Beer Sheva."

R' Hutner and R' Einfeld spent many hours together, after which R' Hutner presented his visitor with a generous donation. "I have given more than usual as a way of trying to make up for what has occurred."

As his guest took leave of him, R' Hutner asked forgiveness once more and invited R' Einfeld to join him at the yeshivah for the Purim *seudah* later that month.

פרשת חיי שרה
Parashas Chayei Sarah

Made in Heaven

וַיֹּאמַר ה' אֱלֹקֵי אֲדֹנִי אַבְרָהָם הַקְרֵה נָא לְפָנַי הַיּוֹם וַעֲשֵׂה חֶסֶד עִם אֲדֹנִי
אַבְרָהָם . . . וַיַּעַן לָבָן וּבְתוּאֵל וַיֹּאמְרוּ מֵה' יָצָא הַדָּבָר לֹא נוּכַל דַּבֵּר אֵלֶיךָ
רַע אוֹ טוֹב.

*And he [Eliezer] said: "Hashem, G-d of my master Avraham,
may You so arrange it for me this day that You do kindness for my
master Avraham . . ." Then Lavan and Besuel answered: "The matter
stemmed from Hashem! We can say to you neither bad nor good."*
(Bereishis 24:12, 50).

E liezer devised a test and prayed that through this test,
Hashem would indicate clearly whom He had chosen as
a partner in marriage for Yitzchak. Hashem answered his
prayer and immediately Rivka came forth to offer water for
Eliezer and his camels — the proof for which Eliezer had
prayed. So clearly evident was Hashem's guiding hand in this
match that even the wicked Lavan and Besuel were forced to
admit, "The matter stemmed from Hashem." From the Torah's
making mention of their response, our Sages derive that every
match is preordained in Heaven (*Moed Kattan* 18b).[1]

❦ ❦ ❦

1. See *Rashba* ad loc.

The room was filled with people and the atmosphere was filled with joy. The place was Har Nof, Jerusalem, and the occasion was the *vort* (engagement celebration) of Avrami Beer and Leah Reisman, a granddaughter of R' Mordechai Gifter, *Rosh Yeshivah* of the Telshe Yeshivah in Cleveland. The two had been introduced to each other by Leah's cousin, R' Michael Sorotzkin, a *Rosh Yeshivah* at Yeshivas Imrei Baruch in Kiryat Telshe Stone. R' Sorotzkin spoke in honor of the occasion and the following was the gist of his message:

"With the help of Hashem, I have now repaid a debt which I have borne for some twenty-three years. Twenty-three years ago, when I was fourteen years old, my father passed away. At that time, my mother felt it best for me to journey to America and enter the Telshe Yeshivah, where I could develop under the loving guidance of my uncle R' Baruch Sorotzkin and our cousin, R' Gifter, to whom we fondly refer as an uncle as well.

"One night, as it approached midnight, I was sleeping in my dormitory room when the *Rosh Yeshivah's* son, Zalman Gifter, awakened me. 'Get up!' he urged. 'My sister has become engaged to Yaakov Reisman![1] My father says that you must come to dance at the *simchah* (celebration)!'

"I cannot describe in words what that message meant to me, a young, lonely orphan, far away from home. The Rosh Yeshivah had a yeshivah of a few hundred *talmidim*, his daughter had just become engaged — and he was thinking of me!

"I got out of bed and, yes, I danced. A few days later, I wrote R' Gifter a letter in which I attempted to express my feelings. Though more than two decades have passed, I have not forgotten that kindness, and I have always felt a debt of gratitude toward him. Now that I have arranged this *shidduch* for the granddaughter of R' Gifter, the eldest child of R' Yaakov Reisman, I feel that the debt has been repaid."

R' Sorotzkin sat down and the next speaker, a brother-in-law of the *chasan* (groom), was introduced. He rose, looked across

---

1. R' Reisman is *Rav* of Agudath Israel of Long Island.

the table at R' Sorotzkin and asked, "Was your father's name R' Yisrael and did he leave this world on 11 Kislev, 5731, (1971)?" Surprised, R' Sorotzkin replied affirmatively. The speaker then related the following:

"I remember that day well. I was driving from Jerusalem to Bnei Brak for the wedding of my roommate at Yeshivas Ponovezh, my closest of friends. I was listening to the news on my car radio as I headed down Highway Four when I heard the following news bulletin:

> A distinguished *rav* is in Tel HaShomer Hospital in critical condition. The *rav* has the rare blood type ___ and is in need of an immediate blood transfusion. Anyone with this blood type who is in the vicinity of the hospital should come there immediately.

"I was not far from Tel HaShomer and I knew that I had that rare blood type. I also knew that by going to the hospital, I would certainly miss the *chuppah* (marriage ceremony) of my friend. Of course, there was no question as to what I should do. I took the exit for Tel HaShomer.

"When I arrived at the hospital, they told me that there was no time for normal transfusion procedures; they would have to do a direct transfusion. They took me to the room in which R' Yisrael Sorotzkin lay and they instructed me to lie down on a bed beside him. They inserted a needle under my skin and began the transfusion. But it was too late; R' Yisrael passed away during the transfusion. Needless to say, I did not go to the wedding that night.

"Twenty-three years ago, I gave a part of myself to your family in a most literal sense. And now, twenty-three years later, Hashem has repaid me by causing you, R' Michael, the son of R' Yisrael, to arrange a *shidduch* between my brother-in-law and a member of your family."

פרשת תולדות
Parashas Toldos

The Power of Prayer

וַיִּגַּשׁ יַעֲקֹב אֶל יִצְחָק אָבִיו וַיְמֻשֵּׁהוּ,
וַיֹּאמֶר הַקֹּל קוֹל יַעֲקֹב וְהַיָּדַיִם יְדֵי עֵשָׂו.

*So Yaakov drew close to Yitzchak his father, who felt him and said,
"The voice is Yaakov's voice, but the hands are Eisav's hands"*
(Bereishis 27:22).

*When the voice of Yaakov is found in the syna-
gogues [lifted up in prayer], then the hands are not the
hands of Eisav [i.e. then Yaakov, and not Eisav, will be
victorious]* (Bereishis Rabbah 65:20).

To most of the world, the Persian Gulf War of 1991 will be
remembered as one of swift, high-tech victory for the
Allied forces over an overconfident, underequipped enemy.
For the Jews of *Eretz Yisrael*, however, the war was viewed
from a far different vantage point. They were living under the
ever-present threat of deadly Scud missiles launched by the
wicked Saddam Hussein and his Iraqi forces. Time and time
again, our brethren hurried to their sealed rooms as the air raid

sirens, signaling a missile attack, were sounded. Time and again, the people of *Eretz Yisrael* were witness to open miracles. As missiles exploded and entire complexes of houses were destroyed, residents walked away with no more than minor injuries.

What was the source of these miracles? Here is the account of one missile-attack survivor:

Night had fallen and I had just ended a special day of fasting and prayer. We had recited *Tehillim* in our neighborhood *shul,* circled the synagogue carrying the Torah scrolls, and sounded the *shofar.* It felt like Yom Kippur.

As I sat down wearily on my bed, the siren sounded and we rushed to our sealed room. There was a terrifying explosion and our entire neighborhood was plunged into darkness. We smelled gas; a propane tank had sprung a leak. But Heaven had caused a water pipe to rupture and the water extinguished a small fire which otherwise would have caused the propane tank to explode.

We were trying to escape the rubble but all exits were sealed off by blocks of fallen concrete. I managed to squeeze through a hole that had been ripped open in our living room wall.

As we climbed up into the darkness outside there was silence all around us. We feared the worst. Had anyone else survived? The scene of devastation seemed to indicate that everyone was lost, G-d forbid. Then suddenly, from all sides, people began to stream out of the rubble. To our amazement and utter exhilaration, everyone was alive and well! — save for minor scratches and wounds from flying bits of plaster and broken glass.

I am sure that the miracle occurred at least partially in the merit of our prayers and fasting that day. Our tears and heartfelt intentions saved us all in both body and spirit.[1]

---

1. From *Mishpachah,* February 1991. For a detailed account of the Gulf War

❀ ❀ ❀

Even in the predominantly secular leadership of the Israeli
Defense Forces, there have been those who recognized the
power of prayer. In 1982, at the height of the war in Lebanon,
the Israeli Air Force was preparing for a major air battle with
Syrian jets over the Bekaa Valley. A request by someone in
the upper echelons of the I.D.F. was conveyed to the Steipler
Gaon, R' Yaakov Yisrael Kanievsky, asking that the *tzaddik*
pray for the success of their mission.

For some two hours, the Steipler recited *Tehillim.* He asked
all those who were with him at the time to pray as well. That
night, he was informed that twenty-three Syrian jets had been
downed, while all Israeli jets had returned safely to base. The
following night, the Steipler was told that another twenty-five
Syrian jets had been downed, and again there were no Israeli
losses. At that time, the Steipler was also given the name of a
soldier who had just been sent to the front, with a request that
he offer his blessings for the soldier's safe return home.[1]

---

miracles, see *Missiles, Masks and Miracles* by Sam Veffer (published by
Yeshivah Aish HaTorah of Jerusalem).
1. From *Toldos Yaakov* by R' Avraham Yeshayahu Kanievsky.

The Power of Torah

וַיֹּאמֶר עֵשָׂו בְּלִבּוֹ יִקְרְבוּ יְמֵי אֵבֶל אָבִי
וְאַהַרְגָה אֶת יַעֲקֹב אָחִי.

Eisav thought: "The days of my father's mourning shall draw near,
then I will kill my brother Yaakov" (Bereishis 27:41).

"The days of my father's mourning shall draw near"
— "When Yaakov will be a mourner, he will be unable
to study Torah, which shields and saves one from
harm — then I will prevail over him" (commentary to
Targum Yonasan).

It was the height of World War I. The German army was
rolling relentlessly onward and the Russian Army was in
desperate need of reinforcements. The streets of Minsk would
soon be swarming with army officers who would stop every
able-bodied man in sight. Whoever could not produce proof of
deferment would be hauled away for immediate induction.

The Chazon Ish was then studying in a *beis midrash* in
Minsk, oblivious to what was transpiring outside. Someone
burst into the *beis midrash* to inform him of the danger and to
advise him to go into hiding, since the Chazon Ish did not
have any papers. The Chazon Ish quickly left the *beis midrash*
and headed for the forests outside the city. However, as he
neared the forests, he saw the area teeming with troops. There
was no choice. Calmly, he walked between two rows of
soldiers. As he later related to his brother-in-law, the Steipler
Gaon, no one so much as looked at him. It was an open
miracle.

Said the Chazon Ish, "The miracle occurred in the merit of my having studied *Masechta Eruvin,* for I had completed my manuscript on the laws of *eruvin* on that very day . . . One who seeks to recognize the hand of Hashem in his life, sees miracles every day and every hour."

❀ ❀ ❀

The Steipler would encourage others to intensify their study of Torah as a source of merit for the sick, and would add that through Torah study, one's prayers are more readily accepted in Heaven. The Sages refer to Torah as *Rachmana,* Compassionate One, said the Steipler, because it is through the merit of Torah that we earn G-d's compassion.[1]

In his younger years, the *tzaddik* R' Moshe Leib Stavisk studied in a *kollel* in Aishishok, Lithuania. It happened that a terrible epidemic struck the province in which Aishishok lies and scores died. Of all the towns and hamlets in that province, only Aishishok was spared, as not one person in the city was stricken! The city's great *Rav,* R' Avraham Shmuel, said privately, "It is the merit of R' Moshe Leib's Torah study which shields our city. He studies for hours on end with incredible diligence, and remains standing the entire time.[2] This is our source of protection."

Some time later, R' Moshe Leib received a telegram from his father-in-law in Lida, insisting that he bring his family to Lida to escape the epidemic which had intensified in the neighboring towns. R' Moshe Leib acceded to this request and, unbeknownst to R' Avraham Shmuel, left Aishishok. Almost immediately, the epidemic struck.

---

1. On Rosh Hashanah, the *baal tokeiah* (one who blows the *shofar*) stands at the *bimah* where the Torah is read, to invoke the merit of Torah study (*Rama, Orach Chaim* ch. 585 with *Mishnah Berurah* §3).

2. The *Mishnah* (*Sotah* 9:15) states, "When Rabban Gamliel the Elder died, the glory of Torah disappeared." *Rashi* (based on *Megillah* 21a) explains that until Rabban Gamliel's time, people were generally strong and healthy, and as a mark of respect, would study Torah while standing. However, with Rabban Gamliel's passing, a general weakness descended to the people and they were no longer able to remain standing throughout the long periods of

Years later, R' Isser Zalman Meltzer wept as he related this episode. He said, "R' Avraham Shmuel was the quintessential *talmid chacham*. In Aishishok's *kollel* were found many outstanding young scholars, who were imbued with awe of Hashem and who toiled diligently in Torah study day and night. Yet R' Avraham Shmuel could perceive that R' Moshe Leib's study was of an entirely different sort, and that it was *his* merit that had shielded everyone" (*B'Derech Eitz Chaim*).

---

time they spent studying Torah. Thus, even though Torah study continued, it lacked the extra measure of honor that it previously had been accorded.

פרשת ויצא
Parashas Vayeitzei

Heightened Perceptions

וַיִּיקַץ יַעֲקֹב מִשְּׁנָתוֹ וַיֹּאמֶר
אָכֵן יֵשׁ ה' בַּמָּקוֹם הַזֶּה וְאָנֹכִי לֹא יָדָעְתִּי.
Yaakov awoke from his sleep and said:
"Surely HASHEM is in this place and I did not know!"
(Bereishis 28:16).

"For had I known, I would not have slept in a holy place such as this"[1] (Rashi).

During the last years of the life of the Steipler *Gaon,* R' Yaakov Yisrael Kanievsky, walking was extremely difficult for him. For this reason, the people of Bnei Brak installed benches upon which to rest along the short route from the Steipler's home to the Lederman *Shul,* where he *davened.*

As Yom Kippur of 5745 (1985) approached, the Steipler's family made preparations for him to spend the night of Yom Kippur in *shul,* so that he would not have to endure the strenuous walk while fasting. A cot was set up in a room adjacent to the Lederman *beis midrash.*

---

1. Earlier (v.11), *Rashi* stated that Hashem had caused the sun to set early, for it was His will that Yaakov spend the night at that place, the site upon which the *Beis HaMikdash* would be built, and there receive his prophetic dream.

On the night of Yom Kippur following *Maariv,* the Steipler went to lie down. However, a few minutes later he returned to the *beis midrash,* where he remained for the rest of the night, reciting *Tehillim.* Later he told someone that he had left the room after only a short while because he had sensed that he was lying in a *makom kadosh,* a sanctified place. It was later discovered that upon that spot where he had lain there had once been an *aron kodesh* (ark) which had held Torah scrolls.

Such perceptions are not inborn. They are developed through a lifetime totally devoted to Hashem's service, especially through immersion in the purifying waters of Torah, and in living a life of spirituality that is totally removed from earthly pleasures.

Amazingly, the Steipler was so removed from material pleasure that he would not allow his family to purchase a fan for his small room in which he spent his days and nights studying and receiving visitors. "Better to have less of this world," was his simple explanation. When he suffered from a respiratory condition, his family wanted to install an air conditioner in his room. He declined this offer for a different reason: Since he did not make use of electricity on Shabbos,[1] he would be able to use the air conditioner only on weekdays. It would not be proper, said the Steipler, to enjoy such comfort on weekdays but not on Shabbos.

Torah study brought him joy and contentment in every situation, under all conditions. A few days before he passed away, the Steipler lost consciousness. His doctors tried all sorts of means to stimulate him and gain some reaction, but to no avail. Then, someone placed earphones to his ears and played a tape of someone reciting *mishnayos.* Immediately, a look of contentment spread across the Steipler's countenance, which remained for as long as the tape was playing, save for the time when the speaker mispronounced a word from the *Mishnah (Toldos Yaakov).*

---

1. Because the electric company operating the generators on Shabbos was staffed by Jews.

An Age-Old Problem

וַיַּעַן לָבָן וַיֹּאמֶר אֶל יַעֲקֹב
הַבָּנוֹת בְּנֹתַי וְהַבָּנִים בָּנַי וְהַצֹּאן צֹאנִי וְכֹל אֲשֶׁר אַתָּה רֹאֶה לִי הוּא.
Then Lavan spoke and said to Yaakov,
"The daughters are my daughters, the children are my children and the
flock is my flock, and all that you see is mine" (Bereishis 31:43).

The Brisker *Rav* (R' Yitzchak Zev Soloveitchik) once visited the Chofetz Chaim and found him discussing our people's travails in exile; in particular, the wave of anti-Jewish edicts that were then being promulgated by the Polish government. The Chofetz Chaim related the following:

A ninety-year old Jew had applied to the Polish government for a passport. When the man told the attending clerk that he did not own a birth certificate, he was told that unless he could produce two witnesses who could attest to where and when he was born, he would not receive a passport. Of course this was impossible, for anyone who was old enough to recall this man's birth would have been past one hundred years of age!

"Such unfairness!" declared the Chofetz Chaim. "Didn't they realize that there was no way the man could fulfill their demands? What were they trying to prove?"

The Chofetz Chaim explained, "When our forefather Yaakov was confronted by his father-in-law Lavan after having fled the latter's house, Lavan demanded an explanation. Yaakov replied by reminding Lavan of the schemes to which he had been subjected for the past twenty years. *'I served you fourteen years for your two daughters, and six years for your flocks; and you changed my wage a hundred times' (Bereishis 31:41).* What was

Lavan's reply? *'The daughters are my daughters, the children are my children and the flock is my flock, and all that you see is mine'* (ibid. v. 43).

"What kind of a reply was that? In no way did it respond to the serious charge with which Lavan had been confronted! This, however, was typical of Lavan. As far as he was concerned, Yaakov's claims did not exist. It was as if they had not been uttered. As such, there was no reason to respond to them.

"Claims and counterclaims can only exist when each party recognizes the other as a claimant. Then, the two sides can bring their case to court for a decision. But when one side does not even respect the other as a claimant, the situation cannot be dealt with."

The Chofetz Chaim continued, "Of course it's unfair to ask a ninety-year-old man to bring witnesses for when he was born. But this can be argued only when the claimant is considered a claimant. As far as the Polish government is concerned, however, we Jews are a non-entity. They govern us with a different set of rules and all our arguments are not reckoned with at all.

"So what can we do?" he concluded. "I cannot offer advice that is better than that of R' Eliezer the Great who said, *'What can a person do to escape the "birthpangs of Mashiach" [i.e. the travails that will precede the Final Redemption]? Let him involve himself in the study of Torah and in performing acts of kindness'* " (*Sanhedrin* 98b).

פרשת וישלח
Parashas Vayishlach

Names

וַיִּשְׁאַל יַעֲקֹב וַיֹּאמֶר הַגִּידָה נָּא שְׁמֶךָ וַיֹּאמֶר לָמָּה זֶּה תִּשְׁאַל לִשְׁמִי?

Then Yaakov inquired and he said, "Tell, if you please,
your name." And he [the angel of Eisav] said,
"Why is it that you ask my name?" (Bereishis 32:30).

"Why is it that you ask my name?" — "We have no
fixed name. Our names change according to the
mission upon which we are sent" (Rashi).

Each soul that descends to this world is entrusted with a specific, lifelong mission which only it can accomplish. Thus, unlike the name of an angel, a person's Hebrew name defines his essence (*Arizal*). *Sefer Me'or Gadol*[1] writes that the higher soul comes to a child when his or her name is given. The *Arizal* is quoted as having said that parents are given a degree of Divine inspiration when choosing a name for their child.[2]

---

1. Cited by *Taamei HaMinhagim* in *Kuntrus Acharon*.
2. See the essay on names in *Bris Milah* by Rabbi Paysach J. Krohn (Mesorah Publications).

❧ ❧ ❧

R' Chaim Moshe Halberstam will always be remembered for his kindness, cheerful disposition and love of children. From meeting him, one would never have imagined the hardships which he had endured during his more than ninety years on earth.

He was the eldest great-grandchild of R' Tzvi Elimelech Spira, the famed Bluzhever *Rebbe,* [1] author of *Tzvi LaTzaddik.* The *Tzvi LaTzaddik* was a Chassidic leader of towering stature and R' Chaim Moshe spent much of his youth in his court. Young Chaim Moshe was present when the *Tzvi Latzaddik* took leave of this world.

The horrors of the Second World War left R' Chaim Moshe bereft of his immediate family. He arrived in America alone, later remarried, and his second wife passed away childless. Despite everything, R' Chaim Moshe never lost his good cheer. He was always smiling and always ready with a joke to bring a smile to someone else.

Twice, he was involved in the engagement of children from families with whom he was particularly close. He was the *shadchan* (matchmaker) of Rabbi and Mrs. Elazar Brodt. While he was not the *shadchan* of Rabbi and Mrs. Dovid Margulis, he was consulted by both families when the match was suggested and helped see the matter through to a successful conclusion.

Soon after the Margulis marriage, R' Chaim Moshe visited the young couple and remarked that he expected *"shad-chanus"* (matchmaker's renumeration) from them. Everyone present, including Mrs. Margulis' parents, Rabbi and Mrs. Yitzchak Spira, smiled at what they perceived as R' Chaim Moshe's typical good humor. Responding in kind, Mrs. Spira said to R' Chaim Moshe, "Well, tell us what you want for *shadchanus."* R' Chaim Moshe turned to the young couple and said with a smile, but in a manner which conveyed some-

---

1. He was the grandfather of R' Yisrael Spira, the late Bluzhever *Rebbe* of New York.

thing other than levity, "I want you to name your third boy after me!"

His words left everyone stunned. What had possessed R' Chaim Moshe to say such a thing? Superficially it sounded like one of his many jokes, but this time there seemed to be something beneath the surface. No one forgot the remark.

In the summer of 5755 (1995), R' Chaim Moshe passed away. A *seudas mitzvah* marking the end of the thirty-day mourning period was held at the Bluzhever *Beis Midrash* in Boro Park. One of the speakers was R' Yitzchak Spira, who remarked that there is a saying, "In every joke there lies a bit of truth." It may have seemed that R' Chaim Moshe was joking when he told the Margulises that their third boy should be named after him, but he may have been hinting that he hoped his memory would be perpetuated through the children who would bear his name. R' Spira called on those assembled to bear this in mind in the coming years when their families would be blessed with new offspring.

The following summer, on the Ninth of Av, 5756 (1996), baby boys were born to Mrs. Elazar Brodt and Mrs. Dovid Margulis. The Brodts already had a boy named Chaim, so they would name their new arrival Moshe Nochum. Faced with the dilemma of whether to name their baby after R' Chaim Moshe or a deceased member of their family, the Margulises forwarded their question to R' Yisroel Mordechai Twersky, the Rachmastrivka *Rebbe* of *Eretz Yisrael*. The *Rebbe* responded that R' Chaim Moshe, it seemed, had been granted a spark of *ruach hakodesh* (Divine inspiration) when he had said that the couple would name their third boy after him. This baby was the Margulis' third boy, and like the Brodts' newborn, his *bris milah* would take place on 16 Av, 5756, *the first yahrtzeit of R' Chaim Moshe Halberstam*. There was no question, the *Rebbe* concluded, that the baby should be named Moshe Nochum.

פרשת וישב
Parashas Vayeishev

Orchestrated From Above

וְהִנֵּה אֹרְחַת יִשְׁמְעֵאלִים בָּאָה מִגִּלְעָד וּגְמַלֵּיהֶם נֹשְׂאִים נְכֹאת וּצְרִי . . .
וָלֹט הוֹלְכִים לְהוֹרִיד מִצְרָיְמָה.

. . . Behold! a caravan of Ishmaelites was coming from Gilad,
and their camels were bearing spices, and balsam, and birthwort
— on their way to bring them down to Egypt (Bereishis 37:25).

Why does the verse publicize what their burden
contained? To make known the reward of the right-
eous. For it is not the way of Arabs to carry anything
but petroleum and resin whose odor is foul, but this
time the cargo was spices, so that Yosef should not
be harmed by the foul odor (Rashi from Bereishis
Rabbah).

R' Chaim Shmulevitz (*Sichos Mussar*) derived from the
above that when Hashem deems it necessary to cause
someone difficulty or suffering, He does so with exact
measure. It had been decreed that Yosef should be sold into
slavery, but it had not been decreed that his journey down to
Egypt should be plagued by the discomfort of traveling in a
foul-smelling caravan. Therefore, Hashem caused it to happen
that the caravan should bear sweet-smelling spices.

Yet another basic lesson can be derived from this episode.
Hashem conducts the affairs of His people through *hashgachah*

pratis, exacting guidance and intervention from Above, in which nothing is left to chance. Because it had not been decreed that Yosef's journey to Egypt should be further aggravated by the foul smell of petroleum, Hashem caused that particular caravan to pass by precisely at the time when Yosef's brothers had decided to sell him as a slave.

In fact, the entire episode of Yosef and the brothers is one of incredible Divine intervention. The brothers thought that by selling Yosef as a slave they were ensuring that his dreams of grandeur would never come true. Hashem planned otherwise. From the abyss of imprisonment, Yosef rose to become viceroy to Pharoah, and ultimately was the sustainer of his father Yaakov and his entire family. To Yosef our Sages apply the verse, "Blessed is the man that trusts in Hashem, then Hashem will be his security" (*Yirmiyahu* 17:7).[1]

The more a person places his trust in Hashem and seeks to go in His ways, the more he merits to witness Hashem's guiding hand in his life.

❈   ❈   ❈

The *Imrei Emes* of Ger, R' Avraham Mordechai Alter, was an outstanding leader of Polish *chassidic* Jewry before the Second World War. After the Germans invaded Poland on September 1, 1939, they launched an intensive search for the Gerrer *Rebbe,* for they knew that the *"Vunder Rabbiner"* ("Wonder Rabbi"), as they referred to him, breathed hope and spirit into his tens of thousands of followers. The *Rebbe's* miraculous escape, which took him across the Polish border and ultimately to *Eretz Yisrael,* involved a series of incredible acts of Divine intervention which came together to ensure his survival.

A key player in the miracle was a Polish gentile who headed the Warsaw office of the Italian National Maritime Corporation. In the years before the war, this man had arranged the *Rebbe's* five sea voyages to *Eretz Yisrael.* For the *Rebbe's* fifth voyage,

---

1. See further in this chapter.

in 1935, this man had provided, on his own initiative and free of charge, two private cabins reserved for dignitaries. After returning home, the *Rebbe,* as a token of gratitude, sent the man two cigars. The gentile gave one cigar to his uncle, who was the Polish Prime Minister, and kept the other one as a "good luck" piece.

When the Germans bombed Warsaw at the war's outbreak, the man's house was reduced to a pile of rubble. Miraculously, he and his family emerged from the ruins unscathed. The only item which was found intact among the ruins was the cigar which the *Rebbe* had given him. The gentile took this as a Heavenly sign that it was the merit of his having helped the *Rebbe* which had saved him, and he dedicated himself to the *Imrei Emes'* rescue.

This gentile managed to procure Italian visas for the *Imrei Emes* and some of his family members. But a major obstacle needed to be overcome. The Germans, well aware that Jews were desperately seeking any means to escape to the free world, issued an order that no visas from any country would be recognized unless they were stamped by a German sergeant named Wenger who headed one of the Gestapo offices in Cracow.

The gentile shipping director saw no way out of the dilemma. He told the Gerrer *chassid* who was directing the attempted rescue of the *Imrei Emes,* "This time, there is nothing that I can do; your great Rabbi will have to bring about a miracle."

The miracle occurred. To everyone's amazement, Sergeant Wenger appeared one day at the Italian shipping office in Warsaw in need of a favor. Two of his Polish acquaintances were in need of passage out of Poland which he could not arrange through his own office. (It would later come to light that Wenger himself was accepting bribes in exchange for handing over sensitive information to the Polish government in exile, and this was why he could not make use of his own office for these "friends" of his.) The shipping director told Wenger that he was prepared to honor his request, but he wanted a favor in return — that a few Italian visas be stamped with his seal of approval. The Nazi agreed and the visas were approved.

❈ ❈ ❈

The guiding hand of Providence can be perceived any time, any place.

Yaakov Leiner[1] was driving through Connecticut on his way home to New York when his car broke down. It was almost evening and there was no chance of getting the car repaired until the next day. Yaakov found his way to the nearest motel and checked in for the night.

Tired and thirsty, he entered the motel lounge and headed for the soda machine. Heading in the same direction was a burly young man, sporting a leather jacket and jeans, with a motorcycle helmet in his hand. He took one look at the *yarmulka*-sporting Yaakov and jeered, "Does that thing on your head keep you good and warm?"

Yaakov shot back, "Have I bothered you in any way? Did I do anything to you that should make you want to ridicule me?" As soon as the words were out of his mouth, Yaakov regretted having said them. Had he ignored the fellow's remarks, the incident might have ended right there. Now that he had answered back, his antagonist would surely have more to say. "Why didn't you keep your mouth closed?" he chided himself.

His antagonist did have more to say. "I'm sorry," the gentile responded. "You're right. You did nothing to me and I was wrong for starting up with you."

Yaakov could not believe his ears. He was even more surprised by the fellow's next words. "Come," he said, "let me buy you a soda and we'll sit down and talk."

They sat down opposite each other. Yaakov recited a *berachah* and sipped his soda as his new-found acquaintance began talking.

---

1. Not his real name.

"My grandfather always used to tell me that I should be nice to Jews. He fought in the Second World War and had a very good experience with a Jew like yourself. The man was a Jewish chaplain in my grandfather's regiment. A real nice, sincere type. My grandfather liked him a lot.

"After the war, the chaplain dedicated his every free moment to finding Jewish children who had been hidden by gentiles during the war. A lot of these gentile families were not too keen on giving the children back.

"One day, the chaplain returned to base looking very upset. 'What's wrong?' my grandfather asked. The chaplain replied, 'There are some families who I know for a fact have Jewish children, but when I went to speak to them, they slammed the door in my face.' "

At this point, Yaakov, who had been listening intently to every word, interrupted.

"Allow me, please, to finish your story. Your grandfather, who as you said, liked the chaplain a lot, suggested, 'You know what, Rabbi? Tomorrow, when you go looking for those children, my buddy and I are going to accompany you.'

"The next day, the chaplain knocked on someone's door. It was opened halfway, but when the person saw the Rabbi standing there, he started to slam the door shut — but your grandfather's foot got in the way.

" 'Just a minute, buddy!' he said, making no attempt to conceal his rifle. 'Don't you go slamming the door. The Rabbi came here for a reason and you'd better listen to what he has to say!'

"And thanks to those two soldiers," Yaakov concluded, "the chaplain succeeded in returning a number of children to their Jewish roots."

The motorcyclist was sitting open-mouthed, seemingly in shock. Finally, he asked, "How did you know what I was going to say?"

"Simple," came the reply. "That chaplain was my uncle and he told me the story."

Yaakov waited a few moments before continuing. "My

friend, I don't know for sure why G-d caused you and me to meet tonight, but I know one thing — it happened for a reason. Perhaps it was a way of telling you that if you ever find yourself in a situation where you can help a Jew, be sure to help him, just as your grandfather did."

The two shook hands and parted.

Levels of Trust

וְלֹא זָכַר שַׂר הַמַּשְׁקִים אֶת יוֹסֵף וַיִּשְׁכָּחֵהוּ.
Yet the Chamberlain of the Cupbearers did not remember Yosef, but he forgot him (Bereishis 40:23).

Yosef languished in an Egyptian prison after being slandered by Potiphar's wife. Sharing the prison pit with him were Pharoah's chief cupbearer and baker. Both dreamt dreams which Yosef interpreted correctly. The cupbearer, Yosef said, would soon be returned to his post; and so it was. After interpreting his dream, Yosef asked the cupbearer to intercede on his behalf when he would be released from prison, but this did not happen. *Yet the Chamberlain of the Cupbearers did not remember Yosef, but he forgot him.*

The *Midrash* states that because Yosef placed his trust in the cupbearer, Heaven decreed that he should spend an additional two years in prison. Paradoxically, the same *Midrash* describes Yosef as one who places his trust in Hashem. " 'Praises to the man who made Hashem his trust' (*Tehillim* 40:5) — this refers to Yosef" (*Bereishis Rabbah* 89:3).

The *Midrash* is telling us that there are infinite levels of emunah and bitachon (faith and trust in Hashem), and a person is expected to live his life according to his level. Yosef lived in Egypt for twenty-two years, one lone Jew among a people mired in the lowest levels of spiritual decadence. He emerged from this incredible trial spiritually unscathed by way of his exalted level of bitachon. Not for a moment did he lose sight of Hashem's Presence and of the exacting Providence through which he was being protected.

For an ordinary person, it would have been wrong *not* to utilize the opportunity presented by the cupbearer being freed. However, someone as great as Yosef should not have sought his salvation through the immoral, arrogant cupbearer, or through any other person. Just as Hashem had caused Yosef to be imprisoned, so would He cause him to be freed, as did ultimately happen.

❦ ❦ ❦

It was 2:00 A.M. and R' Chaim Volozhiner was discussing the concept of bitachon with his talmidim. [1] In those days, few could afford to own a watch. R' Chaim asked if anyone had the time and no one responded. R' Chaim remarked, "If we had true bitachon, then Hashem would cause a watch — even a gold one — to appear."

A few minutes later, the door of the beis midrash opened and in walked a Russian soldier. He came before R' Chaim and began:

"I am a Jew from a village near Lodz and only recently I was drafted into the army. It is now several weeks that I am living at the army base. I live in constant fear since I am the only Jew among gentiles. More than once, I have noticed my fellow soldiers eyeing my beautiful gold watch. I have no doubt that if I keep it with my belongings, it will be stolen sooner or later.

---

1. Since the giving of the Torah at Sinai, the world exists on the strength of Torah study. If, even for an instant, there would be no Torah study in the world, creation would revert to nothingness. Based on this truth, R' Chaim Volozhiner — who discusses it in his classic Nefesh HaChaim — arranged that his students should study in round-the-clock shifts.

"I am presently on a few hours' leave. Passing by, I noticed the light shining in your *beis midrash.* Please let me leave my watch with you."

"My son, I would be more than happy to hold the watch for you," R' Chaim replied, "but I must make clear to you that my house is an open house — people are constantly coming and going. I am reluctant to assume responsibility should anything happen to your watch."

After a moment's hesitation, the soldier replied, *"Rebbi,* I would like to give you the watch as a gift. Better that it should belong to a rabbi than to be stolen by a bunch of thugs."

Without waiting for a response, the soldier placed the watch in front of R' Chaim and hurried out of the *beis midrash.* R' Chaim tried to catch up to him, but could not.

When the excitement subsided, R' Chaim repeated his earlier words, "If we had true *bitachon,* then Hashem would cause a watch — even a gold one — to appear."

פרשת מקץ
Parashas Mikeitz

The Way of a Jew

וַיְצַו יוֹסֵף וַיְמַלְאוּ אֶת כְּלֵיהֶם בָּר
וּלְהָשִׁיב כַּסְפֵּיהֶם אִישׁ אֶל שַׂקּוֹ
וְלָתֵת לָהֶם צֵדָה לַדָּרֶךְ וַיַּעַשׂ לָהֶם כֵּן.

Yosef commanded that they fill their vessels with grain,
and to return their money, each one's to his sack,
and to give them provisions for their journey; and so he did for them
(Bereishis 42:25).

The brothers had come to Egypt during a famine to purchase food for their family. Still posing before his brothers as the viceroy of Egypt who was suspicious of them, Yosef sent them back home to their father with instructions to bring back their youngest brother, Binyamin. Yosef treated them considerately by sending them provisions for the road, in addition to the full vessels of grain which they were bringing home. On the other hand, Yosef secretly instructed his assistants to take the money which the brothers had given as payment, and hide it in their sacks. What was Yosef's motive in doing this?

Kli Yakar explains that when the brothers would find the money they would surely suspect that it had been put there as a pretext to denounce them as thieves and sell them as slaves.

Yosef did this to provide atonement — measure for measure — for his brothers' having sold him as a slave.[1]

R' Shimon Schwab, quoting the Brisker *Rav,* offered a different interpretation. Yosef wanted to ensure that the brothers would return to Egypt. He knew that as descendants of Avraham, Yitzchak and Yaakov, his brothers would not be at peace with themselves knowing that they had someone else's money in their possession. Thus, they would feel forced to return to Egypt if for no other reason than to return the money which was not their own.

R' Schwab himself was renowned for his integrity in all areas. In monetary matters he went far beyond the strict requirements of *halachah,* and in so doing sanctified the Name of Hashem.

Once, R' Schwab visited his son R' Myer when the latter was a student at Mesivta Rabbi Chaim Berlin in Brooklyn. The two then went to a subway station to travel to Manhattan. Not far from the token booth, R' Myer spotted a few quarters lying on the ground. His father instructed him to give them to the clerk at the booth. R' Myer was prepared to obey, but he was puzzled, for a subway station is a public domain and the *halachah* clearly allows one to keep an item such as money (which has no identifying characteristics) when it is found in such an area. Respectfully, he asked his father for an explanation.

R' Schwab explained: "Certainly you are correct that from a halachic standpoint, the money is yours. But in our day and age, we have to utilize every opportunity to be *mekadesh Shem Shamayim* (sanctify the Name of Heaven) and demonstrate what Torah Jews are all about. You hand the money to the man in the booth and I will stick my beard into the window so that he will see who we are!"

---

1. The Torah relates that when one of the brothers opened his sack on the way home and found the money, "Their hearts sank, and they turned trembling to one another, saying, 'What is this that God has done to us?' " (v. 28).

Years later, R' Schwab visited R' Myer in Denver, where he serves as Dean of the city's Bais Yaakov. One day, R' Myer brought home from the cleaners two of his father's suits. Upon examining the receipt and counting his change, R' Schwab realized that he had mistakenly been charged for only one suit. When R' Myer checked the figures, he said, "Yes, it's certainly a mistake. Tomorrow I'll pass by the store and pay the difference."

"It should not wait for tomorrow," his father replied. "We should take care of it right now. I will come along."

In his last years, R' Shimon Schwab was confined to a wheelchair. At the time of his visit to Denver, R' Schwab was still able to walk, but with difficulty. Nevertheless, he insisted on coming along to contribute his share to this *kiddush Hashem.* They arrived at the shopping mall and R' Myer pulled up right in front of the cleaners so that the proprietor could see his father sitting in the front seat. R' Myer entered the store, explained what had happened and paid for the suit. The proprietor turned to looked out the window and R' Schwab smiled and waved at him from the car. The proprietor said to R' Myer, "Rabbi, you didn't have to make a special trip for this — you could have brought the money in tomorrow!"

"I know," R' Myer replied, "but to my father, the matter could not wait until tomorrow; it had to be rectified right away."

פרשת ויגש
Parashas Vayigash

Not a Moment to Spare

מַהֲרוּ וַעֲלוּ אֶל אָבִי וַאֲמַרְתֶּם אֵלָיו כֹּה אָמַר בִּנְךָ יוֹסֵף שָׂמַנִי אֱלֹקִים לְאָדוֹן לְכָל
מִצְרָיִם, רְדָה אֵלַי אַל תַּעֲמֹד.

[Yosef said to his brothers:] Hurry — go up to my father and say to him,
"So said your son Yosef: 'G-d has made me master of all Egypt. Come
down to me; do not delay' " (Bereishis 45:9).

"Hurry" — So that he will not suffer any additional
pain (Sforno).

For twenty-two years, our forefather Yaakov lived with
pain and anguish brought on by his belief that his
beloved son Yosef was dead. The commentators explain why
Yosef did not send his father a message that he was alive and
well as soon as he was freed from prison and appointed viceroy
of Egypt. According to *Ramban,* [1] Yosef considered his dreams
about his father and brothers bowing before him to be
prophecies. Yosef knew that he had to allow these prophecies

---

1. To *Bereishis* 42:9; see also *Haamek Davar.*

to unfold by Divine direction, and thus, he could not reveal himself until the right moment. When Yehudah delivered his impassioned speech for Binyamin's freedom, and even the palace servants appealed for mercy on the brothers' behalf,[1] Yosef knew that the moment had arrived.

As soon as he revealed himself, Yosef's utmost priority was that his father be spared any additional pain. It would be wrong to prolong his father's agony by even one additional minute. And so, Yosef told his brothers, "*Hurry* — go up to my father . . ."

❀ ❀ ❀

For many years, the Sadovner *Rav,* R' Yisrael Sekula,[2] would spend his Purim morning in a rather unusual way. He would pray *Shacharis* and hear the reading of the *Megillah* at an early *minyan.* He would then spend the remainder of his morning making the rounds of the Boro Park synagogues on foot, walking among the congregants at each *minyan* as he collected *tzedakah* for the poor.

One year, he arrived home from his collections shortly before noon, exhausted but exhilarated. It was the *Rav's* custom to partake of two *seudos* (meals) on Purim day and the table was already set for the first meal. However, the *Rav* was not yet ready. His pockets were bursting with assorted change and bills of different denominations, folded and crumpled into various shapes and sizes. The *Rav* emptied his pockets and, assisted by his children, proceeded to unfold and sort out the money.

Suddenly, the *Rav* cried out in dismay, "Look! A hundred-dollar bill!" The *Rav* was one of scores of collectors who made their rounds of the Boro Park *shuls* on Purim morning. It was highly doubtful that an individual would give one collector — even one as distinguished as the Sadovner *Rav* — so large a contribution. "I'm positive that I know who gave this to me. Whenever I come around collecting, he gives me a ten-dollar

---

1. See *Ramban* to 45:1.
2. See chapter on *Parashas Bereishis.*

bill. He probably reached into his wallet for ten dollars and mistakenly pulled out this hundred. He probably thinks that he dropped it somewhere."

The *Rav* donned his coat and headed for the door; he was going to return the money. His wife and children pleaded with him to eat something first. He had exerted himself and was now about to strain himself yet further. Couldn't he partake of the *seudah* first and then attend to the matter?

The *Rav* explained, "If my assumption is correct, and indeed that man did give me this bill mistakenly, then he is surely distressed over its loss. Every minute that I delay in returning it is another minute of anguish that he will suffer. I must return it immediately." With those words, he headed out the door, accompanied by his sons.

They arrived at the man's house and the *Rav* got straight to the point. "Did you lose money today?" he asked. Taken aback, the man responded that he had lost a hundred-dollar bill somewhere. "Did you intend to give me ten dollars this morning?" When the man replied affirmatively, the Sadovner *Rav* handed him the bill and explained what had happened.

However, the man was somewhat embarrassed to accept the money and suggested that the Sadovner *Rav* keep it. The *Rav,* however, would not hear of it. "I only accept *tzedakah* that is given *b'leiv shaleim* (with a full heart). You never intended to give this for *tzedakah*. Please take back your hundred, give me ten dollars and we'll be 'even.' "

Their transaction completed, the *Rav* wished the man "a joyous Purim" and headed home with his children for the Purim *seudah*.

פרשת ויחי
Parashas Vayechi

Of Prayers and Tears

וַאֲנִי בְּבֹאִי מִפַּדָּן מֵתָה עָלַי רָחֵל . . .
וָאֶקְבְּרֶהָ שָּׁם בְּדֶרֶךְ אֶפְרָת הִוא בֵּית לָחֶם.

*But as for me — when I came from Paddan, Rachel died on me . . .
and I buried her there on the road to Ephrath, which is Bethlehem*
(*Bereishis* 48:7).

*"And I buried her there — and I did not even take her to Bethlehem to
bring her into the land, and I know that there is hurt in your heart towards
me. But you should know that by the word of Hashem I buried her there,
so that she should be of aid to her children. When Nevuzaradan would
exile them and they would pass by Rachel's tomb, Rachel would go out
to weep and seek mercy for them . . . and the Holy One answered her,
'There is reward for your act, says Hashem . . . and children shall return
to their boundaries' "* (*Rashi* 48:7 from *Bereishis Rabbah*).

While our prayers and tears may not have the power of
those of our Matriarch Rachel, nevertheless, we
should not underestimate them.

R' Aryeh Levin, the legendary Jerusalem *tzaddik,* was a man
of rare compassion. Once, a distraught, recently widowed
woman came to him and wept bitterly. R' Aryeh did his best to
console the woman, but she continued to weep. After a long

time, she said, "*Rebbi*, I am prepared to accept your words of consolation, but there is something in particular that troubles me. Please tell me, what happened to all my tears? I prayed and prayed that my husband should get well. I recited chapter after chapter of *Tehillim,* and shed countless tears. What happened to them?"

R' Aryeh replied softly, "After a hundred and twenty years, when your soul will return to Heaven, you will see how meaningful were all your prayers and tears. You will then see that Hashem Himself had gathered in and counted every teardrop that you shed and treasured it like a priceless gem. You will then perceive that when harsh decrees hovered over the Jewish people, it was your tears that washed away the evil and saved our people from danger. Even one sincere tear can be a source of salvation!"

When R' Aryeh had finished, the woman began to shed tears anew — tears of gratitude and hope. Some time later, she returned to the *tzaddik* and said, "*Rebbi,* remember what you told me? Please tell it to me again."

※　※　※

When praying on behalf of someone who is seriously ill, ר״ל, and whose condition appears to be worsening, there is a tendency to grow despondent and to be overcome by a feeling that one's prayers are for naught. The Steipler *Gaon* once enumerated five areas in which such *tefillos* achieve significant accomplishment:

a) The *tefillos* may very well diminish the patient's suffering to some degree.

b) The *tefillos* may extend the patient's life by a few months, weeks, days or even a few hours. Even a moment of life, said the Steipler, is of inestimable value and is more precious than gems.

c) Our Sages teach, "Even if a sharp-edged sword is resting upon a person's neck, he should not refrain from beseeching the Heavens for mercy" (*Berachos* 10a). There have been many instances where, through the kindness of Heaven, someone who was gravely ill experienced a full recovery.

d) Even if the prayers effect no change at all in the patient's condition, they still are a source of merit for him, since all those who prayed aroused Heavenly compassion through their prayers, which were uttered because of him. These merits will stand by him in the World to Come and may also protect his offspring in the future.

e) These prayers can bring salvation to other individuals and to the community as a whole. At the End of Days, when all will be revealed, we will learn how each *tefillah* uttered by each individual brought about great goodness and salvation (*Toldos Yaakov*, p. 118-119).

Profitable Partnership

זְבוּלֻן לְחוֹף יַמִּים יִשְׁכֹּן וְהוּא לְחוֹף אֳנִיֹּת וְיַרְכָתוֹ עַל צִידֹן.

Zevulun shall settle by seashores. He shall be at the ship's harbor, and his last border will reach Zidon (Bereishis 49:13).

T hough Zevulun was younger than Yissachar, he was blessed first. Yaakov gave precedence to Zevulun because he used his financial success to support Yissachar and make his Torah learning possible (*Midrash Tanchuma*).

To support the study of Torah is an inestimable source of merit. It is also an obligation. *Ramban* (citing *Talmud Yerushalmi*) states that the verse, "Accursed is one who will not uphold the words of this Torah, to perform them" (*Devarim* 27:26) places an obligation upon every Jew to support Torah study.

Fortunate is the man who views supporting Torah study as a privilege and utilizes his resources for this purpose.

❀ ❀ ❀

"You don't know anyone at Yeshivah Dvar Hashem?[1]"

Yosef Delman replied truthfully that he did not. He was in charge of out-of-town accounts at Achim Food Corporation and Yeshivah Dvar Hashem was an in-town account.

"Well," Mr. Rosen, president of the corporation, went on, "no matter. Dvar Hashem is as fine a yeshivah as they come and I want to help them out. I agreed that our corporation would run their journal campaign for their annual dinner. I myself am tied up right now with other commitments, so I'm appointing you Journal Chairman. It's really quite simple. Contact all your accounts and others with whom you deal, tell them about the yeshivah and ask them to place an ad in the journal."

Yosef took the assignment seriously and was quite successful. As he began his campaign, he thought to himself, "Hashem, You know that I am doing this *mitzvah* for Your sake. I don't know anyone at the yeshivah, and as such I don't stand to gain any honor or recognition for what I am doing. May this *mitzvah* stand by me and my family as a source of merit."

A few weeks later, Yosef received a phone call from one of his largest accounts, a food company in Plainview, Vermont. The company was going out of business and owed Achim tens of thousands of dollars. An honest man, the company owner offered Yosef the only payment he had available — tens of thousands of dollars in perishable stock.

---

1. Names of places and people have been changed.

Yosef hung up the phone and pondered the situation. He had to work quickly to get the stock and then sell it. But to whom could he sell it? It certainly made no sense to bring it to New York for distribution. Yosef took an early flight to Plainview and, upon landing, phoned Steve, a distributor with whom he had a long-standing relationship. They discussed the problem and Steve offered a solution. "There's an Orthodox Jew named Isaac who is a partner in a large food business in a neighboring state. Call him, mention my name and ask if there's any way that he can be of help."

The suggestion proved fruitful. Isaac graciously agreed to buy the entire stock from Yosef and even helped to transfer the goods to his own warehouse. It took until three o'clock in the morning for the transfer to be completed. Wearily, Yosef thanked Isaac for all that he had done for him.

"I'm not finished yet," Isaac replied. "You need a place to spend the night — whatever is left of it, that is. I'm sorry but it's impossible for me to put you up for the night. So I've arranged for you to sleep at the home of my partner and brother-in-law, David."

Isaac's partner was equally gracious. Yosef would have been content to sleep on a couch, but his host insisted on preparing a bed for him. In the morning, the two went to *Shacharis,* then had breakfast together, after which Yosef flew back home.

A few days later, while involved in his work as Journal Chairman, Yosef noticed a familiar name — Mr. David Wallach — whom Yeshivah Dvar Hashem was honoring, along with his wife, as Parents of the Year. The name seemed so familiar, yet Yosef could not place it. He decided to place a call to his new friend, Isaac. "Of course you know David Wallach," Isaac could not help but laugh. "He's my partner and brother-in-law — and you slept at his home not long ago! Yes, he and his wife are being honored as Parents of the Year."

A few weeks later, Yosef sat next to Isaac at the annual dinner of Yeshivah Dvar Hashem. Yosef could not help but marvel at the workings of Providence. He had undertaken to help a place of Torah study, and he had already tasted some of the fruits of his efforts. Hashem had saved him from a financial disaster by sending to his aid a family whose children studied at that yeshivah and who were intimately involved with that yeshivah's support.

פרשת שמות
Parashas Shemos

Sensitivities

וַיֹּאמֶר בִּי אֲדֹנָי שְׁלַח נָא בְּיַד תִּשְׁלָח.
*He [Moshe] replied: "Please, my L-rd,
send through whomever You will send!" (Bereishis 4:13).*

*"Through whomever you will send" — Through the
one whom You are accustomed to send as your
messenger [to the Jewish people], that is, Aharon
(Rashi).*

In Hashem's first revelation to Moshe, Moshe is told to
return to Egypt to become the leader of the Jewish people
and begin the process that would lead to redemption. For
seven days, Moshe contended that he was unsuited for this
calling. He began by stating that he was unworthy, and
concluded by asking that his older brother, Aharon, be granted
this calling in his stead.

The *Midrash* (*Yalkut Shimoni* 172) explains that Moshe was
concerned lest Aharon would feel hurt upon seeing that his
younger brother was returning to replace him as the prophet
and leader of the nation whom he had served faithfully all the
years that Moshe was away in Midian. Hashem assured Moshe
that, to the contrary, "He [Aharon] will see you and he will
rejoice in his heart" (v. 14).

That Moshe did have such concerns at such a time is
remarkable. As R' Chaim Shmulevitz (*Sichos Mussar*) notes,

Moshe was being asked to lead his nation to redemption after it had suffered for so long in bondage. Did the feelings of one individual really matter at such a time? Moshe felt that it did and, explained R' Chaim, Hashem would have approved of his concerns had they been valid. It is only because Hashem knew that Aharon would feel genuine joy in his heart that He reprimanded Moshe.

One of the forty-eight ways through which Torah is acquired (Avos 6:6) is נוֹשֵׂא בְעוֹל עִם חֲבֵרוֹ, sharing a friend's burden, while another is דִּקְדּוּק חֲבֵרִים, exactness with friends. Both of these qualities require the Torah student to be sensitive to the feelings of others, to seek to understand their feelings even when they are not expressed. Such was the way of Moshe and such has been the way of Torah scholars throughout the generations.

❀ ❀ ❀

In the last weeks of his life, R' Isser Zalman Meltzer decided to join a minyan vasikin[1] for Shacharis. He requested that a close talmid awaken him early the next morning to allow him ample time to join the minyan.

The talmid fulfilled his wish as requested. R' Isser Zalman arose immediately, but, to the student's surprise, he did not attend the early minyan. Instead, he went to the later minyan, where he had always prayed. At the conclusion of Shacharis, he explained, "At first, I thought that joining the minyan vasikin was a fine idea. However, upon further consideration, I realized that it would be a mistake for me to leave the minyan where I had prayed Shacharis for so many years. The other members of the minyan have come to expect my presence, and at the conclusion of Shacharis we always wish each other 'Good morning.' Were I to leave the minyan, my absence would certainly cause the others some degree of heartache."

---

1. A minyan vasikin [lit. devoted ones] recites Shemoneh Esrei at sunrise, the most preferred time. See Berachos 9b.

R' Shalom Schwadron of Jerusalem was once walking with his *rebbi,* R' Yitzchak Meir Ben Menachem, when the two met the aged widow of R' Reuven Trop walking with a young man who was probably her grandson. R' Ben Menachem greeted the two, and then inquired as to Rebbetzin Trop's state of health and matters relating to her family. Then, R' Ben Menachem turned to the young man who was the Rebbetzin's escort and inquired as to his personal situation. After they parted and continued on their respective ways, R' Ben Menachem remarked that he did not know the young man and asked if perhaps R' Schwadron knew his name. R' Schwadron did not know him, and commented with amazement that from the conversation he had just heard, he would have surmised that R' Ben Menachem knew the young man quite well! Common practice is to greet a stranger with a simple *"Shalom Aleichem"* when he is with someone whom one knows well.

R' Ben Menachem replied, "Yes, that is common practice, but I seek to emulate the ways of my father-in-law [R' Isser Zalman Meltzer]" (*B'Derech Eitz Chaim*).

※ ※ ※

The Manchester *Rosh Yeshivah,* R' Yehudah Zev Segal, often spent the summer recess at the resort city of Semmering, Austria. One summer, another Torah personality, R' Yitzchak Yaakov Weiss, came to Semmering, accompanied by his son and daughter-in-law. R' Weiss had served as Manchester's *Av Beis Din* before heading the rabbinical court of Jerusalem's *Eidah Chareidis;* he and R' Segal enjoyed a close relationship. Yet R' Segal declined an invitation to join R' Weiss for a Shabbos meal, explaining that this would cause R' Weiss' daughter-in-law discomfort and would probably prompt her to eat alone at a different table. He could not allow this to happen.

R' Segal was once attending a *sheva berachos* meal when his host received a phone call from a single woman who had been unsuccessful for many years in seeking her partner in marriage. The host asked if R' Segal would speak to the woman. He readily agreed, but asked to speak to her on an extension in another room out of concern that the woman's pain might be aggravated by the sounds of wedding music and singing.

❦ ❦ ❦

In 1980, the sixth *Knessiah Gedolah* (World Conference) of Agudath Israel was held in Jerusalem. The gathering was graced by the presence of many Torah luminaries from Israel and abroad, including the venerable R' Yaakov Kamenetsky.

At the conclusion of the *Knessiah,* R' Yaakov headed for Lod Airport in Tel Aviv, accompanied by others who were returning to America, as well as a delegation from Israel that was escorting him to the plane. As they walked through the airport terminal, a young boy ran in front of R' Yaakov, his camera poised to take a picture. Someone next to R' Yaakov felt that this was causing the sage discomfort and he motioned for the boy to go away. The boy's face fell as he lowered his camera and started to move away. But R' Yaakov stopped him. "That's all right," he said with the warm smile that was his trademark, "you can take a picture." R' Yaakov straightened his frock, smiled and said, "Shoot!" The excited youngster snapped the picture.

R' Moshe Sherer, President of Agudath Israel of America, was present at that incident. Years later, he was approached by a young man who said, "I don't know if you remember me, but I was the boy who snapped the picture of R' Yaakov in the airport on his way home from the *Knessiah Gedolah.* The warmth which R' Yaakov displayed towards me made such an impression on me that I decided to devote myself to the study of Torah."

❦ ❦ ❦

R' Yitzchak Hutner, late *Rosh Yeshivah* of Mesivta Rabbi Chaim Berlin, developed a close relationship with scores of his *talmidim. Talmidim* would call to share good news with the *Rosh Yeshivah* and he would rejoice like a father.

Once, a *talmid* called to report that his wife had just given birth to a baby girl. Uncharacteristically, R' Hutner responded, "Yes, call me back in fifteen minutes." When the *talmid* called back, R' Hutner said, "When you called, I had a visitor with me who is still childless after many years of marriage. Had I rejoiced over the birth of your child in his presence, it might have caused him pain over his own plight. Now, I am alone. *Mazel tov!*"

פרשת וארא
Parashas Va'eira

Two of a Kind

הוּא אַהֲרֹן וּמֹשֶׁה.
This is Aharon and Moshe (Shemos 6:26).
הוּא מֹשֶׁה וְאַהֲרֹן.
This is Moshe and Aharon (ibid. 6:27).

"This is Aharon and Moshe" — There are places where the Torah puts Aharon before Moshe and there are places where it puts Moshe before Aharon, to teach that they are of equal significance[1] (Rashi from Mechilta).

Aside from their other great qualities, Moshe and Aharon were both exceedingly humble; each saw the other as more worthy than himself.

---

1. They were equal regarding their characters and good deeds. However, with regard to prophecy Moshe was surely superior, as the Torah states (*Bamidbar* 12:7), ". . .Not so is My servant Moshe; in My entire House he is the trusted one" (*Leket Bahir* citing *Maskil L'David*).

On the eighth day of the dedication of the *Mishkan,* after Moshe had performed the service for seven days, Aharon was instructed to offer the sacrifices of the day as *Kohen Gadol* (High Priest). As *Rashi* relates, "Aharon was embarrassed and afraid to approach. Moshe said to him, 'Why are you embarrassed? This is what you were chosen for.[1]"

Later, after the sacrifices had been offered and the *Shechinah* (Divine Presence) had not yet descended, Aharon said, "I know that the Holy One, Blessed is He, has become angry with me, and because of me the *Shechinah* did not descend.[2]"

Rashi[3] also tells us that when the *Shechinah* did not descend after Moshe's seven days of service, the people became concerned. Moshe told them, "My brother Aharon is worthier and more important than I, for through his offerings and his service, the *Shechinah* will rest among you."

The genuine humility of Torah leaders in all generations causes them to hold their peers in the highest esteem while viewing themselves in a very different light.

❈ ❈ ❈

A year before the passing of the renowned *Rav* of Khal Adath Jeshurun, R' Shimon Schwab, his highly acclaimed *Maayan Beis Hasho'eivah* on the Torah was published. As publication neared, R' Schwab's son, R' Myer, suggested that R' Shlomo Zalman Auerbach of Jerusalem be asked to write a *haskamah* (approbation) for the *sefer.* R' Schwab's initial reaction was reflective of his genuine humility. *"R' Shlomo Zalman should give his haskamah to my divrei Torah?* How can I ask such a thing of him?" It took some effort on his son's part before R' Schwab could be convinced that it was proper to request the *haskamah.* R' Myer contacted R' Yehoshua Y. Neuwirth, author of *Shemiras Shabbos K'Hilchasah* and a confidant of R' Shlomo

---

1. *Rashi* to *Vayikra* 9:7, citing *Toras Kohanim.*
2. *Rashi* to *Vayikra* 9:23. After Moshe and Aharon prayed for Heavenly mercy, the *Shechinah* descended.
3. ibid.

Zalman. Accompanying the request was a sampling of insights contained in R' Schwab's work. A short time later, word was received that R' Shlomo Zalman would be sending his letter of approbation.

However, not long after that, a fax was received from R' Neuwirth, stating that R' Shlomo Zalman had reconsidered the matter and had decided that the Torah thoughts of someone of R' Schwab's stature were not in need of his *haskamah*. In fact, said R' Shlomo Zalman, "it would be a *bizayon* (disgrace)" for a work of such renown to bear the approbation of someone such as himself!

R' Myer Schwab did not inform his father of this development. Instead, he wrote to R' Neuwirth, telling him of how happy his father had been upon hearing that he would be receiving R' Shlomo Zalman's *haskamah*. His father would surely be pained to hear that R' Shlomo Zalman had reconsidered, and in his humility would probably suspect that R' Shlomo Zalman had found fault with some of his writings and had deemed them unworthy of approbation. "Where can I flee from my father's pain?"[1] R' Myer concluded.

A beautiful *haskamah* was soon forthcoming.

❧ ❧ ❧

In his later years, R' Moshe Neuschloss, venerable *Rav* of New Square, suffered from a heart condition and was under the care of a renowned New York cardiologist. As a rule, R' Neuschloss arrived for appointments punctually or early; he was rarely late. On one particular afternoon, he arrived shortly past noon for an appointment that was scheduled for one o'clock. After presenting himself to the secretary, he seated himself in the waiting room, withdrew a *sefer* which he carried on his person and began to learn.

A few minutes later, R' Moshe Feinstein (henceforth referred to here as 'R' Moshe' as he was universally known) entered the doctor's office for his appointment. The two luminaries, who

---

1. Borrowed from *Rashi* to *Bereishis* 37:30.

enjoyed a close relationship and often conferred on halachic issues, greeted each other warmly. Soon after, the receptionist announced that R' Moshe should come to the examination room, explaining that he had arrived on time for his appointment, which was scheduled for twelve-thirty, one half-hour ahead of R' Neuschloss' scheduled appointment.

R' Moshe was visibly distressed. He walked over to R' Neuschloss and said, "The *Rav* should go first; *k'vod haTorah* (honor for the Torah) demands that he go first. And after all, the *Rav* was waiting here ahead of me." R' Neuschloss smiled broadly. *"K'vod haTorah?"* he responded. *"K'vod haTorah* demands that the *Rosh Yeshivah* be first! And as the secretary said, the *Rosh Yeshivah's* appointment is ahead of mine." Very reluctantly, R' Moshe made his way to the examination room. When he emerged some time later, he apologized to R' Neuschloss, who smiled and replied sincerely that, of course, no apologies were necessary.

Late that night, R' Neuschloss received a phone call from R' Moshe. "As I was preparing to retire for the night," he said, "I contemplated what happened today. I feel that I erred in allowing myself to go ahead of the *Rav.* I ask *mechilah* (forgiveness) of him . . ."

פרשת בא
Parashas Bo

Don't Delay

וּשְׁמַרְתֶּם אֶת הַמַּצּוֹת.
You shall guard the matzos (Shemos 12:17).

R' Yoshiya says: "Do not read the word [only] as
הַמַּצּוֹת, the matzos, but rather [also as] הַמִּצְוֹת, the
mitzvos. Just as people do not allow the matzos to
become chametz [leavened], so should they not allow
the mitzvos to become 'chametz' [i.e. to be left
unattended]. Rather, if a mitzvah comes your way, do
it immediately" (Rashi from Mechilta).

R' Yosef Chaim Sonnenfeld, the legendary *tzaddik* who
served as *Rav* of Jerusalem in the early part of this
century, never tarried when a *mitzvah* came his way, even in his
later years.

Once, an acquaintance of his required the assistance of R'
Mordechai Leib Rubin, who served as the city's *av beis din* (chief
judge). The man requested that R' Yosef Chaim speak to R'
Mordechai Leib on his behalf.

That night, a heavy snow blanketed Jerusalem. In the
morning, R' Yosef Chaim donned his overcoat and slowly
trudged his way through the snow to the home of R' Mordechai
Leib. On the way, he passed the home of his acquaintance,
who happened to be looking out the window at the snow-
covered street. The man was shocked to see that an elderly man

resembling R' Yosef Chaim had ventured outside in such treacherous conditions! When the man realized that indeed it *was* R' Yosef Chaim, he rushed outside, tearfully begged forgiveness and insisted that he had never intended that the *Rav* strain himself in such a manner. R' Yosef Chaim did not understand. "Do you think that just because a Jew has a white beard he is forbidden to exert himself to perform a *mitzvah*? 'If a *mitzvah* comes your way do it immediately' — even in snow!"

Once, during a torrential downpour, a young woman stood under an awning for protection clutching her child. It was not long before a horse-drawn carriage came to an abrupt halt. The sole passenger was R' Yosef Chaim, then eighty years of age, who leaped out, took a seat beside the driver, and motioned for the young mother to take his seat inside the carriage. The woman was aghast at the thought of the aged *Rav* becoming drenched on her account, and she was reluctant to accept his offer. She finally yielded when R' Yosef Chaim told her that even were she to refuse to come along, he would not return to his seat inside the carriage, for it had already been dedicated by him for an act of kindness.

פרשת בשלח
Parashas Beshalach

The Sweetest Waters

וַיִּצְעַק אֶל ה' וַיּוֹרֵהוּ ה' עֵץ וַיַּשְׁלֵךְ אֶל הַמַּיִם וַיִּמְתְּקוּ הַמָּיִם.

He cried out to Hashem and Hashem showed him a tree; he threw it into the water and the water became sweet (Shemos 15:25).

The Torah relates that after their miraculous crossing of the Sea of Reeds, the Jews went three days without water. When they finally reached water, they found it too bitter to drink and they complained before Moshe, who cried out in prayer to Hashem. Hashem showed Moshe a certain tree; Moshe took a branch of that tree, threw it into the water and the water became sweet.

Our Sages (*Mechilta*) relate that the tree which Hashem showed Moshe was bitter like the water. That it turned the water sweet was a miracle within a miracle.

The Sages further teach that when the Torah states that the Jews went three days without water it means that they went three days with Torah, which is likened to water. *Kli Yakar* explains that, of course, the literal meaning of the verse is true as well. The Jews *did* go three days without actual water, but this happened *because* their dedication to Torah had become weakened. The fact that the bitter stick turned the water sweet was a lesson to them regarding Torah and *mitzvos*. Living the life of a Torah Jew may be difficult at first, but ultimately it becomes sweet. The more one immerses himself in Torah study, the more one dedicates himself to serving Hashem, the more pleasurable it becomes. Eventually, it becomes so sweet that nothing in the world can compare to it.

One person who truly tasted such sweetness was "R' Beirish the Butcher," whose home was in Jerusalem's Old City during the first half of this century.

※ ※ ※

Near the *Churvah Shul* in the Old City stood a small butcher shop, whose proprietor was a short man with a red, flowing beard and long *peyos.* Over his black *caftan* (frock) R' Beirish wore a white apron as he chopped meat and, at the same time, recited chapters of Mishnah from memory. After the day's meat had been salted, deveined, chopped, weighed and priced, R' Beirish would open a *gemara* and learn. When a customer came in, R' Beirish rarely spoke. Each piece of meat had a tag on it with its type of cut and price, so there was usually no reason for him to interrupt his learning.

When women would come to the store, R' Beirish never gazed directly at them. Once, as he was salting a piece of meat, R' Beirish noticed something about the piece that might have rendered it unkosher. He placed it on the side with the intention of showing it to a *rav* later in the day. Then, a woman customer entered his store and purchased some meat. After she had left, R' Beirish realized that she had taken the questionable piece — but R' Beirish had not looked at her and had no idea who she was!

Without wasting a moment, he closed the store, hurried to *shul* and began to recite *Tehillim* as he beseeched Hashem that he should not be the cause of a Jew inadvertently eating something unkosher. Soon after he returned to his store, the woman appeared to buy more meat. A cat had entered her home, sprung onto her kitchen table and scampered off with the meat that she had bought . . .

On a visit to *Eretz Yisrael,* Rabbi Avraham Mordechai Alter of Ger, author of *Imrei Emes,* passed R' Beirish's store on his way from the *Kosel Maaravi* (Western Wall). The *Imrei Emes* stood in the doorway and watched for a few moments as R' Beirish, unaware that he was being observed, sat immersed in his learning. As he continued on his way, the *Imrei Emes* remarked, "It was worth the entire trip just to see this *Yid* (Jew)."

Where material needs were concerned, he was satisfied with a bare minimum. His meal would often consist of some bread with a piece of onion. For thirty years he wore the same slippers, and for fifty years he *davened* from the same *siddur.* Whatever money he had, he lent to the needy. Very often, the loans were not claimed, for R' Beirish knew that the borrower had no money.

Once, in the middle of the night, R' Beirish's daughter awoke to a strange sight. Her father had awakened and had lit a lantern. He made his way to a closet and withdrew one of his ledgers. R' Beirish ripped out a certain page, disposed of it and started back toward his bed. "What's wrong?" his daughter asked. R' Beirish explained:

"I dreamt that someone whom I know well passed on to the Next World. The Heavenly Tribunal ruled that the man had lived a righteous life and was worthy of a place in *Gan Eden,* save for one fact — he had left this world not having repaid the loan which I had extended to him.

"As soon as I awakened, I resolved with a full heart to cancel the loan. So that no trace of the loan remain, I ripped the page on which it was recorded out of my ledger and discarded it."

In the morning, the news spread that the borrower had died during the night.

As a young man, R' Beirish purchased a burial plot for himself on *Har HaZeisim* (Mount of Olives). Each month on *erev Rosh Chodesh,* a day that is auspicious for repentance and soul-searching, he would stand by the plot and tearfully recite the entire Book of *Tehillim.* When the Jordanians took control of *Har HaZeisim* in 1948, R' Beirish purchased a plot on *Har HaMenuchos,* and there he was buried when he departed this world at age seventy-seven on 19 Shevat, 5714 (1954) (from *Sipurim Yerushalmiyim,* vol. II).

For the Community

וִידֵי מֹשֶׁה כְּבֵדִים וַיִּקְחוּ אֶבֶן וַיָּשִׂימוּ תַחְתָּיו וַיֵּשֶׁב עָלֶיהָ.

Moshe's hands grew heavy, so they took a stone and put it under him and he sat on it (Shemos 17:12).

At a time when the community is suffering, a man should not say, "I will go to my house and eat and drink and peace be upon you, my soul . . ." Rather, a person should suffer along with the community, for we find regarding Moshe, our teacher, that he suffered along with the community [when he sat upon a stone as the nation battled Amalek] (Taanis 11a).

T he face of the Eastern European landscape was altered forever by the Communist rise to power in 1917. Russia, which had been host to scores of thriving Torah communities, became a virtual prison where the practice of Judaism was a crime.

Not for a moment did the two leaders of Lithuanian Jewry, the Chofetz Chaim and R' Chaim Ozer Grodzensky, forget their brethren behind the Iron Curtain. As the persecutions increased, so did their pain. Incredibly, in the last years of his life, the Chofetz Chaim expressed regret at having left Russia to return to his home in Radin, Poland, following the First World War. "I should have remained," he lamented. Had he remained, he would have worked selflessly to preserve Torah life in the Soviet Union; perhaps his efforts would have infused Russian Jewry with a new spirit. "A Jew has to be ready to give his life for Judaism," he reflected. "What would the Communists have done to me — shot me to death? . . . hung me from the gallows? They could only have punished my body and the body is of no importance."

With the rise of Joseph Stalin to undisputed power in Russia in 1928, the sufferings of almost three million Jews increased manifold. The following summer, the Chofetz Chaim was visited by a man who had returned from Russia a few days earlier. The man gave an eyewitness account of the dreadful plight of Soviet Jewry; he told of the brutal decrees that were making life an escalating horror for Jews.

The report devastated the Chofetz Chaim, who was then ninety years of age, and he wasted no time in acting; soon, he was preparing to travel to Vilna to discuss the matter with R' Chaim Ozer.

At that time, the Chofetz Chaim was being visited by his disciple, the *gaon* R' Elchanan Wasserman.[1] Knowing well the Chofetz Chaim's precarious state of health, R' Elchanan prevailed upon his *rebbi* to allow him to travel to Vilna as his emissary. In Vilna, R' Elchanan asked R' Chaim Ozer to travel back with him to the Chofetz Chaim to discuss the situation, as the matter was distressing the Chofetz Chaim to the point that R' Elchanan feared for his life.

It was rare for R' Chaim Ozer to travel because of his frail health and chronic ailments. He caught a cold very easily and even a cold sapped his strength. But when he heard that the situation in Russia was endangering the Chofetz Chaim's health, he left at once. As a result of their meeting, a worldwide fast for Russian Jewry was held on the first day of *Selichos* of that year, and many communities adopted the custom of reciting *Tehillim* on behalf of Russian Jewry every year on the eve of Yom Kippur following *Kol Nidrei*.

---

1. R' Elchanan and R' Chaim Ozer were brothers-in-law.

פרשת יתרו
Parashas Yisro

Honoring Parents

כַּבֵּד אֶת אָבִיךָ וְאֶת אִמֶּךָ
Honor your father and your mother (Shemos 20:12).

R' Shmuel Zvi Kowalsky of Bnei Brak was a harmonious blend of the world of *Chassidus* and the Lithuanian Torah world. He was a *gaon* and *tzaddik* of rare distinction and when he left this world on 23 Sivan, 5752 (1992) at age fifty-seven, his loss was mourned by thousands from various backgrounds and all walks of life.

As a young Torah student, he drew close to R' Avraham Yeshayahu Karelitz, the Chazon Ish. When studying at the Ponovezh Yeshivah, young Shmuel Zvi would make his way to the Chazon Ish's modest home where the two studied privately on a regular basis. The Chazon Ish was extremely fond of his young study partner and guided him not only in Torah learning, but in all areas of spiritual development.

Once, as Shmuel Zvi prepared to travel home for *yom tov,* the Chazon Ish told him, "A Jew is required to begin reviewing the laws of a given *yom tov* thirty days before the *yom tov.* [1] A Torah student who is preparing to return home for *bein*

---
1. *Pesachim* 6a.

haz'manim (intercession) must review the laws of *kibud av v'em* (honoring father and mother) in *Shulchan Aruch.*"

Shmuel Zvi was an ideal student; his performance of this *mitzvah* remains a model to strive to emulate.

His family were Sochatchover *chassidim.* R' Kowalsky's father, who managed a store until his retirement, would travel from Bnei Brak to Jerusalem to participate in the *seudas mitzvah* (*mitzvah* banquet) marking the *yahrtzeit* of the Sochatchover *Rebbe.* In advent of the occasion, R' Kowalsky would phone someone in Jerusalem to prepare a thermos of a particular type of tea which his father enjoyed drinking.

R' Kowalsky delivered a *gemara shiur* (lecture) each morning, which his father, who was then well on in years, attended. Whenever his father would enter while the *shiur* was in progress, R' Kowalsky would rise to his full height, place his own *gemara* before his father and take another volume for himself. When he would respond to a question posed by his father, he spoke as a servant speaking before a king.

After his father passed away, R' Kowalsky visited his mother each morning after delivering his *shiur.* On Shabbos, when his mother joined his family for meals, she sat next to him and was always served first.

His appreciation of this *mitzvah* is perhaps best illustrated by the following story:

A week before R' Kowalsky's passing, he attended the wedding of a son of a primary benefactor of the *kollel* which he headed. Another son of the benefactor, who was married and living in America, came to join his family at his brother's wedding. During the wedding meal, this man suffered chest pains. Afraid to alarm his parents, he asked someone to summon paramedics to examine him in a side room. A doctor was brought in, an electrocardiogram was performed, and after reading the results, the doctor advised the man to go directly to a hospital.

The stricken man was in a quandary. He was afraid to disobey doctor's orders, but he was greatly concerned that his parents would notice his absence and would have to be told what had occurred. Aside from the worry and distress they would endure, the joy which they were now experiencing at their child's wedding would be marred.

As those involved were debating what to do, R' Kowalsky, who was then gravely ill, entered the wedding hall. He was apprised of the situation and after pondering the matter in silence, he told the patient, "Remain here at the wedding. You can relax; all will be well. I take full responsibility for your health."

R' Kowalsky returned home and told his family, "I have assumed a great responsibility!" He then distributed volumes of *Tehillim* to his family, divided the entire Book among them, and they all began to pray. It was 3:00 A.M. when they finished. R' Kowalsky told his family, "This young man came from America only for the sake of his parents, to honor them and bring them joy by participating in his brother's wedding. This *mitzvah* is sufficient to shield him so that he will live long. It cannot be that he will suffer harm for having remained at the wedding to save his parents from distress."

The young man returned to America a few days later and visited a heart specialist. After a thorough examination and a series of tests, the doctor concluded that the man was in excellent health (*Ana Avda*).

---

1. *Pesachim* 6a.

פרשת משפטים
Parashas Mishpatim

Nothing But the Truth

מִדְּבַר שֶׁקֶר תִּרְחָק.

Distance yourself from falsehood (Shemos 23:7).

So much does Hashem abhor falsehood, that we are commanded to stay far away from even an appearance of a lie (R' Simchah Bunim of P'shis'cha).

Each year on the *yahrtzeit* of the Chazon Ish, his brother-in-law R' Yaakov Yisrael Kanievsky, renowned as the Steipler *Gaon*, [1] would deliver a *shiur* at Bnei Brak's *Kollel Chazon Ish.*

A few days after delivering the *shiur* in the year 5745 (1984),[2] the Steipler was visited by R' Nosson Einfeld of *Kollel Chazon Ish.* The Steipler told R' Einfeld:

"I am enduring pain and distress. In the course of the *shiur,* I cited the words of *Birkei Yosef* regarding the laws of *tefillin.* I had come across this comment of *Birkei Yosef* in R' Akiva Eiger's glosses to *Rambam's* laws of the Yom Kippur service. When delivering the *shiur,* I forgot to mention this. Thus, I have

---

1. The Steipler was married to the Chazon Ish's sister.
2. The Steipler passed away two years later at age eighty-four.

been guilty of *geneivas daas* (deceit), for those who attended the *shiur* now think that I am fluent in the writings of *Birkei Yosef* . . .

"What can I do? I am an old man and I forgot to mention it . . ." (*Sichos Chaim*).

❧ ❧ ❧

R' Yeshayah Zev Winograd was a *Rosh Yeshivah* at Yeshivas Toras Chaim in Jerusalem before the First World War[1] and was renowned for his unremitting diligence in study. In the year 1912, with the yeshivah in dire financial straits, he traveled to Eastern Europe on a fund-raising mission.

R' Yeshayah's travels brought him to the city of Brisk where the legendary Torah genius, R' Chaim Soloveitchik, then served as *Rav*.

One day, word spread that R' Chaim would be delivering a *shiur* in his home. R' Yeshayah wasted no time in making his way there and found the *Rav's* small dining room filled beyond capacity with scholars, many of them outstanding in their Torah knowledge. R' Yeshayah found himself a spot in the last row, near the door.

As the *shiur* progressed, R' Chaim expounded upon an original thought related to the topic at hand. As R' Yeshayah listened, it dawned upon him that this idea might be refuted from a passage in *Masechta Chullin* which he had studied that very morning! At first he was afraid to speak up, but finally he said in a barely audible voice, "Perhaps this can be refuted from . . ."

Some in the room did not hide their annoyance at the impudence of this stranger who dared to interrupt the *Rav*. But R' Yeshayah's words had reached the ears of R' Chaim who now sat silently pondering them. He said, "You say, 'Perhaps this can be refuted . . .' It is not 'perhaps.' What I have said is *definitely* refuted from the passage which you have cited." With

1. He later served as a *Rosh Yeshivah* at Yeshivah Eitz Chaim and Yeshivah Shaarei Ziv.

those words, R' Chaim closed his *gemara* and brought the *shiur* to an abrupt end.[1]

Before leaving Brisk, R' Yeshayah paid a personal visit to R' Chaim and introduced himself as a teacher of Torah from Jerusalem. After receiving R' Chaim's blessing for a safe journey home, he asked for advice on how to impart the teachings of Torah to his *talmidim.* R' Chaim had this to say:

"A teacher of Torah must know that if he worked an entire night preparing a *shiur,* and he felt assured that he had prepared something good, and during the course of the *shiur* a *talmid* — even the weakest *talmid* of all — raised a question, and the *rebbi* knows that, with his vast command of knowledge, he can easily respond to the question in a way that will satisfy the *talmidim,* but in his heart he knows that the question is irrefutable and that, in fact, it disproves the very thesis upon which his *shiur* is based, then he must state clearly, 'You have asked correctly, what I have said is wrong and today, I have nothing more to say.' " (*Peninei Rabbeinu HaGriz*).

❧ ❧ ❧

Yitzchak Dellman,[2] a student at Beth Medrash Govoha in Lakewood, was enjoying the pleasant drive on his way to spend Shabbos with his parents. Suddenly, a siren sounded and lights flashed behind him. He quickly pulled over onto the highway's shoulder. Some ten minutes later, he held in his hand a summons for speeding. He couldn't be positive that he had not been going a couple of miles above the speed limit, but he knew that it was no more than that. A hearing date was set.

On the day of the hearing, Yitzchak was delayed and realized that he would be late. He phoned his father, who lived not far from the Motor Vehicles offices, and his father went down to apologize for his son and explain that his delay was unavoi-

---

1. R' Yeshayah later reported that until that day, he had been largely unsuccessful in his fund-raising in Brisk. However, after the episode at R' Chaim's home became known, people held him in high esteem and he accomplished his purpose in coming there.
2. Not his real name.

dable. This must have impressed those present, for when Yitzchak arrived, the police officer who had issued the summons motioned for him to step outside the hearing room so that they could speak privately.

"Listen," the officer said, "I want you to get off easy, so what you should do is plea-bargain. That means, admit to having committed an offense, but not one as bad as speeding. Say that you weren't speeding but that you were driving without wearing a seat belt. The fine will be a lot less and there won't be any points on your license."

Yitzchak's hearing was the last of the day. No one was in the room, save for himself, his father, the judge and the officer. The judge and the officer must have discussed the case beforehand, for the judge began the proceedings by telling Yitzchak, "Listen, we want to let you off easy. Just plea-bargain and say that you weren't wearing a seat belt."

"But I *was* wearing a seat belt," Yitzchak replied.

The judge was annoyed by the young man's apparent naiveté. "Of course you were wearing one, but just say for the record that you weren't. That way we can give you a lighter fine."

"But it's a lie. I can't lie."

"We're not asking you to swear!" The judge was clearly upset — he was trying to be helpful and this young fellow was being stubborn. "Just affirm that you were driving without a seat belt on!"

"As I said before, sir, I cannot lie."

Yitzchak was fined for speeding. Before leaving, his father approached the judge privately and asked, "Is this American justice, that a judge tells the defendant how to lie so that he can get away with it?"

The judge did not respond.

※　※　※

R' Yaakov Kamenetsky was known for his absolute adherence to truth under all conditions. He lived to age ninety-five. When someone asked him in what merit he lived so long, he replied, "I never said a lie."

When R' Yaakov visited a yeshivah, he noticed that on the kindergarten doorpost, the *mezuzah* was affixed low enough so that the young children could reach it without assistance. *Halachah*[1] requires that the *mezuzah* be affixed at the beginning of the doorpost's upper third.

Said R' Yaakov, "It is good to teach children to kiss the *mezuzah*, but the correct way to do it is to place the *mezuzah* in its proper place and have them stand on a stool to kiss it. Otherwise, they will grow up thinking that a *mezuzah* can be placed anywhere on the post. That would be teaching the children a falsehood."

---

1. See *Shulchan Aruch, Yoreh Deah* 289:2.

פרשת תרומה
Parashas Terumah

A Miniature Sanctuary

וְעָשׂוּ לִי מִקְדָּשׁ וְשָׁכַנְתִּי בְּתוֹכָם.

Make for Me a sanctuary so that I may dwell among them
(Shemos 25:8).

Rabbi Akiva taught (*Sotah* 17a) that when a husband and wife live their lives in accordance with Torah and where peace and harmony reign, they bring the *Shechinah* into their midst. This is actually alluded to in the words אִישׁ, *man,* and אִשָּׁה, *woman.* Both words have the identical letters, save for the letters י in אִישׁ and ה in אִשָּׁה which together form the Name of Hashem (*Rashi* ad loc.). Thus do the Sages refer to the Jewish home as a *mikdash me'at,* a miniature sanctuary.[1]

A young man who walked R' Shlomo Zalman Auerbach home one afternoon watched as the venerable *gaon* groomed himself as he prepared to walk up the steps to his apartment. The young man asked R' Shlomo Zalman if he was preparing to

---

1. R' Moshe Wolfson notes that the verse וַיְהִי בְּיוֹם כַּלּוֹת מֹשֶׁה לְהָקִים אֶת הַמִּשְׁכָּן, *It was on the day that Moshe finished erecting the Mishkan . . .* (*Bamidbar* 7:1) has the same *gematria* (numerical equivalent — 1891) as וַיִּבֶן ה' אֱלֹקִים אֶת הַצֵּלָע, אֲשֶׁר לָקַח מִן הָאָדָם לְאִשָּׁה, *And Hashem fashioned the side that He had taken from the man into a woman* (*Bereishis* 2:22), which tells of the fashioning of Eve from the side of Adam.

greet a distinguished visitor who had already arrived at his home. "Actually," he replied, "I am preparing to greet the *Shechinah,* for the *Shechinah* is present whenever a husband and wife live together in peace and harmony."

At the funeral of *Rebbetzin* Chaya Rivka Auerbach on 12 Teves, 5744 (1974), R' Shlomo Zalman revealed the "secret" of the special relationship that he and his wife had enjoyed. It was then that he uttered this astounding statement: "Though it is customary to ask forgiveness of the deceased, I will not do so. My wife and I lived together according to the dictates of *Shulchan Aruch* (Code of Jewish Law). We never offended each other or hurt each other in any way. There is no reason for me to ask forgiveness."

They lived by the *Shulchan Aruch* in every situation. Once, a sister of R' Shlomo Zalman came to him to inquire about a prospective *shidduch* (marriage match). She waited until all visitors had left and then, with no one in the room but R' Shlomo Zalman, his wife and herself, the sister mentioned the boy's name and asked if he would be a suitable mate for her daughter. R' Shlomo Zalman nodded in apparent approval.

In the same neighborhood lived another sister of R' Shlomo Zalman, who had been widowed many years before. R' Shlomo Zalman asked his visiting sister, "Surely you will not return home without visiting our sister?"[2] She replied that, of course, she would call on their sibling. She did, and how surprised she was to find her brother waiting outside for her when she left her sister's home.

"About that boy of whom you inquired before . . . No, you should not pursue the *shidduch;* it is not an appropriate match for your daughter. My words convey a negative impression of the boy and to have uttered them in the presence of my wife — for whom the matter is not relevant — would have been a transgression of the laws of *shemiras halashon* (guarding one's tongue)."

---

2. R' Shlomo Zalman made a point of stopping at his sister's home each morning after *Shacharis.*

פרשת תצוה
Parashas Tetzaveh

Kindness for All

וְנָשָׂא אַהֲרֹן אֶת שְׁמוֹת בְּנֵי יִשְׂרָאֵל בְּחֹשֶׁן הַמִּשְׁפָּט עַל לִבּוֹ בְּבֹאוֹ אֶל
הַקֹּדֶשׁ לְזִכָּרֹן לִפְנֵי ה' תָּמִיד.

Aharon shall bear the names of the sons of Israel on the Breastplate of Judgment when he enters the Sanctuary, as a constant remembrance before Hashem (Shemos 28:29).

In the daily prayers, as well as at other times, we invoke the merit of our forefathers, Avraham, Yitzchak and Yaakov. The *Choshen,* Breastplate, however, bore the names of the Twelve Tribes, the sons of Yaakov.[1]

R' Levi Yitzchak of Berditchev (*Kedushas Levi*) comments that some may have mistakenly thought that Aharon's being chosen as *Kohen Gadol* indicated that *he* had earned Hashem's love and could therefore serve Him, while the Jewish people as a whole had been rejected,[2] and thus had to rely on Aharon as their representative. Hashem therefore decreed that Aharon's Breastplate bear the names of the Tribes, indicating His unconditional love for all the Jewish people.

---

1. The *Choshen* also bore the names of Avraham, Yitzchak and Yaakov (see *Yoma* 73b).
2. Because of the Sin of the Golden Calf.

It was fitting that Aharon should bear this sign of love upon his heart, for it is of him that Hillel the Elder said: "Be among the disciples of Aharon. . .loving people and bringing them closer to Torah" (Avos 1:12). Aharon showed kindness to everyone. If someone did not know how to pray or recite Shema, Aharon would teach him. If a person had difficulty understanding Torah, Aharon would study with him (Tana D'vei Eliyahu ch. 13). In showing love and kindness to all, Aharon emulated the way of his Creator. This quality was surely a contributing factor in his being chosen as Kohen Gadol. [1]

※   ※   ※

One of the forty-eight qualities through which Torah is acquired is אוֹהֵב אֶת הַבְּרִיוֹת, loving [His] creatures (Avos 6:6). One of the great Torah personalities of recent generations who personified this quality was the Kapishnitzer Rebbe, R' Avraham Yehoshua Heschel.

He was recognized as one of the great Torah leaders of his day. When he passed away in the summer of 5727 (1967), he was mourned by Jews of all shades and stripes. He was involved in community matters both in America and in Eretz Yisrael; he was a leader in rescue work during the Second World War and a founding member of Chinuch Atzmai, the government-recognized independent network of Torah schools in Israel. Neither communal leadership nor ill health ever prevented the Rebbe from helping any individual who came his way. He was, in the words of R' Aharon Kotler, the "gadol hador in chesed (giant of the generation in benevolence)."[2]

In the 1950's, a heart condition forced the Rebbe to spend a

---

1. The Midrash states that "the heart that was glad about his brother's greatness will wear the Urim V'Tumim [i.e. the Breastplate which contained the Ineffable Name of God] (Shemos Rabbah 3:17). This refers to Aharon's gladness over the fact that his younger brother Moshe had been chosen as prophet and redeemer of his people (see chapter on Parashas Shemos).
2. See chapter on Parashas Bamidbar for more about the relationship between the Kapishnitzer Rebbe and R' Aharon Kotler.

few weeks at a hotel in Sharon Springs, New York, known for its natural hot springs. One of the hotel waiters, Ari,[1] was a yeshivah student who was working during the summer recess to earn some badly needed pocket money. The *Rebbe* befriended Ari and would spend time conversing with him. He learned that Ari's father had died and that the financial situation at home had forced him to work during his vacation.

The *Rebbe* ate only food that was prepared for him by his family. On weekdays he ate in his room, and on Shabbos he would eat in the hotel dining room, where he was joined by some of his *chassidim.* On the first Friday night of his stay, the *Rebbe* and his entourage were served by Ari, who had already eaten a quick meal and had finished serving his other tables. Following *Kiddush* and the partaking of some *challah,* the meal began with the traditional first course of *gefilte* fish. Ari brought out a large tray with many servings of fish, placed it on the table near the *Rebbe* and was about to begin serving, when the *Rebbe* stopped him. "*Gut Shabbos,* Ari. No, please don't serve yet. Come, sit down next to me." Ari, somewhat uncomfortable, walked around the table and sat down in the chair next to the *Rebbe.* The *Rebbe* then insisted that Ari partake of some food, making him feel that he was more a friend than a hired worker. Only then did he allow the boy to begin serving.

On weekdays, Ari served the *Rebbe* his private meals. Each time that he did, the *Rebbe* thanked him profusely, blessed him warmly and never failed to mention that he held Ari in high esteem.

At the summer's end, as the *Rebbe* prepared to leave for home, he had some "business" to settle with Ari. He carefully calculated how many days the boy had served him and how many guests had joined him for his meals each day, and then presented the boy with an unusually generous tip for his services. Ari was thrilled and attempted to express his appreciation. "So, Ari," the *Rebbe* responded, "you are happy with what I have given you? Good, if you are happy then I shall

---

1. Not his real name.

give you some more!" And he handed the stunned boy a few more dollars.

He then asked Ari when he would be leaving for home and when he would be returning to yeshivah. Ari replied that he was to work for one more week and return home for a two-day break before the beginning of the new *z'man* (semester). The *Rebbe* was not happy with this arrangement. "You are allowing yourself only two days to rest after working hard these past few weeks? One has to be refreshed when beginning a new *z'man*. You must leave here earlier. In fact, I think that you should leave today."

Ari replied that he really had no choice. He had been hired with the understanding that he would work until Labor Day, when he was scheduled to leave. "If your concern is that the hotel owner will consider your leaving today as if you had broken your agreement with him, then you need not worry. I will speak to him about this matter." The *Rebbe* wasted no time in doing this; the owner was very understanding and readily agreed to allow Ari to leave. Ari was thrilled beyond words.

When Ari had come to the hotel, the bus trip from his home in Pennsylvania to Sharon Springs had taken fourteen hours at considerable expense. The *Rebbe* shortened the time of Ari's trip home by half when he invited him to ride in his hired car from the hotel to the train station, from where they would both board a train for Penn Station in New York. The *Rebbe* insisted on paying Ari's train fare, leaving the boy with only the expense of the train ride home from New York.

On the train, Ari sat with the *Rebbe's* grandson, while the *Rebbe* sat alone a few rows away. As they neared their destination, the *Rebbe* motioned that he wished to speak with Ari. "Ari, what sort of gift are you bringing home for your mother?" The question took the boy by surprise; he had not realized that a gift was in order. However, the *Rebbe,* with his exceptional wisdom, boundless *ahavas Yisrael* (love of his fellow Jew) and concern for every individual, had considered the feelings of a lonely widow whom he had never met, and he understood what a gift from her son woulod mean to her.

He explained to Ari how meaningful a gift would be and added, "A nice gift can be expensive, but I have an idea. A *chassid* of mine owns a jewelry store on the East Side. I will write him a note asking that he give you something nice for a good price."

From Penn Station, Ari took the subway to the store, whose owner treated him with utmost courtesy and sold him a beautiful silver pin for a relatively inexpensive price. Ari headed for home with his purchase, and with the fond memories of his days with the Kapishnitzer *Rebbe,* a Jew of rare distinction.

פרשת כי תשא
Parashas Ki Sisa

From Generation to Generation

רְאֵה קָרָאתִי בְשֵׁם, בְּצַלְאֵל בֶּן אוּרִי בֶן חוּר לְמַטֵּה יְהוּדָה

See, I have called by name: Betzalel son of Uri, son of Chur, of the tribe of Yehudah (Shemos 31:2).

Daas Zekeinim[1] relates:

When the Holy One, Blessed is He, told Moshe, "and you shall make . . ." regarding the construction of the *Mishkan,* Moshe thought that he himself would construct everything. Said the Holy One to him, "It will not be as you imagine; rather, the grandson of the *tzaddik* Chur, who was killed because of the Sin of the Golden Calf, will come and construct it, for the *Mishkan* is an atonement for that sin . . ."

As *Rashi*[2] relates, Chur, the son of Miriam, rebuked those who were involved with the Golden Calf. The people responded by murdering Chur. For his self-sacrifice, Chur merited that his grandson be granted the awesome privilege of constructing the *Mishkan,* in which Hashem would rest His Presence.

---

1. *Shemos* 35:30.
2. ibid. 32:5.

A good deed or word is never forgotten Above, although years, even generations, can pass before the reward is realized.[1]

❀ ❀ ❀

Dan was not interested. He simply did not want to hear of it.

He had been born and raised in Tel Aviv. His parents were secular and he had no religious background. One day, he was approached by volunteers of the *Lev L'Achim* outreach organization. Dan enjoyed conversing with these pleasant young men who were about his age, but he politely declined their invitation to learn more about his heritage. He was content to be what he was; connecting with his people's past seemed irrelevant to him. The young men visited him again, with the same results.

As Dan strolled down a Tel Aviv street one afternoon, he heard someone shouting something strange: *"Minchah, minchah!"* A middle-aged man hurried toward him. Realizing that this young fellow seemed confused, the man explained, "We want to begin prayers, but to do that, we need at least ten males over the age of thirteen. You are the tenth. Could you please come inside and join us?"

Dan politely refused. This was not for him. He began to walk away, but the man hurried after him. "Please, you would be doing a very great deed. Really, it will only take fifteen minutes of your time, but I assure you, the dividends are immeasurable. Come, it's getting late . . ."

Dan was annoyed. "What does this guy want from me? Doesn't he understand that this business of praying is not for me?" He did his best, however, to maintain outward calm.

"Now, look here," he countered, "it doesn't bother me if you want to pray, but as I told you, it's not for me."

But the middle-aged man continued to follow him, pleading with a sense of urgency that was difficult to ignore. Grudgingly,

---

1. This point is further elaborated upon in *Inspiration and Insight,* vol. I, p. 153-155.

Dan turned around and followed the man back up the street. They entered the shul and the man handed him a *siddur.*

Dan seated himself on a back bench, apart from everyone else. His *siddur* remained closed, but as the *davening* began, he eyed the others with interest. These nine men were involved in much more than mere lip service. They were totally enwrapped in what they were doing, uttering their prayers slowly, with care and concentration. He became more intrigued when it became quiet, as they stood fixed in their places, swaying ever so slightly, uttering their entreaties in an undertone.

Dan was struck by his discovery. "This is not mere ritual, as I've always been told. These people are really involved in what they're doing . . ."

Davening was over and the people were thanking Dan for joining them. He did not hear what they were saying; his mind was in a whirl.

The next day, he visited the *Lev L'Achim* office.

A few months later, someone was speaking with Dan's father concerning his son's having become a *baal teshuvah.* "I will tell you how it happened," his father said.

"Oh, but I know how it happened," the person replied. "He was the tenth man.."

"No," his father countered, "you *don't* know how it happened. You think that it was his visit to that *shul* that did the trick. I, however, believe that the story started long before that. You see, my father, may he rest in peace, was a fully observant G-d-fearing Jew. When he arrived in Israel from Europe, he settled in Tel Aviv — and he belonged to the very *shul* that Dan was 'coerced' into visiting on that fateful day. That was where my father prayed devoutly, day after day, morning, noon and night, for many years.

"I honestly believe that it was my father's soul which prevented my son from passing that *shul* without coming inside. It was his merit which caused my son to be pressed again and again until he finally gave in and joined the *minyan.* How else can anyone explain the incredible fact that of the hundreds of synagogues which stand in Israel today, this is the one through which my son returned to the ways of his grandfather . . .?"

❧ ❧ ❧

The above point is further illustrated by the following story:

Yair Eitan[1] is the son of a produce distributor in Northern Israel. When Yair's father felt comfortable with his son driving the delivery truck, he began sending him out on his regular route. One of his regular deliveries was at Yeshivah Lev V'Nefesh, a respected center of learning whose student body is comprised primarily of *baalei teshuvah.*

The first time that Yair set foot into Lev V'Nefesh, he was dumbstruck. His parents had carefully shielded him from anything that smacked of religion, and he grew up "free" of any knowledge of tradition or heritage. But the joy and excitement which he saw at the yeshivah aroused his curiosity and he allowed himself to be drawn into conversation with a few students. By his third trip there, he was already sitting down for a few minutes to taste the sweetness of Torah learning for the very first time.

As the days passed, his parents could not help but notice that a change had come over Yair. When Yair unabashedly related what had been going on, his father became enraged. No son of his, he declared, was going to become a backward, bearded *chareidi.* Yair would no longer deliver to that route and he was forbidden to ever visit that yeshivah, or any other yeshivah, again.

Halachah requires that a Jew obey his parents' every instruction, except when they order him to disregard a *mitzvah.* [2]. Yair knew that were he to steer clear of his religious acquaintances, he would remain ignorant of Torah forever. He therefore continued to visit the yeshivah, albeit clandestinely. But his father found out, and he reacted violently. Yair,

---

1. Names of people and places are fictitious.
2. See *Rashi* to *Vayikra* 19:3.

however, was determined to succeed. Discreetly, he inquired about other yeshivos in Israel which would suit his needs. Then, in the middle of the night, he left a note wishing his parents well and informing them why he was leaving, but without revealing his destination.

His father would not make peace with this decision. He discovered Yair's whereabouts and forced him to return home. And he did not rest there. Yair's father blamed the *Rosh Yeshivah* of Lev V'Nefesh as the cause of all his problems. He filed charges against him, accusing him of brainwashing his eighteen-year-old son and of engineering his flight from home. A trial date was set.

The day of the trial arrived and a packed courtroom observed the proceedings with bated breath. The charges were read and the prosecution called Yair to the witness stand. Calm and composed, he was not at all helpful to their case. No, he insisted, he was not coerced in any way. When he made his deliveries to Yeshivah Lev V'Nefesh he had discovered the truth of Torah. It had been his own idea to slip away to another yeshivah in order to escape the harsh treatment to which he was being subjected at home.

Few noticed that while Yair was telling his side of the story, the judge presiding over the case, an elderly man, seemed a bit distracted. Every now and then, he would take his eyes off the speaker to gaze intently at Yair's father. When Yair left the witness stand, the judge announced, "I would like Mr. Eitan to step forward." Surprised but undaunted, Mr. Eitan rose from his seat and came before the judge.

"Your name is Eitan. Are you perhaps of Eastern European origin, and was your name Stark in 'the old country'?"

Clearly taken aback, Yair's father stammered that the judge was indeed correct.

"And are you originally from the town of Pinsk?"

Mr. Eitan nodded meekly.

"Ah, I'm a bit older than you, Eitan, and I remember you well. You come from one of the finest homes of the pre-War Pinsk community. Your father was a deeply religious and highly respected man. Your mother was renowned for her acts of kindness; she would cook meals for the poor and the sick regularly."

By now, the color had completely drained from Mr. Eitan's face. He seemed to be in shock, and could not utter a word.

The judge continued, "I remember well when, as an eighteen-year-old, you openly departed from the ways of your father and mother. I recall vividly the reaction of your parents when you publicly desecrated the Sabbath for the first time. Your father aged overnight; gone was his warm smile, his energetic walk. He seemed to constantly be in mourning. As for your mother, it was said that each Friday night when lighting the candles, she would shed a river of tears.

"I often wondered what became of all those tears. I'm not the most religious person, but I know that there is a G-d Who runs this world, and I could not understand how the tears of so righteous a woman could be ignored in Heaven.

"Today my question has been answered. I see that her tears were not shed in vain. Today, almost half a century later, her grandson has returned to the ways of his ancestors.

"Mr. Eitan, I'm sure you recall that on more than one occasion, friends of your parents pleaded with you that for your parents' sake, you should at least refrain from public transgression. As I recall, your response was, 'I'm now eighteen and I make my own decisions. I can live my life any way I please.' And you dare to file charges because your eighteen-year-old son has returned to the ways that you abandoned?"

"Case dismissed!"

Don't Give Up

וַיִּתֵּן אֶל מֹשֶׁה כְּכַלֹּתוֹ לְדַבֵּר אִתּוֹ בְּהַר סִינַי שְׁנֵי לֻחֹת הָעֵדֻת.

When He finished speaking to Moshe on Mount Sinai, He gave Moshe the Two Tablets of testimony (Shemos 31:18).

The word כְּכַלֹּתוֹ [when He finished] is spelled defectively [without a ו], as if it were vowelized כְּכַלָּתוֹ [like his bride], for the Torah was given to Moshe as a gift like a bride to a groom, because he was unable to learn all of it in such a short time (Rashi).

Joel Leitner[1] had everything a person could have wanted in the way of materialism. His life was exciting; he traveled the world and made big money. All he was missing was a feeling of satisfaction. His life did not have any real meaning.

Then he went to Israel on business. A tourist visit to Jerusalem brought him in contact with an outreach professional, and before long Joel was studying at an Israeli yeshivah for *baalei teshuvah*.

The yeshivah had an excellent and proven program for beginners, but Joel had his problems. No matter how hard he tried, he couldn't grasp the workings of *Gemara*. He attended classes, reviewed diligently and even had some private lessons. But nothing seemed to work. He was growing increasingly frustrated and the thought entered his mind that perhaps he was simply not cut out for learning. But he had been taught that Torah knowledge is G-d's gift to every Jew, and that with proper effort, one is assured that ultimately he will succeed.[2] And so, Joel did not give up.

He finally hit upon an idea. He was having difficulty learning the Talmudic language of Aramaic and at the same time trying

---

1. Not his real name.
2. See *Megillah* 6b.

to grasp the analytical workings of *Gemara*. Perhaps if he channeled all his mental energy toward one of these areas, he would succeed.

He withdrew from the class he had been attending and purchased a volume of the English-language Schottenstein Edition of the Talmud. For the next few months, he spent most of his waking hours hunched over this volume, concentrating primarily on familiarizing himself with the language and style of writing. After a few months, Joel — now known as Yoel — felt adequately proficient in reading and translating the *Gemara,* and reenrolled in the class. It worked! With his new-found familiarity with the Talmudic text, he was able to devote more effort toward its analysis. As time went on and his progress increased, so did his love and devotion to learning. Eventually, he married a fine young woman and the two settled in *Eretz Yisrael,* where he studied in a *kollel* while his wife worked to support them.

Her earnings were rather meager and they could barely afford basic necessities. Nevertheless, they were both quite content with their material situation.

Late one night, a neighborhood man who took pleasure in helping needy scholars entered the *beis midrash* and found Yoel deeply immersed in his studies. The man made some inquiries and was told that while the Leitners certainly qualified for his list, they were known not to accept assistance on principle. The man, however, was not perturbed. He approached Mrs. Leitner's employer and arranged to give her a sum each month which would be given to Mrs. Leitner as a "raise."

A few weeks later, the man was visited by none other than Yoel. "I understand that you help needy people. Well, my wife works for a woman with a large family who really could use some extra money. A few weeks ago, for reasons that we don't understand, she gave my wife a significant increase in salary. But we really don't need this extra money; *baruch Hashem,* we have everything that we need.

"Do you think that if we gave you this additional money, you could find a way to get it back to my wife's employer . . .?"

פרשת ויקהל
Parashas Vayakhel

An Eruv for Toronto

וַיְצַו מֹשֶׁה וַיַּעֲבִירוּ קוֹל בַּמַּחֲנֶה . . . וַיִּכָּלֵא הָעָם מֵהָבִיא.

*And Moshe commanded, and they sounded the proclamation
in the camp . . . and the people were restrained from bringing
(Shemos 36:6-7).*

When Moshe was informed that more materials than
were necessary had already been donated for the
Mishkan, he issued a proclamation that no more should be
brought.

The Talmud (*Shabbos* 96b) explains that bringing materials
involved the labor of הוֹצָאָה מֵרְשׁוּת לִרְשׁוּת, *transferring from
domain to domain,* and derives from these verses that this labor
is forbidden on Shabbos, as are all labors that were performed
in the construction of the *Mishkan.*

The Talmud teaches that a halachically constructed *eruv,*
enclosing an otherwise restricted area, can, in many situations,
make carrying on Shabbos permissible.[1]

---

1. The laws of *eruvin* are extremely complex; an entire Talmudic tractate is
devoted to the topic. In some instances, certain restrictions may make it
halachically impossible for a city to make use of the permit which an *eruv*
provides. For practical application of these laws, one should consult a
competent halachic authority.

The construction of an *eruv* for the city of Toronto was the result of a five-year process which involved much dedication, effort, fund-raising — and, clearly, great *siyata DiShmaya* (Divine assistance).

Upon researching the matter, a group of *rabbanim* ascertained that most of the city's perimeter was surrounded by rail lines which bordered on populated areas. By law, these lines have to be fenced off for safety, and such fences could serve as sections of the *eruv*. However, a train ride around the city showed that in many areas the rail fences were breached, while in other areas there was no fence at all.

A community activist who was then head of a large engineering firm had close ties to the heads of both rail lines, Canadian National and Canadian Pacific, as well as to the Toronto municipal government. Through his efforts, Canadian National appointed the chief of its construction sector, Joe Aktman, to serve as liaison with the *eruv* committee. Though Mr. Aktman was a non-observant Jew, he showed great interest in the matter and was cooperative and helpful at every juncture.

In 1992, Canadian National began construction of new fencing around their rail lines, which stretched across two-thirds of the city's perimeter. The work was supervised by Mr. Aktman, who was given halachic guidance by R' Shlomo Miller. Later, Canadian Pacific began repairs of its lines in the city's southern district. In all, the two rail companies spent more than three hundred thousand dollars on the project. The Jewish community spent seventy-five thousand dollars for the *eruv's* construction.

From time to time, the city's *rabbanim* would tour the city's perimeter to determine which problems had been rectified, which remained and how to deal with them. On an inspection tour in the summer of 1993, Joe Aktman related that on the previous night, his grandfather had appeared to him in a dream and had enjoined him to satisfy the community's every request regarding the *eruv*. "Know," his grandfather had told him, "that this is your purpose in this world."

From then on, Mr. Aktman went about his work for the *eruv* with added intensity, as he strove for both speed and perfection in the fencing work which remained. That summer, the fence repairs were completed. However, numerous other details, much of them bureaucratic, remained.

By Chanukah of 5756 (1996), the *eruv* was completed and ready for use. When the *rabbanim* of Toronto phoned Mr. Aktman's home to inform him of the wonderful news, they were shocked to learn that soon after he had completed his work regarding the *eruv*, Mr. Aktman had died suddenly at age fifty.

His "mission in this world," the *eruv* around the city of Toronto, has certainly enhanced Shabbos observance in the city, and surely is a great source of merit for his soul.[1]

---

1. From an article in *Perspectives*, the publication of Agudath Israel in Toronto and information provided by R' Moshe Mordechai Lowy, *Rav* of Agudath Israel of Toronto.

פרשת פקודי
Parashas Pekudei

The Highest Bidder

אֵלֶּה פְקוּדֵי הַמִּשְׁכָּן מִשְׁכַּן הָעֵדוּת . . .

These are the reckonings of the Mishkan,
the Mishkan of Testimony . . . (Shemos 38:21).

This *parashah* begins with a detailed listing of the amounts of gold, silver, and copper that were contributed for the *Mishkan*. This, writes R' Moshe Feinstein, teaches a profound lesson: Just as the artisans of the *Mishkan* had to account for their use of every ounce of material that was donated for the *Mishkan,* so must we be able to account for how we have made use of Hashem's blessings upon us.

R' Moshe applies this to both time and resources. Do we devote our days and years to Torah and *mitzvos,* or do we squander them on empty pursuits? Do we dedicate a proper amount of our money to *tzedakah?* These are questions that every Jew must ask himself.

The following story tells of the blessings which one can merit through giving of himself or his resources for Torah and *mitzvos.*

R' Shmuel Eideles, known as the *Maharsha,* is best known for his classic commentary to the Talmud. He was *av beis din* of the city of Ostrow, Poland, and headed the city's renowned yeshivah. From far and near, outstanding, budding scholars streamed to Ostrow to drink from the waters of the *Maharsha's* teachings.

With time, the yeshivah outgrew its quarters and the leaders of the Jewish community decided that it was time to erect a new building. On the appointed day, the entire community gathered to lay the cornerstone of the new building. It was announced that the privilege of laying the cornerstone would be sold to the highest bidder. The money pledged would, of course, go towards the building's construction.

Before the bidding began, a quiet, unassuming man approached the treasurer, who would serve as auctioneer, and told him that he was prepared to pay any amount to win the auction, but he did not want his identity revealed. He instructed the treasurer to outbid, on his behalf, any and all bids that would be put forth.

The cornerstone laying was sold for five hundred rubles, a fabulous sum. Everyone crowded around the treasurer to find out who had won, but the treasurer kept his word and said that it had been won anonymously. Later, he approached the purchaser discreetly and asked if he was prepared to lay the cornerstone. The man replied that he wished to bestow this honor upon their *Rav* and leader, the *Maharsha.*

The cornerstone was laid and the people went home not knowing the identity of the man who had honored the *Maharsha.* After everyone had left, the *Maharsha* told the treasurer, "I would like very much to meet the *tzaddik* who gave so much of his money for this *mitzvah.*" When the treasurer conveyed this message to the donor, he wasted no time in coming before the *Maharsha.*

During their conversation, the man said that in truth the five hundred rubles which he had bid were far beyond his means. He had been prompted to offer such an amount because he and his wife had no children and he wanted the new yeshivah to be an eternal source of merit for them. Upon hearing this, the *Maharsha* offered the man his heartfelt blessing that he and his wife should be blessed with a boy who would one day study in the new yeshivah building.

One year later, the wife gave birth to a boy. When the boy was bar mitzvah, his father brought him to the yeshivah to be enrolled. Those in charge, however, did not want to accept a student so young. The man then went to the *Maharsha*. After hearing who the boy was, the *Maharsha* gave instructions that he be admitted into the yeshivah.

In recording the above incident, *Sefer Kehillas Yitzchak* cites the Aggadic teaching that following the dedication of the first *Beis HaMikdash,* every married woman in *Eretz Yisrael* gave birth to a boy (*Moed Kattan* 9a). He suggests that this reward is measure for measure, for the primary "sanctuaries" of the Jewish people are the people themselves.

The Torah states, "And they shall make for Me a sanctuary so that I shall dwell among them" (*Shemos* 25:8). Noting the Torah's use of the term בְּתוֹכָם, *[so that I may dwell] among them,* as opposed to בְּתוֹכוֹ, *[so that I may dwell] in it* (i.e. in the *Mishkan*), the Sages comment: בְּתוֹכָם, *among them, [so that I may dwell] in each and every one of them* (*Seder Olam Rabbah* 6). Every Jew, through his good deeds, causes the *Shechinah* (Hashem's Presence) to dwell within himself.[1] Through proper "reckoning" of his time and resources, he becomes a *"Mishkan"* in a most literal sense.

---

1. See *Nefesh HaChaim* 4:1.

פרשת ויקרא
Parashas Vayikra

For the Sake of Heaven

עוֹלָה הוּא אִשֶּׁה רֵיחַ נִיחֹחַ לַה׳.

It is an olah-offering, a fire-offering, a pleasing fragrance to Hashem
(Vayikra 1:17).

It says "a pleasing fragrance" about an olah-offering
of fowl, and it says "a pleasing fragrance" about an
olah-offering of livestock, to tell you that one who gives
much is the same as one who gives less, as long as his
heart is directed toward Heaven (Rashi from Toras
Kohanim).

R' Yose taught: וְכָל מַעֲשֶׂיךָ יִהְיוּ לְשֵׁם שָׁמַיִם, *And let all your*
deeds be for the sake of Heaven (Avos 2:17). R'
Yeruchom Levovitz (*Daas Chochmah U'Mussar*) explains that
because the human personality is so complex, it can be very
difficult for a person to know which is the path of Torah truth
in any given situation. When a person's intentions are solely
לְשֵׁם שָׁמַיִם, *for the sake of Heaven,* then he is granted Heavenly
assistance to help him arrive at the proper course of action.
Thus did Shlomo state, "In all your paths know Him, and He will
straighten your ways" (*Mishlei* 3:6).

❀ ❀ ❀

When R' Mordechai Twersky, the *Rebbe* of Rachmastrivk, emigrated from Eastern Europe to the Holy Land, he brought along his *succah*. This was not just any *succah;* the *Rebbe* had inherited it from his holy ancestor, the author of *Sefer Me'or Einayim,* and the sanctity that was absorbed in its walls could still be felt when one sat inside it on the festival. Wealthy *chassidim* had offered the *Rebbe* large sums of money for the *succah,* but the *Rebbe* would not think of selling it.

Then an epidemic broke out in Jerusalem. A young girl became seriously ill, and doctors instructed that she be given frequent warm baths. Poverty was rampant, and even basic necessities such as firewood were in short supply.

When the *Rebbe* learned of the girl's condition and what she required, he did not hesitate to do what had to be done. He went to the place where he stored his *succah,* took the *succah's* walls and carefully cut out every Scriptural verse or passage that had been inscribed on the wood. The remainder of the wood he cut into pieces and sent to the girl's parents (*She'al Avicha Veyagedcha*).

❧   ❧   ❧

During the year of mourning which R' Shmuel Zvi Kowalsky[1] observed in memory of his father, there was only one occasion when he missed leading the *minyan* in weekday prayers.

It happened in the *Beis HaKnesses HaGadol* in Bnei Brak, a synagogue where *minyanim* for *Shacharis* pray in succession throughout the early morning. It is the custom there that when someone is in mourning or is observing a *yahrtzeit* and needs to serve as *chazzan,* he stands alongside the *amud* (*chazzan's* lectern) and waits for the *minyan* in progress to end so that he can lead the next one.

One morning, R' Kowalsky stood near the *amud* waiting his turn as the *minyan* in progress neared conclusion. As the

---

1. See chapter to *Parashas Yisro* in this volume.

chazzan completed the *davening* and R' Kowalsky prepared to take over, he noticed an aged man folding his *tallis* and calling to those who were leaving, "Can someone walk me home? I can't walk home alone . . ."

The previous *minyan* was rather small and the few men who were leaving were working men in a hurry to get to their places of work. No one, it seemed, had time to walk this old man home. When R' Kowalsky realized that no one there was responding to the man's request, he walked over to him, gently took him by the hand and said, "Come, I would be happy to walk you home."

Together, they made their way slowly through the streets, with R' Kowalsky whispering to himself every so often, "May this *mitzvah* be a source of merit for my father . . ."

They reached the apartment building where the old man lived. He thanked R' Kowalsky warmly, but the *tzaddik* was not ready to take leave of him. "Come, let me walk you up the stairs . . ."

By the time R' Kowalsky returned to *shul,* a *chazzan* was already standing at the *amud,* leading that morning's final *minyan.* R' Kowalsky took a seat and prayed with the *minyan.*

That night, R' Kowalsky's father appeared to him in a dream. "I am *mochel* (i.e. willing to forgo) your leading the *minyan* at every *tefillah* — as long as in its place you do such *mitzvos.* "

❦ ❦ ❦

When R' Nosson Einfeld[1] served as *Rosh Yeshivah* of Yeshivas Beer Sheva, he chanced upon a visitor to the city who was searching for a kosher restaurant where he could eat lunch. Without offering his credentials, R' Einfeld took the man to his yeshivah, brought him to the dining room and served him lunch. The man thought that he had been served in a cafeteria and upon finishing his meal offered R' Einfeld a five-dollar bill. When R' Einfeld politely refused the money,

---

1. See Chapter to *Parashas Vayeira* in this volume.

the man thought that perhaps he had offered too little, so he took out a twenty-dollar bill.

R' Einfeld smiled warmly and said, "The Torah tells us that when our father Avraham lived in Beer Sheva, he had an inn where he served wayfarers.[1] You, my friend, have come to such an inn! Our yeshivah is accustomed to welcoming guests. It is our pleasure to serve you and no payment is necessary."

The man began to ask R' Einfeld about himself and about the yeshivah. R' Einfeld attempted to ask the man about himself, but at first, he was evasive. Then, suddenly, the man exclaimed, "R' Nosson, you are indeed fortunate! I am a man of means and have come to Israel because I would like to make a generous contribution to a yeshivah somewhere in the land. I have found that yeshivah!"

Later he told R' Einfeld, "Had you accepted the twenty dollars which I offered you, I would not have considered giving a contribution to the yeshivah." Only because R' Einfeld had shown him genuine kindness, without any thought of renumeration, did he decide to contribute generously to the yeshivah.

Before returning home, the man handed R' Einfeld five hundred dollars. After he returned home, he and R' Einfeld corresponded with one another. Eight months after their first meeting, R' Einfeld received a telegram that the man had died and in his will he had bequeathed to Yeshivas Beer Sheva the sum of one hundred thousand dollars.

---

1. See *Bereishis* 21:33 with *Rashi.*

פרשת צו
Parashas Tzav

A Spark Ignited

וְהֵרִים אֶת הַדֶּשֶׁן אֲשֶׁר תֹּאכַל הָאֵשׁ אֶת הָעֹלָה עַל הַמִּזְבֵּחַ.

He shall separate the ash of what the fire consumed of the Olah offering on the Altar (Vayikra 6:3).

The first service of the day in the *Beis HaMikdash* was תְּרוּמַת הַדֶּשֶׁן, *separating the ash,* removing a portion of the previous day's ash from the altar. The ashes removed were from the innermost layers.

R' Meir Shapiro of Lublin taught that the altar's fire symbolizes the soul of man, as it is written, כִּי נֵר ה' נִשְׁמַת אָדָם, *For the lamp of Hashem is the soul of man (Mishlei 20:27).* The ashes which conceal the fire represent the layers of sin which cause the soul to grow distant from Hashem and lose its radiance. The *Kohen's* removing some of the innermost ashes to reveal the fire beneath them symbolizes that even a soul covered with sin retains a spark of holiness that can be re-ignited. No matter how distant a Jew has become from Hashem and His Torah, it is never too late for him to return to his roots.[1]

---

1. R' Shapiro found an allusion to this concept in the verse, "If your dispersed will be at the ends of heaven, from there your God will gather you

It is the *Kohen* whose service represents this teaching, for the *Kohen* is a descendant of Aharon, of whom Hillel the Elder said, "Be among the disciples of Aharon . . . loving people and bringing them closer to Torah"[1] (*Avos* 1:12).

❧ ❧ ❧

The following story tells of one such soul. It is taken from an interview with its subject, and is told in his own words.

❧ ❧ ❧

Until age seventeen, I did not know that I was Jewish.

My mother came from an observant home, where Shabbos and other *mitzvos* were strictly observed. Her father's family was devoutly religious and was highly respected in its community back in Europe. My mother's parents divorced when she was young, and she remained with her mother. She attended public school and grew up in a community where religious observance was weak and assimilation was rampant. During her teenage years, my mother drifted from the religious practices which had been a part of her home. Then she met my father and they married.

I never heard the word "Jew" mentioned by either my father or mother; to their minds, it had absolutely no relevance to them or their son. My parents divorced when I was four years old and I remained with my father on our farm in the Midwest. From that time on, I saw my mother very infrequently.

Around the time I turned seventeen, my mother's mother died and my mother decided to observe the *shivah* mourning period at the house of her only sibling, a brother who had remained fully observant all his life. During that week, a local resident involved in Jewish outreach came to the house a

---

in and from there He will take you" (*Devarim* 30:4). "Heaven" refers, homiletically, to the spiritual part of a person, the soul. Even if one is at the very "end" of his spirituality, meaning that only the tiny, inextinguishable spark of sanctity remains burning within his soul, nevertheless, Hashem can bring him back to the proper path.

1. See chapter to *Parashas Tetzaveh* in this volume.

number of times and spoke with my mother about rediscovering her Jewishness. His words made a profound impact upon her and as soon as the *shivah* ended, she began attending seminars and immersed herself in Torah-related texts. Before long, my mother was fully observant, a genuine *baalas teshuvah.*

❈ ❈ ❈

Shortly thereafter, my mother visited me on my father's farm and, in the course of our conversation, revealed that I was a Jew. She also told me of her own rediscovery of her Jewishness and what this involved.

Her revelation hit me like a bombshell. I discussed the matter with my father after my mother had left. While he did not deny that I was Jewish, he advised me that it was wise to 'stay away from the stuff' which my mother had discussed. Reassured, I gave little thought to whatever she had told me.

But my mother was very persistent. She was in frequent contact with me and when summer vacation aproached, she paid my fare so that I would join her on the East Coast and spend two weeks with her. I was eager to see that part of the country for the first time in my life and accepted my mother's offer.

During those two weeks, I spent a lot of time with my mother's brother, who introduced me to many of my observant relatives. This was my first exposure to observant Jews. While they impressed me as nice, sincere people, I did not feel comfortable with them. "This is not for me," I kept assuring myself. My world was elsewhere.

But a bridge had been built. Upon my return home, my mother put me in touch with an outreach professional in my area who opened his door to me and even had me over for meals from time to time.

❈ ❈ ❈

While still in high school, I signed up for army reserve training and duty. Out of one hundred thirty students in my graduating class, close to eighty signed up for the service. My friends and

I were used to physical work and, as country boys, we were eager to "see the world." Upon graduating from high school at age eighteen, I headed for Georgia to an army training school from which I graduated a few weeks later. Before graduation, I was offered various options for pursuing my army career; the rule is that once an option is chosen and the soldier signs the necessary papers, the choice is final. I signed up for more training, this time in Germany.

My mother, however, had other plans for me. While I was in Georgia, she phoned me a number of times, imploring me to come to the East Coast after graduation and spend some time in something called a "yeshivah," a term that was new to me. I really had no interest in this and, as I told my mother truthfully, my decision to go to Germany was irrevocable, if I had any intention of realizing my goal of becoming an army officer.

But Hashem has His ways of reversing the irrevocable. Somehow, the army misplaced all my papers and I was told to submit new ones. I now had an opportunity to review my options anew. I still very much wanted to go to Germany, but for some reason which, to this day, I cannot explain rationally, I opted for reserve duty back home.

I returned to my father's farm. That same afternoon, I drove into town for some errands and, while I was there, I went to the bus station and bought a ticket to go visit my mother. I cannot explain why I bought that ticket when I had been so certain that this is not what I wanted to do. In fact, I still recall that as I drove back to the farm that day, I was telling myself, "I really don't know why I bought this ticket."

I spent the next six months commuting between a yeshivah on the East Coast and my weekend reserve duty in the Midwest once a month. At yeshivah, I learned to read Hebrew and put on tefillin, and I attended Torah classes. I was not academically oriented and I found the studying quite difficult. However, I compensated for this somewhat by helping people in the community with things like building succahs and other chores which put my physical abilities to good use.

I felt like my feet were planted in two worlds at once — and they were. When the six months were up, I still saw myself as a future army officer. I did not see myself becoming observant. However, I did feel that what I had learned in those six months was important. As I prepared to leave for Germany, I packed the expensive *tefillin* my mother had purchased for me, a *siddur* and a few *yarmulkas*.

※　※　※

I went through seven months of intense training in Germany. The maneuvers we practiced were performed on rugged terrain which prepared us well for the eventuality of battle. One day, on a training mission in Bergen-Belsen, we received word that our unit was being deployed to the Persian Gulf to take part in Operation Desert Shield, which later developed into Operation Desert Storm.

The days before our departure were hectic indeed. We were quickly trained in the art of battle under the threat of chemical warfare. I was taken to a rifle range where I practiced using an M-60 automatic weapon while dressed in a protective anti-chemical suit. At that time, I was designated team chief of communications for our unit, which had in it some fourteen M-109 howitzers. Each howitzer was wired with four or five radios that ensured proper coordination among our guns. Without proper coordination, a shell cannot be fired. My responsibility was awesome and my work was made more difficult by the fact that the quick turn of events in the Gulf brought fresh recruits into my unit who had received far less training than I had. I was all of nineteen at that time.

Throughout my stay in the Gulf, I never let a day go by without putting on *tefillin* and reciting *Shema*. My fellow soldiers, both black and white, respected me for wearing my "teflons," and would stand at a distance and gaze in silence as I wrapped myself in these sacred articles and prayed.

My unit was stationed at a tactical assembly area in the middle of the desert, while we waited for the ground war to begin. One day, I received a package in the mail from one of my observant cousins in the States. It contained a batch of home-baked cookies and a beautiful ArtScroll *Siddur,* which I use to this day. The strange thing was that by the time the package reached me, its cover had been completely ripped off and my name was not on it. It seems that all the mail for my brigade — of some thirty-five hundred soldiers — had been thrown onto an open truck and had been severely damaged in a rainstorm. One of the men handling the mail recognized the *siddur* as a Hebrew prayer book, and as far as he knew, I was the only Jew in the brigade.

❦ ❦ ❦

After weeks of training and anticipation, we finally received word that only four hours remained until the ground war would begin. Beginning with that moment, I was to go three consecutive days and nights without sleep.

The ground war erupted. Again and again, the same scenario was repeated: We would reach a particular spot, communications would quickly be set up and formations arranged, guns would be fired and enemy positions destroyed, communications would then be dismantled and we would move on. I kept my *tefillin* and *siddur* in what I considered the safest place in the truck that I was driving: under the driver's seat, wrapped in many coverings, with a sandbag underneath in case we would go over a landmine.

On the second night of the ground war, we were moving along in column formation, which was particularly vulnerable to attack since all our vehicles were very close together. We had stopped for some reason when suddenly I spotted two T-72 Soviet-built tanks coming over a sand dune. My truck was at the very rear of our column and in all probability was first to be targeted. But one of our tanks spotted them in the nick of time. The Iraqi tanks went up in flames and the explosions of their ammunition went on for another fifteen minutes. I could feel the heat on my face. There was something else I felt — God's closeness in that time of great danger. I had experienced my first real taste of battle and I knew that Hashem was with me.

❧ ❧ ❧

After seventy-two hours without sleep, we were in Kuwait and just about ready to wrap things up. Iraq's Elite Republican Guard was in our range of fire and we had received the coordinates of their positions. I was hooking up the last radio before the firing could begin when an officer came running towards me and ordered that the radios be dismantled. A cease-fire had been declared.

As we drove down Basra Highway toward Kuwait City, I beheld a sight too awesome to depict. Miles away in all directions, fire was shooting out of the ground and the once-blue sky was thick with black clouds. These were the oil fires which the Iraqis had set before they fled for their lives. But that was not all. As our truck snaked its way down the highway, the sides of the road for about eight miles or more were one huge scrap heap. Twisted, burnt-out Iraqi army vehicles were sandwiched between the world's most expensive cars, which the Iraqis had taken from the Kuwaitis at gunpoint when they invaded months before. Gold-plated Mercedeses, luxurious Porsches and elegant Cadillacs had become heaps of garbage.

As we drove along, my buddies were excitedly commenting on which one of these luxury cars they would love to own. I listened in silence, astounded at their reaction which was so different from my own. I was witnessing the destruction of materialism, seeing with my own eyes how in so little time, trillions of dollars in oil were going up in smoke and the cars of our dreams had joined billions of dollars in modern weaponry to become the largest scrap-metal heap in the world. All of it was worthless — and so was its pursuit.

After a few more miles of driving, we stopped our truck, pitched our tents and fell into an exhausted sleep. I awoke three hours later and the first thing I did was to pray. Wrapped in my *tefillin* and holding my *siddur,* I took a look around to make sure that I had not been hallucinating out of exhaustion. Nothing had changed. The destruction was still very much visible everywhere I turned. That moment is still deeply etched in my memory. It was then that I decided that at the very first opportunity, I would return to yeshivah.

After the war, I completed my tour of army duty and, immediately afterwards, enrolled in a yeshivah. And that is where I have been ever since.

My first weeks back in yeshivah were very hard for me. After being a soldier in combat, I found it extremely difficult to sit and study for even an hour at a time, let alone an entire day. However, army life had, in a sense, prepared me for this next struggle. In the army I had learned that "orders are orders." No matter how difficult the task, no matter how tired I was, I was expected to carry out whatever was expected of me — and I did. Now, as I reentered the world of Torah, I felt a sense of obligation to try my hardest. I perceived clearly that I now was treading the path of truth and as such, I had to strive to succeed, no matter how difficult the task.

And with Hashem's help, I have succeeded thus far. Today, I can taste the sweetness of Torah and experience the joy of living a life that is truly meaningful.

פרשת שמיני
Parashas Shemini

In the Way of Aharon

וַיֹּאמֶר מֹשֶׁה אֶל אַהֲרֹן הוּא אֲשֶׁר דִּבֶּר ה׳ לֵאמֹר בִּקְרֹבַי אֶקָּדֵשׁ וְעַל פְּנֵי כָל הָעָם אֶכָּבֵד וַיִּדֹּם אַהֲרֹן.

Moshe said to Aharon: "Of this did Hashem speak, saying, 'I will be sanctified through those who are nearest Me, thus will I be honored before the entire people' "; and Aharon was silent (Vayikra 10:3).

J ust when the joy of the *Mishkan's* dedication reached its peak, tragedy struck. Aharon's two oldest sons, Nadav and Avihu, performed an unauthorized service and lost their lives. This double tragedy occurred on the very day when Aharon was inaugurated as *Kohen Gadol* (High Priest). The Torah testifies that Aharon reacted to his losses with silent acceptance of the Divine judgment. In reward for this, the next *mitzvah* in the Torah was communicated directly to him rather than to Moshe,[1] which was always the case with this one exception.

When a Jew acts in the way of Aharon, he sanctifies Hashem's Name by demonstrating his unflinching faith that everything that occurs on this world is orchestrated from Above. Through unquestioning acceptance of the Divine

---

1. See verses 8-11.

decree, the person also makes clear his belief that all Hashem's ways are perfect, and ultimately are for the good.

Only three years ago, our generation witnessed how a father and mother, during a time of great trauma and tragedy, acted and spoke in a way which surely ranks them among the great "disciples of Aharon".[1]

On Monday, October 10, 1994, it became public knowledge that Nachshon Waxman, הי"ד, a soldier in the Israeli Defense Forces, had been kidnapped by Hamas terrorists. From the start of the ordeal, Nachshon's parents, Yehudah and Esther Waxman, spoke with powerful *emunah* (faith), as they stressed repeatedly in interviews which were broadcast throughout Israel that only Hashem could save their son, and as they beseeched the entire nation, religious and secular alike, to pray that their son be saved.

Throughout the week that followed, Mrs. Waxman told her country that all the leaders involved in trying to secure her son's release were but messengers of Hashem and one could only *daven* (pray) that He put into their minds the wisdom to take the steps which would ensure her son's survival.

It was unprecedented. In a land where, unfortunately, secular and religious societies do not co-exist peacefully, all Jews were united in praying for one of their sons. There was an intense feeling of brotherhood. Schools across the spectrum recited *Tehillim* and even small children at home organized groups of friends to say *Tehillim*. On Thursday of that week, over fifty thousand people assembled at the *Kosel* for the heartfelt recitation of *Tehillim*.

On Friday afternoon, Mrs. Waxman spoke on the radio. "Nachshon," she said, "we are going to have our usual Shabbos meal, perhaps heightened by your absence. Please — you, too, try to have a regular Shabbos."

That night, Nachshon Waxman joined the ranks of Rabbi Akiva and the other martyrs of our people. When the news of his murder became known, all of *Eretz Yisrael* felt as if it had lost

---

1. From *Avos* 1:12.

a brother. A friend of the family, R' Mordechai Elon, came to the house that night to comfort the family. Nachshon's father told him:

There is no need to say anything. Just one thing worries me: Nachshon succeeded in raising the Jewish people to a high level of *emunah* (faith) and *tefillah* (prayer). Now we have the responsibility to maintain this heightened level.

People will ask: How is it that we were not answered from Above in spite of all the countless *tefillos*? But, you know, I asked Hashem for many things in my life, and He always granted them. I asked Him for good health and He gave it to me. I asked Him for a family such as I have merited, and He gave it to me. Now, if they will ask why our *tefillos* did not earn us the reply we sought from our Father in Heaven, I will tell them, "We did receive a response, we did get an answer. The answer was 'No,' because sometimes a father can answer, 'No.'

In an interview on the day following the funeral, Mr. Waxman said:

The cruel and vicious band of thugs who kidnapped my son was a group that did not care even for its own lives — they were barricaded behind booby-trapped steel doors. It is clear that the *tefillos* were not in vain. Many soldiers could have lost their lives [in the rescue mission launched on Friday afternoon]. The many *tefillos* were a factor in sparing their lives.[1]

I'm telling you again, most of the time when I have asked Hashem for something, I received 'Yes' for an answer. This time, the answer to me personally was, 'No,' but the answer to the *tefillos* in general was a positive one.

Mrs. Waxman had this to say:

We are an ordinary family with ordinary ups and downs. We aren't special. This could have happened to anyone.

---

1. See chapter on *Parashas Vayechi* in this volume for a discussion of the concept that no *tefillah* is in vain.

The only thing that kept us sane and functioning through all this was our faith. We believe that our years are numbered. When a person fulfills his mission, then that is the end . . . Our faith tells us that these were the years allotted to our son and he fulfilled what he was supposed to fulfill. Our faith is what kept us going.

Yes, true disciples of Aharon.[1]

In the Way of Moshe

וַיִּשְׁמַע מֹשֶׁה וַיִּיטַב בְּעֵינָיו.
Moshe heard and he approved (Vayikra 10:20).

Moshe had confronted Aharon and his surviving sons and asked why they had not eaten from the *Rosh Chodesh* offering. Aharon responded by demonstrating correctly that the deaths of Nadav and Avihu prevented them from partaking of this offering.

As soon as he heard Aharon's reasoning, Moshe conceded that he was right. As *Rashi* teaches, Moshe did not attempt to defend his position. Instead, he admitted without embarrassment that Hashem had instructed him only that the special one-time inauguration offerings should be eaten on that day, just as Aharon and his sons had assumed — but Moshe had forgotten this fact.

It seems difficult to understand why the Torah must inform us that Moshe immediately admitted his mistake and did not

---

1. From an article by Rabbi Pinchas Meyer in *The Jewish Observer* (December 1994).

attempt to defend his position. Would we have expected any less from the greatest prophet of all time, the humblest of men, through whom Hashem transmitted the Torah to our people?

R' Chaim Shmulevitz explains that it is precisely because of his unparalleled stature that Moshe might have been tempted to deny that he had erred. He might have reasoned, "How can I admit that I have forgotten a law? If I admit to this, people might say that if I erred in this instance, I may have erred in other areas as well. All that I have taught them may become subject to doubt and the truth of the Torah which I have transmitted may come into question."

Moshe made no such rationalizations. He knew that "the seal of Hashem is truth," and that there could be no deviating from it. If in this one instance Moshe erred, then he was prepared to admit his mistake without hesitation and without fear of repercussions. It was through such strength of personality that Moshe merited to be the teacher of all Israel forever, whose word remains sacred and unchallenged for all eternity.

❧ ❧ ❧

R' Yisrael Salanter is known as the founder of the *Mussar* Movement because he introduced daily ethical study as an indispensable part of the yeshivah student's Torah curriculum. He also taught that *mussar* study must be done with total involvement of one's spirit and emotions so that the ethical teachings of the Sages will effect a lasting impact on one's *neshamah* (soul).

Today, R' Yisrael's approach is practiced in yeshivos the world over. However, more than a century ago when R' Yisrael began to publicize his philosophies, he was met with stiff opposition from some who considered his approach somewhat revolutionary and unnecessary.

It happened once that R' Yisrael came to a certain city to deliver a Talmudic lecture open to the public. In the audience were some of his antagonists who were eager to find some flaw in his lecture and thereby damage his image in the community. In the course of the lecture, one such fellow interjected with a question which challenged the premise put forth by R' Yisrael. R' Yisrael was silent for a few moments. Then, those near him heard him murmuring to himself, "R' Yisrael, you are, after all, a *baal mussar* (one who lives by and preaches the teachings of *mussar*)." He then announced, "The question put forth has refuted my premise. I have nothing more to say." With those words, he closed the volume before him and descended the pulpit.

While R' Yisrael's antagonists smiled with satisfaction, his disciples approached him to ask what he had meant by those words which he had whispered.

"You see," R' Yisrael explained, "I actually had three possible ways by which to answer his question. Had I chosen any of these three responses, I highly doubt whether he would have had anything more to say. But in truth, I know that none of these three approaches is correct, for each can be refuted, though with great difficulty. For a moment, I considered using one of these responses, for if I were to admit defeat, this might do damage to my cause of spreading the idea of *mussar* study.

"However, I then reflected, 'R' Yisrael, you are, after all, a *baal mussar*. Does not *mussar* stress the quality of truth and disparage those who stray after falsehood? How can you in good conscience suggest an answer which in your heart you know to be false?!'

"That is why I descended the podium without responding."

פרשת תזריע
Parashas Tazria

Like One Man, With One Heart

אָדָם כִּי יִהְיֶה בְעוֹר בְּשָׂרוֹ שְׂאֵת אוֹ סַפַּחַת אוֹ בַהֶרֶת וְהָיָה בְעוֹר בְּשָׂרוֹ לְנֶגַע צָרָעַת.

If a person will have on the skin of his flesh a se'eis or a sapachas, or a baheres, and it will become a tzaraas affliction on the skin of his flesh
(*Vayikra* 13:2).

The year 1911 saw the entire Jewish world in an uproar over the infamous "blood libel" case against Mendel Beilus, an unassuming Russian Jew who was falsely accused of murdering a Christian child in order to use its blood for Jewish ritual. In the course of its efforts for the cause of "justice," the prosecution sought some sort of proof that although it was virtually unheard of for Jews to commit acts of violence, it was not beneath them to perpetrate such crimes against those of other faiths.

It is told that Grunzenberg, Mendel Beilus' defense attorney, asked the Chortkover *Rebbe* how to respond if he was asked to explain the Talmudic teaching, "You, Israel, are called *Adam,* Man, but the nations of the world are not called *Adam*" (*Yevamos* 61a). Does this not imply, the prosecution might charge, that Jews consider men of other faiths sub-human, and as such can be killed like any beast of the forest?

The *Rebbe* told him: "Ask the judge: If an Italian were

arrested in Poland or a Frenchman in Germany, would the entire Italian nation or all Frenchmen be praying for his acquittal and release? But when one Jew, such as Beilus, is put on trial, the entire Jewish people is at his side. The Jewish people are like a single אָדָם. When one limb is suffering, the entire body feels the pain."

R' Shlomo Ganzfried (*Sefer Apiryon*) discusses why in our verse the Torah uses the term אָדָם, as opposed to some other term referring to *man*. He explains that other terms which refer to man, such as אִישׁ, have a plural form (אֲנָשִׁים, *men*), but אָדָם exists only in the singular form. Only the Jewish people are likened to a single אָדָם, for their souls are bound together in Heaven as one and their fortunes affect one another as with no other nation.

Our verse introduces the passages dealing with *tzaraas,* an affliction which comes upon a person as a punishment for speaking *lashon hara* (evil talk). *Lashon hara* destroys peace and harmony among Jews, it harms relationships and creates divisiveness. *Lashon hara* contradicts the quality of אָדָם, the special degree of oneness, that is unique to the Jewish people.[1]

❈ ❈ ❈

The Manchester *Rosh Yeshivah,* R' Yehudah Zev Segal, lived by the principle that the Jewish people are like a single body composed of many organs. His heart ached whenever he learned that a Jew was suffering, even if he had never met that person and was separated from him by thousands of miles.

Someone once watched as R' Segal listened by phone to the details of a patient's condition. His face was contorted with pain, he wept, and finally conferred his blessing. When he

---

1. In this vein, R' Yitzchak Isbee, ז״ל, suggested that the Torah uses the term אָדָם here because when Adam was created, he was described as a נֶפֶשׁ חַיָּה, *living being,* which *Targum Onkelos* translates as a *speaking spirit* (*Bereishis* 2:7). Thus the power of speech defines man's essence, and one who speaks *lashon hara* has profaned this power (see preface to *Sefer Shemiras HaLashon*).

hung up the phone he was asked, "Was that call about someone close to the *Rosh Yeshivah*?" R' Segal replied matter-of-factly, "I have never met the patient and I have no idea who he is."

On an *erev Shabbos* minutes before candle-lighting, R' Segal received a call from New York informing him that a young man whom he did not know had been in a serious car accident. There was only enough time to write down the victim's Hebrew name. Throughout Shabbos, R' Segal prayed for the person's recovery. As soon as *Havdalah* had been concluded at Shabbos' end, R' Segal instructed his *talmidim* to call the major hospitals in the New York area and ask whether a young Jewish man who had been in an automobile accident had been brought in on Friday afternoon. When the correct hospital was finally located, inquiries were made until the family was contacted, R' Segal was informed of the patient's condition and he was satisfied that the patient was being cared for by expert physicians.

When the last phone call had ended, R' Segal remarked, "Imagine the pain of a young mother, waiting for her husband to come home before Shabbos, only to learn that he had been in a terrible accident, ר״ל. Could we possibly have gone to sleep tonight without first learning of his condition?"

Once, after a *talmid* had poured out his troubles to him, R' Segal said, "You have not fulfilled it." The *talmid* responded, "I don't understand." R' Segal explained, "Our Sages have taught that if someone has a worry in his heart, he should share it with others.[1] However, in sharing your concern with me, you have not really shared it with 'others,' for I feel your pain as if it were my own."

---

1. *Yoma* 75a.

פרשת מצורע
Parashas Metzora

A Man of Principle

זֹאת תִּהְיֶה תּוֹרַת הַמְּצֹרָע בְּיוֹם טָהֳרָתוֹ.

This shall be the law of the metzora on the day of his purification
(Vayikra 14:2).

R' Yehoshua ben Levi said: "The term תּוֹרָה appears five times in the chapters which discuss the *metzora* (whose afflictions are a result of his having spoken *lashon hara*). This teaches that one who speaks *lashon hara* is considered as if he has transgressed the Five Books of the Torah" (*Vayikra Rabbah* 16:6).

Yalkut Shimoni states that the malady of *tzaraas* afflicts not only the *metzora's* body, but his soul as well. Thus, writes the Chofetz Chaim,[1] one who is in the habit of speaking *lashon hara* should bemoan the state of his soul. Though Hashem has mercy on him and does not reveal his shame in this world, such will not be the case in the World to Come.[2]

---

1. *Sefer Shemiras HaLashon, Shaar HaZechirah,* ch. 6.
2. The Chofetz Chaim (ibid.) discusses why since the Destruction of the *Beis HaMikdash* those who speak *lashon hara* are not smitten with physical *tzaraas.*

Conversely, *Zohar*[1] states that one who is careful in avoiding forbidden speech becomes enveloped in a spirit of sanctity. And the Vilna *Gaon*, quoting the *Midrash*, writes that for every moment that a person refrains from speaking the forbidden, he merits a hidden light that even angels cannot fathom.[2]

❦ ❦ ❦

R' Mordechai Grossman, *Rav* of the Galician city of Kaminka, was respected for his vast Torah scholarship, as well as for his exemplary character. He was a devoted *chassid* of R' Yisrael of Rizhin, one of the towering Chassidic personalities of nineteenth-century Galicia. The Rizhiner, as he was known, had high regard for R' Mordechai and would go for walks with him when R' Mordechai visited Rizhin.

The Rizhiner conducted himself as befits royalty. He lived in a beautiful home, dressed in expensive clothing and traveled in a horse-drawn carriage. But those who were close to the Rizhiner knew that though he wore expensive boots, the boots had no soles, and when he walked, his feet would become bruised and sore. His display of royalty may have been a way of uplifting his followers, many of whom were constantly being abused by their gentile neighbors. Or, the Rizhiner may have felt that a Torah leader is a representative of Hashem on earth, and therefore must conduct himself in a way that will earn him the greatest respect. Whatever his reasons were, the Rizhiner was recognized by the Torah leaders of his day as a great *tzaddik* and miracle worker.

The *shochet* (ritual slaughterer) of Kaminka did not understand the way of Rizhin, and he would openly speak critically of

---

1. *Parashas Chukas.*
2. When his grandson became a bar mitzvah, the Steipler *Gaon* encouraged the boy to choose one *mitzvah* which he would undertake to observe in all its fine details, even under the most difficult circumstances. "In our days," he said, "the *mitzvah* which one should choose to observe meticulously is *shemiras halashon* (guarding one's tongue), to accept upon oneself to observe its laws in all situations and under all conditions" (*Toldos Yaakov*).

R' Yisrael. R' Mordechai tried to explain to the *shochet* that *Chassidus* is only one of a variety of paths through which service of Hashem can be accomplished, and within *Chassidus* many divergent paths exist as well. The *shochet* did not have to subscribe to the path of Rizhin, but he certainly had no right to criticize the *tzaddik* who was its leader.

However, the *Rav's* words fell on deaf ears. The *shochet* was warned that if he did not cease his *lashon hara* (evil talk), then R' Mordechai would have no choice but to refrain from eating the meat he had slaughtered. This warning, too, was ignored. R' Mordechai then made it known that he would no longer eat the *shochet's* meat, unless the man began adhering to the laws of proper speech.

Unfortunately, the *Rosh HaKahal* (Community President), not a very learned man, sided with the *shochet* and demonstrated his displeasure with the *Rav's* decision by withholding the *Rav's* salary. Almost overnight, the *Rav* and his family were reduced to poverty.

Over the next two years, R' Mordechai's material situation went from bad to worse. He turned to borrowing money so that his family would not starve or freeze in the frigid winters. His debts continued to grow but his humility and pursuit of peace would not permit him to fight back against those who had wronged him.

Even on his visits to Rizhin, he could not bring himself to make mention of the matter to his *rebbe,* R' Yisrael. Then, one day, the Rizhiner asked R' Mordechai to serve as his emissary on a mission to the renowned Chassidic *tzaddik,* R' Meir of Premishlan.

R' Meir'l (as he was known) was then old and weak, and R' Mordechai spoke to him as he lay in bed. The two discussed the matter for which R' Mordechai had been sent and then, after two years of silence, R' Mordechai unburdened himself.

R' Meir'l lay on his bed, listening to this young man's sad tale of mistreatment, deprivation and debt. The brim of R' Mordechai's hat concealed most of his forehead. When R' Mordechai finished telling his story, R' Meir'l reached up and lifted up the hat, revealing R' Mordechai's forehead. Gazing at it intently, he said, "Meir'l sees that you owe nothing in the World of Truth [i.e. that R' Mordechai was wholly righteous]. And one who owes nothing in the World of Truth, owes nothing in this world."

A surprise awaited R' Mordechai upon his return to Kaminka. The *Rosh HaKahal* had experienced a change of heart; he regretted his mistreatment of the *Rav*. R' Mordechai was given two years of unpaid salary, and was paid regularly from then on.

And he was rewarded from Above with a spiritual legacy of descendants who to this day follow in his ways, by combining Torah greatness with outstanding character.[1]

---

1. The renowned Jerusalem *Rav*, R' Yisrael Grossman, is his great-grandson.

פרשת אחרי מות
Parashas Acharei Mos

Serve Hashem With Joy

וּשְׁמַרְתֶּם אֶת חֻקֹּתַי וְאֶת מִשְׁפָּטַי אֲשֶׁר יַעֲשֶׂה אֹתָם הָאָדָם וָחַי בָּהֶם.

You shall observe My decrees and My laws, which man shall carry out and by which he shall live (Vayikra 18:5).

Chiddushei HaRim interprets the words וָחַי בָּהֶם, *lit., and by which he shall live,* homiletically: A Jew should be full of *life* when performing a *mitzvah,* doing it with joy and enthusiasm, and demonstrating that it is from Torah and its observance that he derives vitality and fulfillment.

☙ ☙ ☙

R' Nissin Pilchik viewed himself as a plain working man, no different from anyone else. But anyone who knew him personally, or observed him as he prayed and studied Torah in the *beis midrash* of Karlin-Stolin in Brooklyn, knew that this was no simple man. His soul was aflame with love of Hashem, His Torah, and His people. His face shone with a joy and excitement which stemmed from an appreciation of *mitzvos* and a sense of purpose. Anyone who stood in his presence could not help but be drawn closer to his Creator.

Once, at the conclusion of *Shacharis,* a group of *chassidim* arrived in *shul* from overseas. The group immediately donned *tallis* and *tefillin* and formed a *minyan* of their own. When they reached the chapters of Psalms recited as part of *Pesukei D'Zimrah*, R' Nissin, who had already *davened*, began to pray along with them in his lively, heartfelt way. He continued in this way until the conclusion of *Pesukei D'Zimrah*. When questioned about this, R' Nissin explained, "When I heard these *Yidden* (Jews) saying those holy, sweet words, I simply couldn't hold myself back — I had to *daven* along with them! Those sacred words are so filled with life!"

He once asked, "How was King David able to request, '. . . that I dwell in the house of Hashem all the days of my life'? Such a request does not seem humanly possible; after all, one must eat, sleep and earn a livelihood.

"The answer to this is that if one eats as a Jew should eat, sleeps as a Jew should sleep and does business as a Jew should do business, then he takes the 'house of Hashem' with him wherever he goes."

Once, he was overheard saying to himself, "Six, six, six . . ." He later explained, "I had witnessed something which had aroused anger within me. But anger is a most shameful trait and one must work to overcome it. So at such times I remind myself: One who demonstrates anger is liable to transgress six Scriptural commandments. With this in mind, I am able to remain calm."

Toward the end of his life, he told someone, "In three areas my vigilance never slackened: In keeping the Shabbos, in guarding my eyes [from witnessing an improper sight] and in keeping my hands clean of other people's money."

During the Great Depression years, he fell into huge debt, but he refused to declare bankruptcy. It was then that he experienced what, to his mind, may have been the biggest test of his life.

R' Nissin was struggling to keep his linen business afloat. One day, a man named Mr. Nelson came to his store and offered to sell him enormous quantities of linen at an incredibly low price. R' Nissin calculated that the expected profits from the subsequent retail sales of such a purchase would wipe out his entire debt after fifteen weeks. But one thought nagged at him: How was this man able to sell his merchandise at so low a price? Nelson claimed that his contacts in the United States Navy afforded him the opportunity to purchase quality merchandise rock-bottom prices, but R' Nissin knew that it was possible that Nelson was dealing with stolen goods. Nevertheless, even if this suspicion proved to be true and Nelson was caught, R' Nissin could have said, in all honesty, that he did not know the goods were stolen.

However, R' Nissin reasoned, "If the goods are indeed stolen and Mr. Nelson is caught, they will ask him, 'With whom do you do business?' He will reply, of course, 'With Mr. Pilchik.' Though I will not be found guilty, people will still say that an observant Jew was in the middle of all this — and a *chillul Hashem* (desecration of Hashem's Name) will occur. And so, *Ribono shel Olam* (Master of the Universe), for the sake of Your honor, I will forgo this deal!"

Every Shabbos, R' Nissin was in a constant state of elation; from observing him, one could actually perceive the Sages' description of Shabbos as "a semblance of the World to Come."

He scrupulously observed the chassidic custom of napping on *erev Shabbos*. "The whole week," R' Nissin would say, "is dependent on the *erev Shabbos* nap." He would explain: "If one naps on *erev Shabbos*, then he will have the necessary energy to *daven* with *geshmack* (gusto) and conduct his Friday night meal, with its singing and words of Torah, as he should. If his Friday night will be as it should, then his recital of *Nishmas* [1] on Shabbos morning will be of an altogether different [i.e. more spiritual] nature. If his *Nishmas* will be as it should, the rest of Shabbos will be of a higher nature. Now, the *Zohar* states that the spiritual quality of the coming week is dependent on the

---

1. The beautiful prayer which follows the Song at the Sea in the morning prayers of Shabbos and Yom Tov. It depicts our utter dependency on Hashem's mercy, our inadequacy to laud Him properly, and our deep resolve to dedicate ourselves to His service.

way in which one experiences Shabbos — and it all begins with the *erev Shabbos* nap! So the entire week is dependent on that nap!"

During the Depression, the Pilchiks lived in abject poverty. Nevertheless, R' Nissin managed to put aside five dollars each week for the purchase of his Shabbos needs. With that money, his devoted wife would purchase fish and other delights, and would bake *eighteen challos.* Their table was always filled with guests and each guest would receive his own *challah.* As R' Nissin explained, "Some guests were shy, and we wanted every one to eat as much as he wanted without having to ask. Also, we wanted to demonstrate to our guests that they were truly welcome and that we considered it a privilege to have them at our table."

On one *Motza'ei Shabbos,* R' Nissin and his guests enjoyed a particularly uplifting *Melaveh Malkah* together. For hours on end they sang, exchanged words of Torah and related stories of *tzaddikim.* By the time they finished, it was nearing dawn. As R' Nissin walked to the *mikveh* in preparation for *Shacharis,* he met R' Shmuel Kushelevitz, a *Rosh Yeshivah* at Mesivta Torah Vodaath. "I have some good news for you!" R' Nissin exclaimed. "In six more days, it will be Shabbos again!"

Virtually nothing could dampen his joy in life as a servant of Hashem. Once, only a few days before Pesach, he misplaced his dentures. His only concern was that without dentures he could not possibly fulfill the *mitzvah* of eating *matzah* on the *Seder* night. With the help of a grandson, he searched his house but was not successful. He told his grandson, "It seems that it is Hashem's will that I should not eat *matzah* this Pesach. If this is Hashem's will, then I accept it with love and joy!" With that, he took hold of his grandson's hands and began to sing and dance. Suddenly, he stopped and said, "We are obligated to do everything that we can before assuming that there is no solution to my problem." He then phoned his dentist, who told him that it would be impossible to have a new pair of dentures made in time for Pesach. After hanging up the phone, R' Nissin again broke out in joyous song.

The dentures were found before the start of Pesach. Some fifteen minutes after they were found, R' Nissin's grandson found him sitting on his bed, clapping his hands and exclaiming again and again, "Thank You, Hashem, for helping me find my dentures."

He once related that decades earlier, a widow, who was known as a difficult person, came to his house each week to do housekeeping. One year as Pesach approached, the woman asked him, "Mr. Pilchik, could you get me some *matzah* for the *Seder*?" R' Nissin replied affirmatively. However, he later reflected, "I can give her three *matzos* and she'll be satisfied — but would that be the right thing to do? Can I allow a Jewish daughter to sit at her *Seder* all alone?" He then considered the other side of the problem. "She is a very difficult person to get along with. If she will sit at my table, it will very possibly lead to problems . . . I cannot afford to sacrifice my *Seder* — I derive spiritual sustenance from it which lasts me the entire year!" In the end, the first argument won. "I could not allow a Jewish daughter to conduct her *Seder* all alone."

R' Nissin concluded, "She joined us for the *Seder* — and it was the most uplifting *Seder* of my entire life!"

Toward the end of his long life, in 1989 (5750), R' Nissin spent the High Holy Days in Jerusalem, where he prayed at the Karlin-Stolin *Beis Midrash* with the Stoliner *Rebbe.* That year, Yom Kippur in the Holy Land was a torridly hot day; even young people found fasting more difficult than usual. During the afternoon recess, someone said, "R' Nissin, only three more hours and the fast will be over." R' Nissin was visibly upset by this remark. "You consider that good news?" he chided the fellow. "All year long I wait for this *heiliger tog* (holy day)! Each moment of Yom Kippur is precious beyond words — and you are trying to make me feel good by telling me that only three hours remain?!"

The following Yom Kippur, which was the last he spent in *Eretz Yisrael,* R' Nissin remained in *shul* after *Maariv* to recite the entire Book of *Tehillim* with a *minyan*. He related to someone that in his younger years, he and a friend studied Torah together for many hours on Yom Kippur eve following *Maariv*. They experienced such upliftment from their learning that, upon closing their *sefarim* for the night, the two joined hands in a joyous dance.

A month before his passing, when he was extremely ill and weak, he told his son, "What have I left? I am no longer able to learn, I am no longer able to *daven*. Do you know what I am still left with? My faith . . . my faith is still strong."

On the day of R' Nissin's funeral, a man approached one of his grandsons and said, "R' Nissin was your grandfather? Let me tell you a story.

"You recall, I'm sure, that seven years ago, your grandfather underwent gall bladder surgery. I, too, was hospitalized at that time; your grandfather and I spent much of our time enjoying each other's company.

"On the third day following your grandfather's surgery, he came to see me in my room, wheeling along his intravenous pole. 'Tonight is the last night of *Sefiras HaOmer* (Counting of the Omer). It is my custom to dance on this night (in celebration of the completion of the *mitzvah*). I need advice — what should I do?'

"I replied, 'Fine. Come back here tonight and we will dance together.' Your grandfather responded, 'Only the two of us? —that is no dance! I will go around to the other rooms and invite *Yidden* to join us in my room tonight.'

"What shall I tell you?" the man concluded. "Your grandfather was a flaming fire that night; it was a dance to remember. There was one Jew who, unfortunately, had had a foot amputated. Yet he was so caught up in the joy of the evening, that he insisted on joining the circle in his wheelchair!"

To Stoliner *chassidim*, R' Nissin was fondly known as 'Zeidy' (Grandfather). He once remarked, "It is correct that everyone calls me 'Zeidy' — I love everyone like my very own grandchild!"

פרשת קדושים
Parashas Kedoshim

The Case of the Missing Snack

בְּצֶדֶק תִּשְׁפֹּט עֲמִיתֶךָ.
With righteousness you shall judge your fellow (Vayikra 19:15).

One must always give people the benefit of the doubt (Rashi from Sanhedrin 34b).

It was lunchtime at Yeshivah Darchei Torah in Far Rockaway. The eighth graders ate a quick lunch and then headed outside for some ball-playing. Only one boy, Yosef Levy,[1] requested permission of his *rebbi,* R' Moshe Grossman, to remain in their second-floor classroom and spend his recess reading.

When recess ended, the students returned to their room. One boy, Shlomo Friedman, hurried to his desk and reached inside for his bag of cookies so that he could grab a quick snack before class resumed.

"Yosef!" he yelled. "You were here during recess. Who ate my snack?"

---

1. The names of the two boys in the story have been changed.

"No one," Yosef shot back. "I was here the whole time and no one else entered the room — and I certainly didn't eat it!"

"Well, I left a bag of cookies in my desk and they're gone! If no one else was here, then you're the only one who could have eaten them!" Shlomo was clearly agitated.

But so was Yosef. "Are you accusing me of stealing your cookies? What do I need your cookies for? I have plenty of my own!"

The boys continued their war of words until R' Grossman entered the room. Immediately, the two hurried over to the *rebbi's* desk. Shlomo voiced his accusation, while Yosef hotly denied the charge.

As R' Grossman questioned each boy to ascertain the facts, the door of the room opened and another *rebbi*, R' Moshe Mandel, entered. "R' Grossman!" he exclaimed. "You've got to hear this!"

"Please," R' Grossman replied. "I want to hear it, but not now. I'm in the middle of trying to resolve something."

"Well, perhaps I can resolve it for you," R' Mandel responded. "I walked by your room during recess and you won't believe what I saw! A squirrel was scampering along on the window ledge outside, and suddenly it hopped in through the open window. It scampered to the fourth row of desks, went inside a desk, and came out holding a bag of cookies." R' Mandel pointed to Shlomo Friedman's desk. "I could not believe how it knew exactly which desk held the 'loot.' Either squirrels have an unusual sense of smell, or they have uncanny eyesight. In any case, it quickly scooted back out the window with the bag of cookies. Can you believe it?"

Everyone believed it, including Shlomo, who went over to Yosef and meekly apologized.

A Message From Heaven

וְכִי תָבֹאוּ אֶל הָאָרֶץ וּנְטַעְתֶּם כָּל עֵץ מַאֲכָל וַעֲרַלְתֶּם עָרְלָתוֹ אֶת פִּרְיוֹ,
שָׁלשׁ שָׁנִים יִהְיֶה לָכֶם עֲרֵלִים לֹא יֵאָכֵל.

When you shall come to the Land and you shall plant any food tree,
you shall treat its food as forbidden; for three years they shall be
forbidden to you, they shall not be eaten (Vayikra 19:23).

All fruits of the first three years of a newly planted tree or its grafted shoots are known as *Orlah* (lit. closed off) and are forbidden for use in any way. As the Torah continues, those of the fourth year are holy and are to be eaten in Jerusalem.[1]

♚ ♚ ♚

Mr. Ben Chaim[2] is an Israeli farmer who was not fully observant until an episode occurred which would change his life forever.

In 1971, Ben Chaim planted a large area of his fields with new peach trees. By the third year of its growth, the orchard had developed beautifully and was producing fruits fit for marketing. What Ben Chaim did not realize was that these fruits were *Orlah* and that it was forbidden to benefit from them.

He and his workers packed the peaches into crates and he practically danced his way to the market, so certain was he of earning a huge profit. The price of peaches was high at that time and Mr. Ben Chaim returned from his trip to the market very pleased.

---

1. Although in general land-related commandments apply only in *Eretz Yisrael, Orlah,* through a tradition taught at Sinai, is an exception (*Kiddushin* 36a-b).
2. Not his real name.

That same evening, his happiness was marred by the mysterious death of a number of his cows. While he was upset over the loss, Ben Chaim viewed it as a natural, though unusual, loss which farmers suffer every now and then.

Two weeks later, the second harvest of peaches was ready for the market. Once again, the farmer happily returned home from the market with a handsome profit in hand. That night, the roof of his turkey coop caved in, killing most of his turkeys. Later that night, a very concerned Mr. Ben Chaim totalled up his losses from the two "accidents" and compared it with the profits of his peach sales. The two totals were almost identical; this was no coincidence.

After much soul-searching and discussion with some of his more observant neighbors, Mr. Ben Chaim went to the legendary R' Binyamin Mendelsohn, late *Rav* of *Moshav Komemius,* a *kibbutz* founded by Agudath Israel which to this day is run completely in accordance with Torah law. R' Mendelsohn began by patiently teaching the farmer the basics regarding the Torah's agricultural laws — including the laws of *Orlah.* Later, he provided Mr. Ben Chaim with a tutor who taught him the details of these laws, as well as general *mitzvah* observance. Slowly but surely, the farmer began to observe *mitzvos* more meticulously.

As the first *Shemittah*[1] following this episode approached, R' Mendelsohn spoke to Mr. Ben Chaim. Through some merit,[2] Heaven had deemed fit to send him a clear message regarding *Orlah.* Would it not be proper for the farmer to see this as a message regarding the Torah's other agricultural laws as well, and observe the laws of *Shemittah*?

For a farmer, especially one who had been non-observant

---

1. The seventh and concluding year of the agricultural cycle, when planting is prohibited and all crops which grow naturally are free for anyone's taking. The laws of *Shemittah* are detailed in *Vayikra* ch.25 and Mishnah *Shevi'is.*

2. While no one can know for certain why Mr. Ben Chaim meritred this sign, he does descend from illustrious lineage. One of his forebears was R' Baruch Mordechai Lifschitz, the Shedlitzer *Rav,* whose approbation is printed in the preface to the Chofetz Chaim's *Sefer Shemiras HaLashon.*

most of his life, it is no small undertaking to accept upon himself to let his land lie fallow for a year's time every seventh year. Mr. Ben Chaim felt equal to the challenge. He faithfully observed that *Shemittah* and every one that has followed. And he has never regretted it.

The Torah promises that if we observe the laws of *Shemittah,* then Hashem will bestow His blessing in the sixth year of the agricultural cycle, and we will not lose out. Mr. Ben Chaim reports: "It's miraculous. One has to be blind not see it. In the merit of *Shemittah,* each sixth year we see tremendous blessing."[1]

Today, one of Mr. Ben Chaim's sons is a *dayan* (rabbinical judge) in a large Israeli city, a second son studies in a *kollel,* and a third studies in a yeshivah.

---

1. From an article by R' Shmuel Bloom in *The Jewish Observer* (October 1993).

פרשת אמור
Parashas Emor

Teaching By Example

אֱמֹר אֶל הַכֹּהֲנִים בְּנֵי אַהֲרֹן וְאָמַרְתָּ אֲלֵהֶם . . .

Say to the Kohanim, the sons of Aharon, and you shall say to them . . . (Vayikra 21:1).

Rashi (citing *Yevamos* 114a) writes that the apparently redundant *say* in "and say to them," teaches that the *Kohanim* were enjoined to ensure that their young children [i.e. those under the age of bar mitzvah] not transgress the laws of ritual purity which are unique to *Kohanim*.

R' Moshe Feinstein (*Darash Moshe*) notes that while the Sages seem to be interpreting the second term as a warning from the *Kohanim* to their youngsters, the plain meaning of the verse does not indicate this. R' Moshe, therefore, explains that the term אֱמֹר, *say,* is a command to teach the laws to the *Kohanim,* while the term וְאָמַרְתָּ, *say to them,* is a command that the *Kohanim* be taught to observe the laws in a way of love which will, by example, influence their children in a positive way.

When a parent's words and deeds demonstrate his love for the *mitzvos* and that he views their observance as a privilege, this will influence his children to love the *mitzvos* and observe them steadfastly. However, when a parent conveys an attitude that *mitzvah* observance is a burden which he accepts for lack of a choice, then there is a real danger that his children will not want to bear what he considers a "burden."

❧ ❧ ❧

During the early years of this century there lived a wealthy Jew named R' Binyamin Beinush Denus, who was one of the main supporters of Torah study in Lithuania, both before and after the First World War.

R' Binyamin's father had been snatched away at the tender age of seven to serve in the Czar's army. It was during the period of the infamous Cantonist decrees, which were designed to tear Jewish boys from their families and heritage and erase any vestige of Jewishness from their souls. Army emissaries would force young boys from their homes to "serve the motherland" for as long as twenty-five years.

Incredibly, when R' Binyamin's father was discharged from the army as a young man in his twenties, he returned home as a Jew deeply committed to his faith. Providence had arranged that throughout his first years in the army, a deeply religious boy some five years his senior was part of his battalion. This boy cared for him like a brother, both physically and spiritually, and ensured that he, as well as other Jewish boys, remained faithful to Hashem and His Torah. Every day this boy gathered his young charges, and together they would recite the *Shema*, declaring their belief in the one and only Hashem.

In his later years, pained by the fact that he had been denied the opportunity to study Torah, R' Binyamin's father hired for himself a *melamed* (Torah teacher), who would normally teach children, to study with him regularly. The lessons of his pure faith and love of Torah were absorbed well by his son, R' Binyamin.

Though R' Binyamin was a man of wealth, he would not carpet the floor of his home. Upon his wife's request, he purchased a new carpet — and then had it placed in his attic for storage! "I can't have carpeting in my home!" he argued. "I want the poor to feel welcome here; if they see carpeting on my floors they will hesitate to enter for fear of soiling the carpet with the mud on their boots. But I *did* purchase the carpet, so that you would not suspect that I was just being stingy."

Once, he fell deathly ill. It seemed as if his end was near and the *chevra kadisha* (burial society) was summoned. When they came to his bedside, R' Binyamin asked the leader, "So how much do you reckon my burial will cost?"[1] The startled man found it difficult to respond, but did manage to name a sum. "Fine," said R' Binyamin, and he instructed his family to pay the sum immediately. Soon after, he experienced a miraculous recovery. To those who suggested that his payment to the *chevra kadisha* had been the result of *Ruach HaKodesh* (Divine Inspiration), R' Binyamin replied, "Not at all. As I lay there stricken, I considered the possibility that my judgment was somehow linked to the needs of the *chevra kadisha*. Perhaps they had pleaded to the One Above that He grant them sustenance, and Heaven had decreed that their request be granted through the revenue which my demise would generate. So I said to myself, 'Why postpone benefiting these people until after death? Perhaps by paying them now, the *kitrug* (Heavenly accusation) against me will be removed! Apparently, it worked."

His home was frequented by the outstanding Torah personalities of the Lithuanian Torah world, whose yeshivos received major support from R' Binyamin. One *rosh yeshivah* would receive a particularly large donation. R' Binyamin explained, "When a solicitor seems very impressed with my elegant home and fine furnishings, I find it hard to be overly generous. You see, if my wealth is so impressive, than parting with it is no simple matter.

"However, when observing this *rosh yeshivah* in my home, I can tell that my wealth leaves him wholly unimpressed. He

---

1. In those days, it was common for the *chevra kadisha* to charge according to what the deceased's family could afford. Accordingly, R' Binyamin's burial would have earned them a hefty fee.

makes me understand that my material possessions are of little permanent value — it's Torah and *mitzvos* that really count. With this kind of understanding, how can I not give him a very large donation?"

It is told that once a *rosh yeshivah* traveled through a fierce storm to solicit a donation from R' Binyamin. When he arrived at his destination, his coat was drenched and his boots were caked with mud. Not wanting to track water and mud all over R' Binyamin's floor, the *rosh yeshivah* entered the house through a back door. R' Binyamin was visibly upset by this, and he explained:

"My two daughters are growing up amid wealth; this is something that I cannot help, for Hashem has blessed with me with prosperity. My house is frequented by wealthy businessmen who come to deal with me, and this too does not go unnoticed by my children. My dream, however, is that my daughters should marry true *talmidei chachamim*. How can I instill in them a love and appreciation for Torah? By teaching them by way of example that Torah is worth more to me than all the money in the world.

"My daughters know that when it is time for me to attend one of my daily *shiurim* (Torah lectures), I stop whatever I am doing and head for the *shiur*. Even a room full of businessmen cannot prevent me from keeping to my daily learning schedule. And my daughters know something else — that no one receives more honor in this home than a *talmid chacham*. When a *talmid chacham* enters my home, I drop everything and hurry to tend to him with the greatest respect and concern.

"Now, I fear, my daughters will think that I value my furnishings more than the honor of a *talmid chacham*. Quite possibly, they will assume that the *Rosh Yeshivah* was merely honoring my wishes by coming in through the kitchen. And if they will think this way, then what will become of them?!"

"I appreciate your feelings," said the *Rosh Yeshivah*, "but did you really expect me to track mud all over your house?"

R' Binyamin replied, "Nevertheless, I have a favor to ask of the *Rosh Yeshivah*. Please allow me to escort you to my dining room near the front door while you are still wearing your coat and boots. I am really not concerned about my floors and furniture. I am far more concerned that my children learn to revere the Torah and its scholars." And with those words, he escorted the *Rosh Yeshivah* to the front of the house.

It is no wonder that his daughters did grow up with a heightened appreciation for Torah and its students. They married two of the leaders of the Telshe Yeshivah in Telshe, Lithuania — R' Shmuel Zalman Bloch and R' Avraham Yitzchak Bloch.[1] And for three years, R' Binyamin Denus single-handedly sustained the Telshe Yeshivah.

---

1. R' Shmuel Zalman Bloch was the father-in-law of the Telshe *Rosh Yeshivah,* R' Mordechai Gifter. R' Avraham Yitzchak Bloch was the father-in-law of the late Telshe *Rosh Yeshivah,* R' Baruch Sorotzkin.

A Single Mitzvah

לְנֶפֶשׁ לֹא יִטַּמָּא בְּעַמָּיו.

. . . to a [dead] person, he shall not become impure among his people
(*Vayikra* 21:1).

The term בְּעַמָּיו, *among his people,* teaches that a *Kohen* may not defile himself by coming in contact with a corpse when that corpse is "among his people," that is, when there are others who can attend to it. This comes to exclude the case of a *meis mitzvah* (unattended corpse), which even a *Kohen Gadol* (High Priest) may attend to (*Rashi* from *Toras Kohanim*).

❈ ❈ ❈

In 1959, a woman was killed instantly when hit by a car as she crossed a street in Bnei Brak. No one recognized the woman and a search through her pocketbook revealed that she lived in a secular neighborhood in the city of Holon. No one knew why she had come to Bnei Brak. When her neighbors in Holon were contacted, they said that the woman lived alone and had no family as far as they knew.

A meeting of *rabbanim* was held in Bnei Brak and it was decided that the deceased had the status of a *meis mitzvah,* and therefore it was the responsibility of the Bnei Brak community to conduct a funeral and give the woman a proper burial.

As preparations got underway, the deceased lay in the Great Synagogue of Bnei Brak, where *talmidei chachamim* and commonfolk gathered to recite *Tehillim.* Then, the police arrived at the scene and demanded that the body be handed over to them. They admitted that before burying the deceased, the body would be given to pathologists so that they could perform an autopsy and remove organs for laboratory work. Representatives of the community explained that Jewish law prohibits such practices and that they were halachically responsible to ensure that the woman be given a burial which would be in accordance with Jewish law.

The police sent in reinforcements and threatened to remove the body by force. At the same time, a few thousand residents assembled outside the synagogue, while scores inside continued to recite *Tehillim* for the deceased. The situation grew tense and many feared the worst. Finally, after lengthy discussion between community activists and the police hierarchy, permission was granted for the people of Bnei Brak to go ahead with the funeral and burial as planned. The police left the scene and the funeral got underway, with thousands in attendance.

Tehillim was recited and *Kaddish* was said in memory of the deceased. A huge crowd accompanied the body to its resting place. Each time that the procession passed a synagogue, another *Kaddish* was said. Someone undertook to recite *Kaddish* for the entire year of mourning.

Some wondered: This woman had lived a secular existence and she was not even a resident of Bnei Brak. Why had Heaven arranged that she should die in Bnei Brak and be accorded a funeral which thousands attended and where *Tehillim* was recited by hundreds, and that she be given a traditional burial which she would not have otherwise merited?

A resident of Bnei Brak came forward to say that he remembered this woman from the ghetto in Poland where they and thousands of others had been incarcerated by the Germans. This man remembered well how this woman risked her life to bury Jews who had been killed in the ghetto or who had died of hunger and disease.

Though man may forget with the passage of time, Hashem does not forget. Every good deed brings with it fitting, inestimable reward (*Sichos Chaim*).

פרשת בהר
Parashas Behar

Watch Your Words

וְלֹא תוֹנוּ אִישׁ אֶת עֲמִיתוֹ.

Each of you shall not aggrieve his fellow man (Vayikra 25:17).

Here the Torah cautions us regarding אוֹנָאַת דְּבָרִים,
causing hurt through words (Rashi).

Sefer HaChinuch (§338) writes: "This commandment prohibits us from causing pain or embarrassment to others in any manner. We must be careful not to insult others even by way of hints or motions. The Torah is extremely stringent regarding אוֹנָאַת דְּבָרִים because it causes so much pain to people."

The *Midrash* (*Vayikra Rabbah* 33:1) relates that once, Rabbi Yehudah *HaNasi* (the Prince) held a feast for his disciples at which tongue was served. Rabbi Yehudah watched as his disciples passed over the tougher pieces of meat in favor of those that were tender. He used this to teach a lesson: When one uses his tongue for speech, he should be careful to express himself in a gentle and respectful manner and refrain from words that are sharp and possibly hurtful.

❃ ❃ ❃

R' Yaakov Yosef Herman was a unique individual. At the age of bar mitzvah, he found himself all alone in America, a young immigrant from Russia with no one to care for him. Nevertheless, he overcame all obstacles to earn a livelihood and, at the same time, strive ever higher in his service of Hashem and become an outstanding *talmid chacham*. After he married, his house on the Lower East Side became a center of Torah and *chesed*.

In 1939, R' Yaakov Yosef and his devoted wife emigrated to *Eretz Yisrael* where they lived for the rest of their lives. There, too, they continued their tradition of spreading Torah, welcoming guests and strengthening *mitzvah* observance. Everyone who came in contact with them knew that these were people who possessed a rare level of faith and who lived their lives on a higher plane.

For a time after Mrs. Herman passed away, a relative lived with R' Yaakov Yosef. One night, R' Yaakov Yosef had difficulty falling asleep, which for him was most unusual. A person who carefully weighed his every word and deed, he was sure that his inability to fall asleep had to be related to some spiritual problem in his home. He lay in bed thinking of what he might have done wrong that day that was causing his insomnia, but he could not come up with anything of substance. Finally, he saw no choice but to awaken his companion.

"What happened here today?" he asked his sleepy relative.

"Nothing, nothing at all."

"Did anyone visit today?"

"Yes, your grandson Avremal."

"Did anything happen during his visit?'

"Not really."

"Tell me the truth," R' Yaakov Yosef pressed. "Did anything at all happen while Avremal was here?"

"Well, nothing really terrible. Avremal and I had a bit of an argument, and for a joke I told him that he should not come here any more."

R' Yaakov Yosef was most disturbed by this. "Get dressed," he instructed. "Avremal is an orphan and your words may have offended him. We will go to his house and you will ask him forgiveness."

"But it's the middle of the night!" the relative protested. "Avremal is surely sleeping — I will go to speak with him first thing in the morning. I'm sure that he did not take me seriously."

But R' Yaakov Yosef was adamant. "When a wrong is committed, it must be corrected immediately. We are going now."

They walked through the quiet Jerusalem streets until they reached the apartment complex in which Avremal lived. Looking up at the windows of his third-floor apartment, they saw that a light was on in his dining room.

They climbed the stairs and knocked softly on the door. Avremal opened the door and exclaimed, "*Zeidy* (Grandfather), what are you doing here in the middle of the night?"

"And what are *you* doing up in the middle of the night?" R' Yaakov Yosef responded.

"I could not sleep; something was troubling me," was Avremal's response.

R' Yaakov Yosef then motioned to his relative, who had been standing in the hallway. The relative rushed in and exclaimed, "Avremal, surely you did not take me seriously when I said that you were not welcome any longer in your *zeidy's* apartment. If you did, then please forgive me." Avremal replied that he forgave him.

Then, turning to R' Yaakov Yosef, Avremal said with deep emotion, "*Zeidy,* you have lifted a heavy weight from my heart. I could not imagine that I would not be welcome in your house, where I grew up."

R' Yaakov Yosef and his companion returned home. As soon as R' Yaakov Yosef returned to his bed, he fell asleep.[1]

✿ ✿ ✿

Torah sages throughout the generations have always exercised great caution in speech, choosing words which help

---

1. Adapted from *All for the Boss: The Life and Impact of Yaakov Yosef Herman, a Torah Pioneer in America* by Ruchoma Shain (published by Feldheim).

instead of harm, and always taking into account the particulars of a given situation.

R' Gedaliah Schorr, late *Rosh Yeshivah* of Mesivta Torah Vodaath, was traveling with a professor who had no yeshivah background but who attended a *Daf Yomi* class each morning. The professor had not been able to attend that morning's class and was attempting to learn "the *daf*" (daily page) on the train. "Would you mind if we learned together?" R' Schorr asked him. "I haven't learned today's *daf* either." The professor later said, "He surely didn't need me to study the *daf*. He knew that I was struggling, so he gave up his time to teach me the *gemara,* and made me feel as if I was doing him a favor!"

※   ※   ※

R' Yisrael Spira, the late Bluzhever *Rebbe,* was a man of deep sensitivity towards others. He had a keen understanding of human nature and always found the right words when conversing with people.

Once, a man spoke with him concerning his elderly father. The father had taken ill and doctors had cautioned him to restrict his activity. One practice which they insisted be stopped was his daily immersion in a *mikveh.* The man was of chassidic stock and he steadfastly insisted that he could not give up this practice. The *Rebbe* agreed with the son that his father had to obey doctors' orders and he arranged to discuss the matter with him.

Soon after, the elderly man called on the *Rebbe.* He came prepared with an argument. "Does not the *Rebbe* immerse himself in the *mikveh* each morning? Well, I am younger than the *Rebbe,* so surely it is all right for me as well!"

The *Rebbe,* who was then well past eighty, did not immediately respond. He knew that the man's logic was seriously flawed. Of course he was older than the man. But the man was in a poor state of health, while he was in good health. The *Rebbe* knew, however, that to tell this to the man would surely cause him hurt and would weaken his spirit. Then, an idea came to him.

"What you say is true, for indeed I am older than you. But what can I do? I am a *Rebbe* of *chassidim*. Now, what will *chassidim* think of a *Rebbe* who does not immerse himself in a *mikveh* every morning? *I* really have no choice; I must do it for my livelihood!"

The elderly Jew was convinced and agreed to follow doctor's orders.

❊ ❊ ❊

When R' Yaakov Kamenetsky, late *Rosh Yeshivah* of Mesivta Torah Vodaath, was in his seventies, his *rebbetzin* of many years passed away. When he later remarried, he would invite *talmidim* to join him at his table as he had done in the past. For the first Shavuos holiday following his remarriage, he invited three *talmidim* to join him and his new *rebbetzin* for *kiddush* on the first morning of the *yom tov*.

R' Yaakov entered his home, greeted his *rebbetzin* and led his students to the dining room table, which was already prepared with cups, wine and an assortment of cheesecake and *blintzes*, as is customarily served on Shavuos. When the *rebbetzin* went into the kitchen for something, the *talmidim* noticed that R' Yaakov seemed preoccupied.

He explained, "It is my *minhag* (custom) not to eat cheese on Fridays — but I forgot to mention this to my new *rebbetzin*. A *minhag,* as you know, has the strength of a vow, which must be observed. On the other hand, if I do not partake of the delicacies which my *rebbetzin* has taken so much trouble to prepare, it will surely cause her hurt."

With his *rebbetzin* still in the kitchen, R' Yaakov asked his *talmidim* to serve as a *beis din* (rabbinical court) so that they could perform *hataras nedarim* (annulment of vows) for him. This was accomplished before his *rebbetzin* returned to the room.

When she returned, R' Yaakov recited *Kiddush,* partook of the delicacies and brought happiness to his new wife by complimenting her on her fine baking. After *yom tov,* R' Yaakov informed her of his custom regarding cheese.

פרשת בחוקתי
Parashas Bechukosai

The Blessing of Torah (I)

אִם בְּחֻקֹּתַי תֵּלֵכוּ . . . וְנָתַתִּי גִשְׁמֵיכֶם בְּעִתָּם . . .

If you will follow My decrees . . . then I will provide your rains in their time . . . (Vayikra 26:3-4).

If you will follow My decrees — that you will toil
intensively in Torah study (Rashi from Sifra).

The year was 1951, and America was at war in Korea, when
the draft notice arrived. Understandably, Daniel[1] was
more than a bit apprehensive.

He had grown up in the Willamsburg section of Brooklyn and
had attended Mesivta Torah Vodaath. After developing a heart
condition, Daniel's father sought an alternative to the fast-
paced city life. He purchased a farm in Farmingdale, New
Jersey and moved his family there. The farm was near an
Orthodox *shul* and was only a few miles from the city of

---

1. Not his real name.

Lakewood, which since 1941 was home to Beth Medrash Govoha, the great yeshivah of higher learning headed by R' Aharon Kotler.

Some of R' Aharon's *talmidim* had studied at Torah Vodaath and Daniel was friendly with them. He spent most of his day working on his father's farm, and at night would take a bus to Lakewood where he would spend a few hours studying Torah.

Soon after the draft notice arrived, Daniel went to see R' Aharon. Upon being told of the notice, R' Aharon spent some time trying to allay the young man's fears, even telling him of friends of his who had been drafted into the Russian Army during the First World War and had returned home safely.

As their conversation drew to a close, Daniel asked, "Could the *Rosh Yeshivah* please give me a *berachah* (blessing)?"

R' Aharon was clearly uncomfortable with the request. With genuine humility, he responded that he was not one from whom people sought blessings. Daniel, however, persisted with his request. R' Aharon sat in thoughtful silence for a short while and then said, "Accept upon yourself that throughout your army service, you will study Torah every day without exception."

Daniel was taken aback by the suggestion. *Study Torah every day — in the army?* It seemed impossible. In the army "orders are orders"; surely, in the thick of battle, a soldier's time is not his own. There might be days when it would simply be impossible to open a *sefer*.

Daniel attempted to explain his views on the matter, but now, it was R' Aharon who was persistent. No, he contended, it *was* possible to fulfill such a commitment. He was not asking Daniel to commit himself to *a specific amount* of learning time, only that *he would learn* each and every day.

Bowing to R' Aharon's wisdom, Daniel committed himself to daily study. Certain that R' Aharon had intended this as a precondition to granting his request, he said, "Now, can the *Rosh Yeshivah* please bless me that I should return home safely?"

R' Aharon responded with emotion, "You don't understand — *dos alein is der berachah,* this itself is the *berachah!* Once you have accepted to study Torah daily, there is no need for any further blessings."

Daniel reported for induction with a duffle bag which contained, among other items, his *tefillin,* a *siddur* and a few *sefarim.* He endured weeks of grueling training as part of an infantry battalion. He kept to his word; no matter how exhausted, he would not retire for the night without first studying from his *gemara.*

When their training was completed, Daniel's group was assembled and told their assignments. Out of two hundred soldiers, one hundred and eighty were sent to fight in Korea. Daniel, however, was sent to Ft. Belvoir, Virginia, where he was assigned to a desk job. For the next two years, until his honorable discharge, he handled paperwork for a few hours a day and spent the remaining hours at his desk studying Torah. As he jokes about it now, "I was studying in *'kollel'* . . ."

But before entering his private *"kollel,"* Daniel had undertaken a crucial commitment. As R' Aharon had put it, *"Dos alein is der berachah."*

The Blessing of Torah (II)

There is a tradition that the occasion of a *siyum* (completion) of a Talmudic tractate is an auspicious time for one's prayers to be accepted and one's hopes to be realized. Stories are told of *tzaddikim* in earlier generations whose blessings, when conferred at the time of a *siyum,* achieved miraculous results.

In Jerusalem some four decades ago lived a couple that was childless for many years. R' Velvel Tchetchik, a renowned *tzaddik* and scholar, offered them the following advice: The Brisker *Rav,* R' Yitzchak Zev Soloveitchik, was soon to complete *Masechta Zevachim* with a study group which met regularly in his home. R' Tchetchik advised that on the evening of the *siyum,* the wife should request that the *Rav* confer his blessing that she and her husband be granted a child.

The night of the *siyum,* after the members of the *Rav's* study group had gone home, the *Rav's* daughter approached him to say that this woman had come seeking his blessing. The *Rav* responded, "May Hashem help her."

Ten months later she gave birth to a boy (*P'ninei Rabbeinu HaGriz*).

Toiling in Torah

Once, the late Telshe *Rosh Yeshivah* R' Baruch Sorotzkin was studying with a student in his home. R' Baruch was offering his understanding of a comment of *Rashba* when the phone rang. It was another *rosh yeshivah,* calling to request of R' Baruch that he send some of his married *talmidim* to help start a *kollel* somewhere. R' Baruch replied that he could not honor the request at that particular time. However, the caller was not satisfied with this response and the discussion continued for a long time. The call finally ended with R' Baruch remaining with his decision not to honor the request.

Upon hanging up the phone, R' Baruch turned to his student and asked, "Am I not correct?" The student was caught off guard. Why was the *Rosh Yeshivah* asking *him* if he agreed with his decision? If he felt that he could not send *talmidim* away at that time, then certainly he was correct!

While the student tried to find the words with which to respond, R' Baruch posed his question again. "Am I not correct? Is it possible to explain the *Rashba* any other way . . .?"

❧ ❧ ❧

In his later years, R' Chaim Ozer Grodzensky, the great *Rav* of Vilna, had to undergo surgery, but due to his poor physical condition, doctors felt that it would be dangerous to administer anesthesia. Before the operation was to begin, R' Chaim Ozer asked for a certain *sefer.* Throughout the surgery, he remained immersed in the text, seemingly oblivious to the pain. As his wife later related to R' Shimon Schwab, the doctors could not believe that such a phenomenal power of concentration was possible. The doctors could not know that such concentration was possible only because R' Chaim Ozer's *neshamah* (soul) was firmly and eternally bound to the Torah's sacred words.

The Will to Live

The Tchebiner *Rav,* R' Dov Beirish Weidenfeld, was recognized as one of the generation's outstanding Torah personalities until his passing in 1965. In his eulogy of the *Rav,* the Mirrer *Rosh Yeshivah,* R' Chaim Shmulevitz, related the following:

The Tchebiner *Rav's* guidance was often sought by *Eretz Yisrael's* religious community as it faced the issues of the day. It was known that the *Rav* would almost never take leave of his studies, in which he toiled ceaselessly. When asked, he would readily analyze a current issue and state his opinion, but he would not attend rabbinic conferences on the matter.

It happened once that the Torah leaders of the land were to meet regarding an issue of paramount importance and they agreed that the Tchebiner Rav should be asked to participate. R' Chaim, together with another luminary of that day, went to personally call on the *Rav.*

The Tchebiner *Rav* welcomed his distinguished guests and listened to their request. He responded, "This surely is a matter of major importance; the meeting is absolutely necessary and participating in it is surely a great *mitzvah.* However, I am sorry but I cannot attend."

R' Chaim and his companion were somewhat taken aback. If the *Rav* did agree that the matter was so pressing, then why would he not participate? They repeated their request.

The Tchebiner *Rav* was silent for a few moments. "I'll tell you," he finally said. "Thirteen years ago I was dangerously ill; it appeared as if my end was near. At that time, I followed the example of King Chizkiyahu in his time of illness — 'And Chizkiyahu turned his face toward the wall and he prayed to Hashem' (*II Kings* 20:2). I cried out, '*Ribbono shel Olam! Ich vil lernen Dein heiliger Torah! Ich vil lernen Dein heiliger Torah!* Master of the Universe! I want to study Your holy Torah! I want to study Your holy Torah!' Hashem heeded my cries, and miraculously, I was cured.

"So you see, I am alive today because I begged Hashem to be allowed to continue to study Torah. Therefore, I cannot allow anything — not even a pressing communal matter — to take me away from my studies. As I said before, the meeting *is* important and attending it is certainly a great *mitzvah* and not in the realm of *bitul Torah* (disruption of Torah study). Nevertheless, I cannot attend."

In relating the above, R' Chaim concluded: "The *pasuk* (verse) states that after Chizkiyahu had concluded his prayer, G-d appeared to the prophet Yeshayahu and informed him that the king would be healed from his illness three days hence. The prophecy continued: '[Say to Chizkiyahu:] And I shall add to your days fifteen years' (ibid. v. 6).

"And the Tchebiner *Rav* passed away two years after the above incident, fifteen years after he fell ill and uttered his prayer, like Chizkiyahu."

פרשת במדבר
Parashas Bamidbar

More Than Meets the Eye

אִישׁ עַל דִּגְלוֹ בְאֹתֹת לְבֵית אֲבֹתָם יַחֲנוּ בְּנֵי יִשְׂרָאֵל.

The Children of Israel shall encamp, each man by his banner according to the insignias of their father's household (Bamidbar 2:2).

Hashem commanded that the Twelve Tribes encamp around the *Mishkan* in formations of three tribes each. These formations were known as דְּגָלִים, *banners,* and each "banner" was led by a designated tribe.

As *Rashi* relates, these formations had actually been transmitted by our forefather Yaakov before his death some two hundred years earlier. On his deathbed, Yaakov had instructed his sons to occupy specific positions when they would carry his coffin from Egypt to *Eretz Yisrael* for burial. The דְּגָלִים in the Wilderness were arranged according to this formation.

Picture a casual observer at the funeral of Yaakov, as he watched the grieving sons take up specific positions around their father's coffin. Why make an issue over such a matter, the person may have wondered. Did it really matter if Yehudah, or Shimon, or Naftali, stood on the right, the left, the middle or the front? Yet centuries later, as the tribes encamped in formation around the *Mishkan,* the specific position of each tribe took on tremendous significance. For example, the greatness in Torah of the tribes of Yehudah, Yissachar and Zevulun had much to do with the fact that they were encamped on the east, and were neighbors with Moshe, Aharon and his sons.[1] When Yaakov blessed his sons before he departed this world, he foretold the greatness in Torah of Yissachar. Yaakov saw what others did not, and his instructions regarding the bearing of his coffin reflected his greater sense of "vision."

A *tzaddik* can often see what others cannot. Therefore, his words and instructions which may seem unimportant today may take on great significance at some future time.

❀ ❀ ❀

R' Yisrael Zev Gustman, who passed away in Jerusalem in 5749 (1989), was a link to the glorious days of Torah greatness of pre-War Lithuania. At age twenty-two, he began serving on the Vilna rabbinate headed by the generation's leader, R' Chaim Ozer Grodzensky. R' Chaim Ozer held the young *rav* in great esteem and forwarded halachic questions to him which were posed by the some of the greatest *poskim* of the day.

When R' Gustman arrived in *Eretz Yisrael* after the War, he called on the world-renowned Tchebiner *Rav,* who was considerably older than him. The *Rav* recognized the name "Gustman" from a correspondence which he had once received when he had sent a question to R' Chaim Ozer. "Perhaps," the Tchebiner *Rav* asked him, "you are the son of *HaRav* Gustman from Vilna?" When the *Rav* realized that *he was speaking to HaRav Gustman,* he put on his hat and coat and recited the blessing one says when seeing an exceptionally great Torah personality.[2]

Especially in his last years, R' Chaim Ozer's health was frail. On most afternoons, he was taken for a wagon ride in the forests on the outskirts of the city so that his lungs could

---

1. *Rashi* to 3:38 citing *Midrash Tanchuma.*
2. *See Shulchan Aruch, Orach Chaim* 224:6.

inhale the fresh country air. Very often, he asked young R' Yisrael Zev Gustman to accompany him, and the two would spend their time together discussing Torah topics.

One afternoon, for reasons which he did not explain, R' Chaim Ozer broke with his usual practice and instead used the wagon ride to give his escort a "guided tour" of the forest. "Over there," he pointed out, "is a cave . . . That plant over there is poisonous . . . The one over here, on the other hand, is *not* poisonous, and can in fact provide some sustenance . . ." R' Gustman listened and nodded in understanding, but did not understand the purpose of all this information.

September 1, 1939 arrived. The Second World War erupted as Poland was invaded by Germany from one side and Russia from the other. Vilna, which was officially the capital of Lithuania, had been under Polish control since 1919. Now, in what proved to be one of the great hidden miracles of the Second World War, Russia announced that it would be returning Vilna to Lithuania, and allowed that country to maintain its independence for the time being. Until the transfer officially took place, the border between Poland and Vilna would remain open.

R' Chaim Ozer recognized this as an opportunity for rescue, and sent messages to the yeshivos in Poland to flee to Vilna even on Shabbos, in the hope that they could escape Russian tyranny and possibly depart from Lithuania for the free world. The *roshei yeshivah* heeded R' Chaim Ozer's call and, along with thousands of yeshivah students, streamed into Vilna. R' Chaim Ozer, ill and often confined to bed, directed the massive organization and relocation of these yeshivos. By fleeing to Vilna before the border between Poland and Lithuania was sealed shut, many *roshei yeshivah* and students were able to flee Eastern Europe, be saved from the horrors of the Holocaust, and play a major role in the revival of Torah study after the war.[1]

---

1. The escape through Vilna and R' Chaim Ozer's efforts in that episode are recorded in *Reb Chaim Ozer: The Life and Ideals of Rabbi Chaim Ozer*

Less than a year after the war's outbreak, in the summer of 1940, R' Chaim Ozer lay deathly ill. By that time, Russian troops had entered Lithuania and the situation had deteriorated. It would become considerably worse when the Germans declared war against Russia and invaded Lithuania.

As Jewry entered the month of Av, when we mourn the Destruction of both Temples, as well as other national tragedies of this long and difficult exile, it appeared that R' Chaim Ozer's time to leave this world had come. The *rabbanim* of Vilna were permitted to enter R' Chaim Ozer's room and take leave of him individually.

When R' Gustman's turn came, R' Chaim Ozer grasped his hand and said, "You will overcome them — both the East and the West." To no one else did R' Chaim Ozer say these words.

Soon after the Nazis entered Vilna, they declared a certain day "Rabbis' Day," when they made a special effort to track down and eliminate every *rav* in the city, for they understood that the teachers of Torah infuse their people with faith and spirit. R' Gustman was seized by a Nazi soldier but miraculously escaped. He, his wife and their little daughter fled to the forests of Vilna. It was then that R' Gustman recalled the day when R' Chaim Ozer had pointed out certain facts about the forest and its vegetation and he now put that knowledge to use in trying to keep his family alive and well.[1]

For almost five years they hid, and on numerous occasions were a hairsbreadth away from death. More than *one hundred times* during the war, R' Gustman recited *Vidui* (the confessional prayer), certain that his final moments had arrived. In more than one incident, bullets creased his scalp. In several instances, Nazi soldiers looked straight at him but apparently did not see him. R' Gustman later said, "It was more than a miracle; it was a decree from Heaven. The *Ribono shel Olam* Who decrees who shall die also decrees who shall live."

Grodzensky (Mesorah Publications).

1. R' Gustman would personally water the garden of his yeshivah in *Eretz*

He and his family were among the very few to return to Vilna when the war ended. One night, a Jewish Communist knocked on R' Gustman's door to warn him that the Soviet regime which had regained control of Lithuania was planning to deport him the next day. That night, R' Gustman fled with his family, and eventually arrived safely in America.

As R' Chaim Ozer had foretold, he had overcome the "East" — the Russians of Eastern Europe — and the "West" — the Germans of Western Europe.[1]

Yisrael to display his gratitude for having survived by eating grasses and shrubs.

1. Author's note: In the summer of 1987, while writing *Reb Chaim Ozer,* I placed a call to *Eretz Yisrael* and had the privilege of speaking with R' Gustman, זצ״ל. I related the above episode in concise form, asked whether the story was true and requested permission to publish it. R' Gustman replied that it was true and that he would allow me to publish it, on condition that I not use his name, but say that it happened to "a *rav* in Vilna." At that time, I followed his instructions. Now, after his passing, and when the account has already been published elsewhere with R' Gustman's name, it was deemed proper to use his name.

פרשת נשא
Parashas Naso

Mutual Admiration

זֹאת חֲנֻכַּת הַמִּזְבֵּחַ בְּיוֹם הִמָּשַׁח אֹתוֹ מֵאֵת נְשִׂיאֵי יִשְׂרָאֵל.

This was the dedication of the Altar, on the day it was anointed, from the leaders of Israel (Bamidbar 7:84).

The Torah records each of the *Nesi'im's* (Princes') dedication offerings, though all were identical. The *Midrash* and commentators explain that the *Nesi'im* did not confer with one another and decide to bring the same offering. Rather, each one had different reasons and intended different symbolisms, and Heaven ordained that through their reckonings and symbolisms, they would all arrive at the identical offering.

The Ponovezher *Rosh Yeshivah,* R' Eliezer Menachem Shach, saw an important lesson in this. In authentic service of Hashem, there is more than one path. What is crucial is that one's way of life and outlook be rooted in authentic Torah law and tradition. If such is the case, then all paths will ultimately lead to the same result — a firm attachment to Hashem and His Torah.

We can take this lesson one step further. Since there is more than one path in serving Hashem, then it is important that members of different paths respect one another, and certainly not denigrate one another.

The *Midrash* states that one of the miracles at the crossing of the Sea of Reeds was that each of the twelve tribes had its own path, crossing between walls of frozen water on either side. The *Midrash* tells of yet another miracle: the walls of frozen water were transparent, so that the tribes could see one another as they crossed. Some explain that this was meant to teach the Jewish people: Hold firm to the traditions and ways of your "tribe" — your family, your community — but always view those of other groups with respect and love.

❧ ❧ ❧

Torah leaders of variant backgrounds and schools of thought have always held each other in great esteem.

The relationship between R' Avraham Yehoshua Heschel, the *Rebbe* of Kapishnitz, and the outstanding luminaries of the Lithuanian Torah world was one of true love and deep admiration. The *Rebbe* was extremely close with the legendary leader of Torah Jewry in America after the Second World War, R' Aharon Kotler.

The *Rebbe* once said, "If R' Aharon would tell me to run a hundred miles, I would do it."

R' Aharon referred to the *Rebbe* as "the *gadol hador* in *chesed* (leader of the generation in lovingkindness)."[1]

At the Friday night meal at an Agudath Israel Convention, R' Aharon shared a table with R' Yaakov Yitzchak Ruderman, who was accompanied by his *talmid* at Yeshivas Ner Israel, R' Shmuel Bloom. At a nearby table sat the Kapishnitzer *Rebbe* and other chassidic leaders. R' Aharon marveled at the *Rebbe's* level of *chesed.* He related that one summer, he and the *Rebbe* were guests at Lederer's Hotel in Fleischmanns, New York. At the Friday night meal, the *Rebbe* had hurried over to R' Aharon with *challos* and wine for *Kiddush,* in the way of a child who eagerly serves an adult.

Someone who had spent a summer in Fleischmanns related that he was once walking with the *Rebbe* near the forest when

---

1. See chapters on *Parashas Tetzaveh* and *Parashas Devarim.*

they heard a voice of someone learning Torah with unmistakable joy and excitement. It was the voice of R' Aharon. The *Rebbe's* companion exclaimed, "Listen to how R' Aharon learns!"

"And how else can one become a R' Aharon?!" the *Rebbe* retorted.

During his summer respite, R' Aharon would deliver a *gemara shiur* at the hotel. The Kapishnitzer *Rebbe* would attend the *shiur,* remaining on his feet the entire time.

R' Aharon was a dynamic proponent of the *Chinuch Atzmai* school system in Israel. He served as president of the system's American fund-raising organization and worked tirelessly for it. The Kapishnitzer *Rebbe* was a founding member of *Chinuch Atzmai's* American organization and worked hand-in-hand with R' Aharon on its behalf. R' Aharon would say that were it not for the Kapishnitzer *Rebbe,* he would have been unable to cope with the pressure of his commitment to ensure *Chinuch Atzmai's* existence and growth.

Once, R' Aharon visited the *Rebbe* and asked that he accompany him on some fund-raising visits. Though the *Rebbe* was not feeling well that day, he immediately donned his coat and headed out the door. Concerned for the *Rebbe's* health, someone present asked, "But isn't the *Rebbe* feeling ill today?" The *Rebbe* responded, "I am a soldier — if the "General" of *Klal Yisrael* asks one to go, one goes!"

Mr. Heshy Jacob was present when R' Aharon asked the *Rebbe's* personal *gabbai* (secretary and attendant) to write a *kvittel,* [1] which R' Aharon took with him when he entered the *Rebbe's* private room to see him. The two spent a long time together. When R' Aharon emerged, another *rosh yeshivah,* who was waiting to see the *Rebbe,* expressed surprise that R' Aharon, who was of Lithuanian origin, would engage in the

---

1. A *kvittel* is a note on which one writes the Hebrew name (example: יוסף בן רחל, Yosef son of Rachel) of the person for whom he seeks the *tzaddik's* blessing, along with the specific request for what the person needs. In our day, it is not uncommon to make use of a *kvittel* even when petitioning non-Chassidic *tzaddikim.*

Chassidic custom of having a *kvittel* written. R' Aharon responded, "If you would know the *Rebbe* as I know him, you would also write a *kvittel.*"

Once, the Kapishnitzer *Rebbe's* ill state of health required him to leave New York for a short time in order to rest. He traveled to Lakewood, New Jersey, home of R' Aharon's yeshivah, where a scholarly Chassidic Jew owned an egg farm. One day, R' Aharon approached one of his *talmidim* and said, "The Kapishnitzer *Rebbe* needs to go for a walk for health reasons. Go to the egg farm right now and take him to the park for a walk."

The student drove down to the farm and brought the *Rebbe* to Rockefeller Park in Lakewood. They had walked together for only a short time when a disheveled-looking fellow approached them and began speaking to the *Rebbe* in incoherent English, a language with which the *Rebbe* was not fluent.

"Please don't disturb us," the well-meaning student told the man.

"No," the *Rebbe* told the *talmid* in *Yiddish*. "He wants something. Find out what he wants."

"He doesn't seem to be making any sense," the *talmid* replied. "I think there's something wrong with him."

"Nevertheless, listen to what he's saying and repeat it to me," the *Rebbe* insisted.

The student listened to the fellow's half-sentences and repeated them to the *Rebbe* in *Yiddish*. The *Rebbe* listened carefully and then told his companion, "Tell him that I said he should not worry. He should take care of himself and everything will be all right." When the student repeated this in English, a noticeable change came over the fellow. He seemed heartened by the *Rebbe's* words and appeared relaxed.

R' Aharon passed away on 2 Kislev, 5723 (1962) after a short illness. When the news of his passing reached the *Rebbe's* family, they decided to break it to him slowly. The *Rebbe's* son, R' Moshe Mordechai (who later succeeded him as *Rebbe*), entered his room and said, "The situation with R' Aharon is very grave . . ." The *Rebbe* responded, "And who says that there is still something to pray for?" His heart had perceived the truth.

At the *shivah*, the *Rebbe* told R' Aharon's son and successor, R' Shneur, "The *Rosh Yeshivah* was like a father to me."

Six months after R' Aharon passed away, the *Rebbe* met R' Yaakov Weisberg, who has worked for decades on behalf of Beth Medrash Govoha and was very close to R' Aharon. The *Rebbe* grasped R' Weisberg's hand and began to weep. *"Es felt mir ois ai'ereh R' Aharon . . ., * Oh, how I miss your R' Aharon . . ." he cried.

R' Moshe Feinstein and the Kapishnitzer *Rebbe* both lived in New York's Lower East Side. One year on *erev* Succos, the city was struck by a severe rainstorm. R' Moshe's *succah,* which had no protective covering, was not fit for use that night. His family, therefore, arranged for him to eat the *yom tov* meal at the *Rebbe's succah.* When R' Moshe entered the *succah* that night, the *Rebbe* was already seated, surrounded by his family and *chassidim.* The *Rebbe* exclaimed, "The *Mishnah*[1] states that rain on Succos is not a good omen. However, for me it *is* a good omen, for because of the rain, I have the *zechus* (privilege) to have *HaRav* Moshe, שליט"א, join me in my *succah!*"

The Ponovezher *Rav,* R' Yosef Shlomo Kahaneman, also enjoyed a very close relationship with the *Rebbe.* The *Rebbe* was once spending a few weeks in Miami during the winter when the Ponovezher *Rav* arrived there to raise funds for his yeshivos in *Eretz Yisrael.* The *Rav* joined the *Rebbe's* private *minyan* for *Shacharis* and *Maariv* every day.

It was the Ponovezher *Rav* who arranged the *shidduch* (marriage match) between the granddaughter of the Kapish-nitzer *Rebbe* and the son of R' Shlomo Zalman Auerbach.

---

1. *Mishnah Succah* 2:9.

When the *Rebbe* came to *Eretz Yisrael* for the wedding, he and R' Shlomo Zalman met for the first time. By the time he was preparing to return home following the week of *sheva berachos,* these two Torah giants had forged a close relationship.

On his way to the airport, the *Rebbe* came to R' Shlomo Zalman's home to take leave of him. A taxi was called, and when they heard a car horn outside, R' Shlomo Zalman escorted the *Rebbe* outside and down a flight of steps to the street. However, the taxi had not yet arrived; the horn was that of another vehicle.

R' Shlomo Zalman sent someone into his apartment to bring down a chair on which the *Rebbe* could sit until the taxi arrived. The chair was placed on the pavement and R' Shlomo Zalman invited the *Rebbe* to be seated, but despite R' Shlomo Zalman's entreaties, the *Rebbe* refused to be seated. He explained:

"When I was young, my father, of blessed memory, once told me: 'Before you do something, imagine that there is a photographer snapping pictures of you. Years later, you will take out these pictures and examine them. Will you be proud of how you appear? If yes, then go ahead and carry out your plans. Will you be ashamed of such pictures? Then cancel your plans!'

"Now, how would I feel years from now were I to look at a picture of myself *sitting* on a chair while *HaGaon* R' Shlomo Zalman Auerbach is *standing* next to me . . .?!"

When the Kapishnitzer *Rebbe* passed away on 16 Tammuz, 5727 (1967), R' Yaakov Yitzchak Ruderman was vacationing in upstate New York. R' Ruderman made the three-hour bus trip to New York City for the funeral. He told a *talmid* who accompanied him, "I would walk from Baltimore, if I had to, to attend the Kapishnitzer *Rebbe's* funeral."

פרשת בהלותך
Parashas Behaalosecha

Powerful Notes

עֲשֵׂה לְךָ שְׁתֵּי חֲצוֹצְרֹת כֶּסֶף.
Make for yourself two silver trumpets (Bamidbar 10:2).

In discussing the command that trumpets be sounded upon the offering of Temple sacrifices and at times of community distress, *Sefer HaChinuch* writes: "Among the roots of this *mitzvah* is. . . that a human being requires a great deal of spiritual awakening and nothing will awaken him like the sounds of music. . ."

R' Yisrael of Shklov, quoting his master and teacher, the Vilna Gaon, [1] writes that in music lies the power to effect *techias hameisim,* the resuscitation of the dead.

Torah study is the greatest *mitzvah* of all. Our Sages relate that King David's nighttime study was preceded by song: "A harp was suspended over David's bed. At midnight, a north wind would blow, causing it to play. When David heard the music, he would arise and engage in the study of Torah" (*Berachos* 3b).

Music and song contain awesome spiritual power.

R' Nachman,[2] a senior lecturer at a respected American

---

1. Introduction to *Pe'as HaShulchan.*
2. Not his real name.

yeshivah, became a *baal teshuvah* as a young man when he was pursuing a professional career. He had been introduced to the late R' Yehudah Davis, *Rosh Yeshivah* of Yeshivah Zichron Mayir, who, through the course of his long and productive life, was highly successful in reaching out to non-observant American young Jewish men. R' Nachman related what he views as the turning point in his return to the way of Torah.

"R' Davis took us to a remote area in upstate New York so that we could experience Shabbos in an atmosphere of utter calm and serenity. Friday night, we were sitting around the table enjoying a wonderful blend of Torah thoughts, Shabbos food and heartfelt singing. R' Davis then asked that we sing a stirring tune to the words, . . . אַחַת שָׁאַלְתִּי מֵאֵת ה', *One thing I asked of Hashem . . .* [1] 'Sing it again and again,' he told us. 'Let the words become a part of you.'

"I recall that as I sat there, singing intently with my eyes closed, I made up my mind to dedicate my life to the study and teaching of Torah."

❧   ❧   ❧

Eddie, formerly known as Ephraim,[2] had been born into an observant family but drifted away from Torah and *mitzvos*. Eventually, he joined the wayward society of Manhattan's Greenwich Village and totally severed any connections with his religious past.

One night, his father, who was no longer living, appeared to him in a dream. "Return to yeshivah," his father pleaded. "But it is false!" Eddie responded adamantly. "I never saw falsehood there," his father countered. Eddie woke up, deeply troubled. He had no intention of changing his lifestyle, but why had he had such a dream?

---

1. . . .*that shall I seek: That I dwell in the House of Hashem all the days of my life, to behold the sweetness of Hashem and to bask in His Sanctuary (Tehillim 27:4).*
2. Not his real name.

The next day, he met a friend, Elaine, who noticed that he was troubled. The girl was Jewish but was totally ignorant of even basic Jewish tradition. After hearing the details of his dream, she asked innocently, "What exactly do they do in a yeshivah?" After Eddie offered a description of what a yeshivah is, Elaine replied, "Your father seems to be right. There's nothing that you described to me which sounds false." Eddie became incensed. "If you think yeshivos are so wonderful, then why don't you join one?!"

Elaine took his advice. After making some inquiries, she headed for Jerusalem and enrolled in a seminary for girls who were returning to the path of Torah. She became deeply observant, returned to America and eventually married a young man who was engaged in the full-time study of Torah. During the week of *sheva berachos* following their wedding, Elaine told her husband, "You know, it's all thanks to Eddie that I've reached this day. If not for him, I might have remained ignorant of Judaism my entire life! Wouldn't it be proper to invite him to one of the *sheva berachos* meals as a sign of gratitude?" Her husband agreed and chose to invite Eddie to the *sheva berachos* that his fellow yeshivah students and their wives were hosting.

The *rosh yeshivah* of the yeshivah had a strong feeling for Jewish song. He inspired his students to appreciate song and to select tunes which were soul-stirring and appropriate for the occasion. In the middle of the *sheva berachos,* during a particularly heartfelt tune, Eddie burst into tears. The song had reached the depths of his soul. Ultimately, he returned to his roots.

פרשת שלח
Parashas Shelach

A Meaningful Rip

וְעָשׂוּ לָהֶם צִיצִת עַל כַּנְפֵי בִגְדֵיהֶם לְדֹרֹתָם. . .
*. . . that they shall make themselves tzitzis on the corners
of their garments, throughout their generations (Bamidbar 15:38).*

R' Yekusiel Yehudah Halberstam, the Klausenberger
Rebbe, was unique among the giants of his day. He
emerged from the Holocaust the only survivor of his immediate family, having lost his wife and eleven children, ר"ל. The
Rebbe's pure, deep-rooted faith enabled him to overcome his
personal losses and be a pillar of strength to his suffering
brethren. After the war he remarried, raised a new family, and
among many accomplishments, renewed the *chassidus* of
Klausenberg into a thriving, G-d-fearing community both in
America and in *Eretz Yisrael.* He founded the international *Mifal
HaShas* program whereby large portions of Talmud are studied
monthly by scores of students the world over.

As soon as the war ended, the *Rebbe* made his way to
various Displaced Persons Camps, where he infused the
people with hope and helped them renew their commitment to
Torah and *mitzvos.* In one episode, he was responsible for

ensuring that a large group of teenage girls, who were in danger of being lost as observant Jews, be brought back into the fold before it was too late.

The *Rebbe* worked hard to provide the survivors with religious articles such as *tefillin, tzitzis, siddurim* and *chumashim*. In one camp, he would stand for hours each morning supervising as men and boys lined up to don a single pair of *tefillin*.

Once, the *Rebbe* walked into a camp and announced that he had four sets of *tzitzis* threads which could be attached to a four-cornered garment, as *halachah* requires. One hundred and fifty men came forward for a chance to receive the *tzitzis*. The *rebbe* announced that he would draw lots to determine which four of the one hundred and fifty would receive the *tzitzis*.

But before the lots could be drawn, a teenaged boy named Mendel, a Gerrer *chassid*, stepped forward. "*Rebbe*," he cried, "I should be entitled to receive one of the pairs without a lot being drawn!"

"And why is that?" the *Rebbe* asked.

"Because the strict Scriptural law states that one is required to wear *tzitzis* if he wears a four-cornered garment, but he is not guilty of transgression for not wearing a four-cornered garment at all.[1] And I am the only one here who wears a four-cornered garment!" With those words, Mendel grabbed hold of the hem of his shirt — possibly the only one he owned at the time — and ripped it in such a way that the shirt became a four-cornered garment which required *tzitzis*.

The *Rebbe* looked kindly at this young survivor, whose suffering had not weakened his love for Hashem's *mitzvos*. "Nevertheless," the *Rebbe* said gently, "it would not be fair to the others to give you the *tzitzis* without a *goral* (lot). If your

---

1. Note, however, the words of *Shulchan Aruch*, "It is proper for every person to be careful to wear a small *tallis* all day . . . One who is meticulous regarding the *mitzvah* of *tzitzis* will merit to see the Shechinah" (*Orach Chaim* 24:1,6). Such has been the practice of Jewish males throughout the ages.

intentions in doing what you have just done were purely *l'sheim Shamayim* (for the sake of Heaven) — as it appears to be — then Heaven will see to it that your lot should be drawn."

The lots were drawn — and Mendel was a winner.[1]

1. This story was drawn from *Lapid Eish,* the recently published Hebrew biography of the Klausenberger *Rebbe.* A chapter concerning the *Rebbe's* efforts in the Displaced Persons camps appears in *Lieutenant Birnbaum* by Meyer Birnbaum with Yonason Rosenblum (Mesorah Publications).

פרשת קרח
Parashas Korach

The Greatness of Jewish Women

וַיִּקַּח קֹרַח בֶּן יִצְהָר בֶּן קְהָת בֶּן לֵוִי
וְדָתָן וַאֲבִירָם בְּנֵי אֱלִיאָב וְאוֹן בֶּן פֶּלֶת בְּנֵי רְאוּבֵן.

Korach son of Yitzhar son of Kehas son of Levi separated himself, with Dasan and Aviram, sons of Eliav, and Ohn, son of Peles, the offspring of Reuven (Bamidbar 16:1).

Korach led a heinous rebellion against Moshe and Aharon, claiming that Aharon's appointment as *Kohen Gadol* was not Divinely ordained. For challenging Moshe's authority, Korach and his people met a terrible end.

In the Torah's account of the rebellion, no further mention is made of Ohn ben Peles, for ultimately Ohn left the camp of Korach, and therefore his life was spared.

The Sages (*Sanhedrin* 109b) teach that it was Korach's wife who instigated his rebellion against Moshe, and it was the wife of Ohn who actually saved his life by convincing him to withdraw from the rebellion. The Sages conclude by quoting the verse, "The wisdom of women can establish her home, and the foolish woman destroys it with her own hands" (*Mishlei* 14:1).

Torah study, our Sages teach, is the greatest *mitzvah* of all, the force which keeps heaven and earth in existence. The wise and righteous women of Israel dedicate themselves to ensuring that their husbands study Torah daily and that their sons become proficient in knowledge of Hashem's wisdom.

The final Mishnah in the Oral Law states: "The Holy One, Blessed is He, is destined to bequeath to each *tzaddik* 310 worlds" (*Mishnah Uktzin* 3:12). Three hundred and ten is half of 620, which is the total number of Scriptural *mitzvos* (613) plus the seven Rabbinic *mitzvos*. [1] Another 310 worlds are reserved for the *tzaddik's* wife, who shares equally in her husband's reward (*Chasam Sofer*).

❧ ❧ ❧

Until the Second World War, the city of Vilna was a center of Torah learning and scholarship, and was known as the "Jerusalem of Lithuania." After the war, the great scholar and *posek* R' Yisrael Zev Gustman, his wife and their young daughter were among only 800 Jews to return to the city. [2]

On the day of their return, the three wandered through the remaining structures of the Jewish sector of the city. They came upon a room filled with *sefarim* which, for unknown reasons, the Nazis had not destroyed.

R' Gustman looked at his wife and daughter. They had eaten very little that day. He told his wife that he would try to procure some food, and began making his way to the door. His wife stopped him.

"Are you serious?" she asked in wonderment. "It has been *years* since you have seen a *sefer,* let alone studied from one! First learn, then find us some food."

❧ ❧ ❧

For as long as anyone can remember, it has been the way of

---

1. They are: 1) Washing one's hands before eating bread. 2) The requirements of *eruvin* (related to carrying on Shabbos). 3) Purim. 4) Chanukah. 5) The recitation of blessings before and after eating (with the exception of *Bircas HaMazon* which is Scriptural). 6) The kindling of the Shabbos and *yom tov* lights. 7) The recitation of *Hallel.* (See commentary of *Tiferes Yisrael* to *Mishnah Uktzin* 3:12).

2. See chapter to *Parashas Bamidbar.*

the renowned *posek* of Jerusalem, R' Yosef Shalom Elyashiv, to arise well before dawn to begin his daily study. For all their married life, R' Elyashiv's wife, *Rebbetzin* Chaya Sheina, would arise when he did so that she could prepare a cup of coffee for him before he began his learning.

Toward the end of her life, the *Rebbetzin* was suffering from illness and was very weak. Her children attempted to convince her that it was not necessary for her to arise so early. They would purchase a percolator in which to store hot water, so that their father could easily prepare a hot drink for himself. The *Rebbetzin,* however, would not hear of it.

"Had I wanted to teach your father how to prepare a cup of coffee, I could have done it fifty years ago. I get up to make his coffee because I want to have a share in his learning — and you want me to give that up . . .?"

❧ ❧ ❧

R' Meir Shapiro, *Rav* of Lublin, Poland and *Rosh Yeshivah* of Yeshivas Chachmei Lublin, is best known as the originator of *Daf Yomi,* the daily study program of one *daf* (page) of Talmud a day, through which one completes the study of the entire Talmud in seven and a half years.

R' Shapiro introduced the concept of *Daf Yomi* in 1923 at the first *Knessiah Gedolah* (World Assembly) of Agudath Israel in Vienna. The idea was received with tremendous excitement. More than half a century later, the late Bluzhever *Rebbe,* R' Yisrael Spira, who was present at that *Knessiah,* recalled that scene as "a semblance of the scene at Sinai" when the Torah was given.

The leaders of the generation decided that the study of *daf Yomi* would begin on Rosh Hashanah of that year. On the night of Rosh Hashanah, R' Meir Shapiro's sister dreamt that she saw her mother in her place in Heaven being presented with a golden crown. Later, someone asked R' Shapiro what particular merit had earned his mother that crown. He replied:

"When I was a little boy, my family was forced more than once to move to a different city. What bothered my mother more than anything was that my Torah learning was being interrupted.

"Once, as we were preparing for our next move, my mother had an idea. She contacted a *melamed* (Torah teacher) in the city of our destination and arranged that he should meet our wagon as soon as it arrived.

"We arrived in the city, but for some inexplicable reason, the *melamed* was nowhere to be found. My mother sat down near the wagon and cried for a long time. I attempted to calm her, "Mama, please do not cry — I will learn tomorrow!"

"My mother looked at me through her tears and said, 'Meir'l, Meir'l, you are too young to understand what it means to miss a day of Torah learning . . .' "

פרשת חקת
Parashas Chukas

A Priceless Lesson

זֹאת הַתּוֹרָה אָדָם כִּי יָמוּת בְּאֹהֶל.
This is the teaching regarding a man who would die in a tent
(Bamidbar 19:14).

In its plain meaning, this verse discusses the laws of *tumah* (ritual contamination) from a corpse. However, our Sages also derive a homiletical teaching from it: "Torah can endure only in a person who dies [כִּי יָמוּת] over it" (*Berachos* 63b). This means that to make Torah a part of one's very essence, it is necessary that it be studied with what the Sages call עֲמֵלוּת בַּתּוֹרָה, dedicated, unremitting toil and self-sacrifice. Only through such study can one's soul become bound to the Torah's awesome sanctity so that its sacred words will impact on his being and transform him into a higher, more refined individual.

❈ ❈ ❈

R' Mordechai Gifter, the Telshe *Rosh Yeshivah,* once found it necessary to travel far from his yeshivah in Wickliffe, Ohio, to raise funds. He came to a city where there lived a very wealthy Jew who was known to contribute generously to worthy causes. R' Gifter called the man's house a number of times to arrange an appointment, but the man was never home. Finally, he contacted the man's secretary and was given an appointment at the office for the following morning at 7:30!

R' Gifter *davened* early and arrived at the office punctually. When he entered the office, the man was in the middle of a phone conversation and motioned for his guest to be seated. The phone call ended and the man extended his hand in greeting, adding an apology for not terminating the phone call as soon as the *Rosh Yeshivah* had arrived. "Please forgive me," he said, "but it was a trans-Atlantic call — I was speaking to Paris!"

R' Gifter responded, "There is something that I must ask you. I tried reaching you at your home many times, but was unsuccessful. Finally, someone told me that it is almost impossible to reach you at home because you arrive home from work at a very late hour. Now, I see that you also *leave for work* at a *very early* hour.

"I am told that your home is something truly exquisite, a 'landmark' in the community. But what pleasure do you have from your home if you are never home to enjoy it?"

The man responded, "Rabbi, you make a very strong point. But what can I tell you? You think I have the house for *my* pleasure? It is for my wife and children. As for me, I'm forever at work. In fact, there in front of you is the sofa I sleep on. What can I do? — that's business, אז מען וויל מצליח זיין אין גישעפט דארף מען ליגען אין גישעפט, *If one wants to succeed in business, he has to lie [i.e. be totally involved] in his business!*"

R' Gifter was thoughtful for a moment and then smiled broadly. "It was worth coming for this lesson alone," he said excitedly. "What I have learned from you is worth far more than money.

"You see, in the morning Blessing of the Torah, we express our praise of Hashem Who commanded us לַעֲסוֹק בְּדִבְרֵי תוֹרָה, *to engross ourselves in the words of the Torah*. The word לַעֲסוֹק, *to engross*, is related to עֵסֶק, which can mean a *business venture*. The way to truly succeed in Torah study is to approach it as you approach your business — אז מען וויל מצליח זיין אין גישעפט דארף מען ליגען אין גישעפט!"

A Man of the People

בְּאֵר חֲפָרוּהָ שָׂרִים . . . וּמִמִּדְבָּר מַתָּנָה
A well that the princes dug . . . a gift from the Wilderness
(*Bamidbar* 21:18).

What is the meaning of ". . . a gift from the Wilderness"? If a person makes himself like this wilderness which everyone treads upon [i.e. he is genuinely humble], then the Torah is given to him as a gift[1] (*Eruvin* 54a).

R' Shlomo Zalman Auerbach's halachic expertise, wise counsel and warm blessings were sought by count-less Jews of all types. It was crucial to R' Shlomo Zalman that he have a fixed amount of time each day when he could learn undisturbed. Thus, every afternoon he would go to a small *sefarim*-lined room in his Shaarei Chesed neighborhood and study there alone. Few people outside of the neigborhood knew the room's location and those that did would not disturb R' Shlomo Zalman when he studied there, except for emergencies.

On at least one occasion, R' Shlomo Zalman invited someone into that room. A neighborhood boy of about ten had been rummaging through some drawers in his apartment when he came upon an old camera, which his parents said he could use. Excitedly, he ran into the street to find something worth photographing. Just then, R' Shlomo Zalman was making his way to his private retreat. The boy ran over, held the camera

---

1. And he will retain what he learns (*Rashi*).

up and asked, "May I take a picture of the *Rosh Yeshivah*?" "Certainly," replied R' Shlomo Zalman, "but I would prefer not to do it here in the street." He led the boy into his study room, sat down and posed for the picture.

R' Shlomo Zalman served as *sandak* at countless *brisim.* At one *bris,* the *mohel* announced the name of each person who was accorded an honor. He called out, "Honored with being *sandak* is *Maran* (Our Guide) *HaRav* Shlomo Zalman Auerbach, שליט"א!" In a public setting, the term *'Maran'* is usually reserved for a leader of the generation.

That night, the *mohel* received a phone call. "Good evening, this is Shlomo Zalman speaking."

"Shlomo Zalman? I know many Shlomo Zalmans! To whom do I have the pleasure of speaking?"

"*Maran* Shlomo Zalman!" came the reply. The *mohel* realized immediately who the caller was. R' Shlomo Zalman then continued, "Please, I beg of you, if I am *sandak* again at a *bris* where you are *mohel,* do not announce me as *'Maran.'* If it happens again, I fear that I will have to think twice before being *sandak* when you are doing the announcing."

Once, a unique situation forced R' Shlomo Zalman to refer to himself as a person of prominence. A teenaged boy who was mentally disturbed had to be placed in an institution for such children. However, when the boy's parents informed him of this, he became unruly and insisted that he would not allow himself to be brought there. The parents sought the counsel of R' Shlomo Zalman, who agreed with their decision. R' Shlomo Zalman asked that the boy be brought to him.

R' Shlomo Zalman took the boy's hand in his own and said lovingly, "You know, I am a great rabbi, and therefore, I have the authority to confer *semichah* upon you and make you a rabbi as well. And now that you are a rabbi, I am assigning you a very important job: When you go to live in that school with other children, you will check on the *kashrus* of the food that is served, and you will also make sure that the children learn." The boy was very happy with this idea and the problem was solved.

In Jerusalem some two years ago, on the morning of *erev Pesach,* Menashe Cohen[1] suddenly realized that he had not taken a haircut. *Halachah* prohibits cutting hair on *erev Pesach* from midday.[2]

Menashe rushed down the stairs of his home and headed for the local barber shop. As he expected, the shop was crowded with customers, each one waiting his turn. Menashe was tense; there was so much to do in preparation for *yom tov.* He certainly could not afford to wait an hour until his turn came. He approached the barber, a pleasant, non-*Chareidi* Jew, and asked if he could take care of some errands and return in time for his turn.

"I'm sorry," the man replied, "but that's not how it works in this barber shop. If you leave, you lose your turn."

"But you must understand!" Menashe pleaded. "I have so many things to take care of . . ."

"Let me tell you something," the barber replied kindly. "Every month, R' Shlomo Zalman Auerbach comes here for a haircut. I know that it is not easy for him to walk here, and therefore I offered to go to his house and give him the haircut there. He told me, 'As long as my feet can carry me, I will come to you, and not the other way around.'

"In all the years that he is coming here, not once did he ever permit himself to take his haircut out of turn. As far as he is concerned, he is no different from anyone else. And you are asking me to make an exception for you?

"You know, when R' Auerbach passed away, I made it my business to tell all my friends that they simply had to stop whatever they were doing and come to his funeral."

Given the impression which R' Shlomo Zalman's personality left upon others, it is not surprising that three hundred thousand people attended his funeral. And it is not surprising that this humblest of men was among the very greatest Torah luminaries of his time.

---

1. Not his real name.
2. See *Mishnah Berurah* 468:5.

פָּרָשַׁת בָּלָק
Parashas Balak

The Right Words

וַיָּבֹא אֱלֹהִים אֶל בִּלְעָם לַיְלָה וַיֹּאמֶר לוֹ אִם לִקְרֹא לְךָ בָּאוּ הָאֲנָשִׁים קוּם
לֵךְ אִתָּם, וְאַךְ אֶת הַדָּבָר אֲשֶׁר אֲדַבֵּר אֵלֶיךָ אֹתוֹ תַעֲשֶׂה.

Hashem came to Bilam at night and said to him, "If the men came to summon you, arise and go with them, but only the thing that I shall speak to you — that you will do" (Bamidbar 22:20).

Bilam, in his greed, sought Hashem's permission to accompany the emissaries of Balak, who wanted Bilam to confer his curse upon Hashem's Chosen Nation. Bilam requested this despite the fact that Hashem had already told him not to accompany them. This time, Hashem told Bilam that he was free to accompany Balak's people if such was his desire — but his efforts would prove futile, for Hashem would not permit a curse to leave his mouth. Instead, beautiful blessings and praises of the Jewish people poured forth from his lips.

The wisest of men said, "It is for man to arrange his feelings, but eloquent speech is a G-dly gift" (*Mishlei* 16:1). Like everything else in life, the words we say and the impact which they leave are very much dependent upon the degree of *siyata*

DiShmaya (Heavenly assistance) we merit.

Sometimes, an individual wants to help someone with kind, meaningful words but does not know how to express himself. His sincere efforts may earn him special *siyata DiShmaya* (Divine assistance) so that he will find the right words to say.

❧ ❧ ❧

It had been an inspiring gathering. Reuven[1] was enthralled by the speakers, who had delivered impassioned pleas, spiced with beautiful Torah insights, on the importance of going out on door-to-door missions to return our estranged brethren to the path of Torah. Everything that had been said rang of truth. The dais had been graced by the presence of some of *Eretz Yisrael's* leading Torah personalities, whose participation in the gathering was their clear endorsement of its purpose.

But Reuven was troubled by something. As the gathering ended and the crowd filed out, he made his way to the dais and approached R' Tzvi Eliach, who had delivered the evening's keynote address on behalf of *Lev L'Achim.* "I understand everything that the *Rav* said," the young man said shyly, "but I have a problem. You see, I really don't think that I'm cut out for this kind of work. I can knock on people's doors, but then I'll be stuck — I can see myself being very ill at ease. I'll be at a loss for what to say!"

R' Eliach responded, "You have already heard my feelings on this. It is for you to do as you see fit."

That month, when a group of young scholars went out to knock on doors in the city of Ramallah, Reuven went along. As he walked up the path leading to a front door, about to begin his first *kiruv* (outreach) venture and still unsure of what he would say, his heart pounded.

He rang the bell. A woman opened the door. "Can I help you?" she asked pleasantly. Without hesitation, Reuven responded, *"Bati lilmod Torah im baaleich,* I have come to study Torah with your husband." The woman turned toward an inner

1. Not his real name.

room and shouted, "Uri — shut the television and put on a *kipah* (skullcap); someone is here to study Torah with you!"

As a matter of practice, Reuven carried with him a small volume of *mishnayos* from which he studied whenever he traveled. He sat down, opened the *mishnayos,* and the two became engrossed in the world of Talmudic law.

One half-hour later, Reuven rose to leave. Uri, his eyes reflecting love and gratitude, said, "I will allow you to leave so soon only if you promise to return next week."

Three months later, Reuven and his wife came to Ramallah for a Chanukah celebration in Uri's home — which was now strictly kosher. And Uri's children were already enrolled in yeshivah.

פרשת פנחס
Parashas Pinchas

Measure for Measure

וְהָיְתָה לוֹ וּלְזַרְעוֹ אַחֲרָיו בְּרִית כְּהוּנַת עוֹלָם תַּחַת אֲשֶׁר קִנֵּא לֵאלֹקָיו וַיְכַפֵּר עַל בְּנֵי יִשְׂרָאֵל.

And it shall be for him and his offspring after him a covenant of eternal priesthood, because he took vengeance for his G-d and he atoned for the Children of Israel (Bamidbar 25:13).

Pinchas risked his life to carry out Divine justice at a time when the heinous sins of his people had caused the death of twenty-four thousand Jews. Pinchas saw how the prince of the tribe of Shimon was committing a terrible sin with a Midianite princess and he remembered that Moshe had taught that one who commits such a sin can be killed on the spot without a trial. Pinchas took spear in hand and killed both the Jewish prince and the Midianite princess. Immediately, the plague of death ceased.

For his great act of self-sacrifice, Pinchas was rewarded with בְּרִית כְּהוּנַת עוֹלָם, *a covenant of eternal priesthood,* that he and his descendants forever would be *Kohanim* who would perform the Priestly service in the *Beis HaMikdash.*

The commentators discuss how this reward was appropriate for the deed that Pinchas had carried out. R' Zalman Sorotzkin (*Oznaim L'Torah*) explains that according to one opinion, a *Kohen* who performs the priestly service is acting as both a representative of Hashem and of the Jewish people. Thus, this reward was most fitting for Pinchas, who acted for the sake of Heaven and in so doing saved the Jewish people from further deaths.

Divine reward is always bestowed מִדָּה כְּנֶגֶד מִדָּה, *measure for measure.* The reward one receives for a good deed is appropriate for that particular deed.

❦ ❦ ❦

In the spring of 1996, Abe Kimmel[1] was admitted to the Metropolitan Jewish Geriatric Center in Boro Park. Mr. Kimmel was suffering from a debilitating illness and it had become impossible for his family to care for him at home. Until then, he had been living with his married daughter, Mrs. Rachel Stein, in Somerset, New Jersey.

Three months later, Mr. Kimmel passed away. The family was contacted and arrangements for the funeral began. That day, R' Dovid Grossman, Chaplain at the Geriatric Center, received a phone call from Mr. Kimmel's daughter. Their rabbi was bedridden and was unable to officiate at the funeral. Would it be possible for R' Grossman to officiate? R' Grossman agreed, and asked if someone could provide him with some information about the deceased which could be used in his eulogy.

Mrs. Stein gave the phone to her husband, who told R' Grossman, "For forty years — until his deteriorating health made it impossible — my father-in-law arose each morning at three o'clock to recite the entire Book of *Tehillim.* After that, he would join the early *minyan* in *shul* — but he never *davened* with them. He preferred *davening* with the second *minyan.* He would join the early *minyan* so that he could serve as the tenth man if necessary. The early hour did not make for very good attendance and it happened many times that, indeed, my father-in-law was the tenth man."

R' Grossman thanked Mr. Stein and said that it was not necessary for him to hear anything more.

---

1. Names of people and places, except for that of R' Dovid Grossman, are fictitious.

At the funeral the next day, the local rabbi spoke briefly, saying that he had felt it necessary to leave his sickbed simply to mention how Mr. Kimmel had been a pillar of the *shul's* prayer services for the past four decades. His speech was followed by R' Grossman's eulogy. Then, R' Grossman approached Mrs. Stein and said, "There is a special *Kaddish* to recite at the cemetery after a burial. However, if you think that there will not be a *minyan* there, then we can recite a chapter of *Tehillim* now which will be followed by the regular Mourner's *Kaddish*." Calculating quickly, Mrs. Stein replied that only eight men, including R' Grossman, would be going to the cemetery. *Tehillim,* followed by the regular Mourner's *Kaddish,* was recited, then the small procession proceeded to the cemetery.

It was a torridly hot day. The small group stood sweltering in the heat as the gentile gravediggers went about their work. R' Grossman turned to the family and said, "It would be a great *mitzvah* if you would take spade in hand and cover the coffin with earth. I realize that you may not feel up to it in this heat; in that case, we'll let the gravediggers finish."

The men conferred briefly and decided to undertake the *mitzvah.* The extreme heat, coupled with their inexperience, made the task take very long. As the last shovels full of earth were being placed onto the grave, a car drove into the cemetery with two obviously religious Jewish men, who had come in observance of a *yahrtzeit.* R' Grossman hurried over and told them, "If you would join us, the special *Kaddish* at a burial could be recited." The two readily obliged.

R' Grossman later phoned Mrs. Stein. "Do you realize what happened at the cemetery?" he asked. "For forty years, your father dedicated himself to ensuring that others would have a *minyan* when they needed it. And so Heaven ensured that when a *minyan* was needed for *Kaddish* to be recited in memory of your father, those two strangers appeared at precisely the right moment."

Mrs. Stein was too overcome with emotion to respond.

פרשת מטות
Parashas Matos

Gratitude

נְקֹם נִקְמַת בְּנֵי יִשְׂרָאֵל מֵאֵת הַמִּדְיָנִים.
*Take vengeance for the Children of Israel
against the Midianites (Bamidbar 31:2).*

It would seem that the above command to Moshe should have required him to lead the battle against the Midianites. Yet the *Midrash* tells us that Moshe reasoned, "Since I was made great in Midian, it is not right to harm those who have been good to me" (*Yalkut Shimoni, Bamidbar* §31).

R' Chaim Shmulevitz (*Sichos Mussar*) explains that *hakaras hatov,* gratitude, is a most essential trait of a Jew; so essential that in this instance, Moshe used it to determine the interpretation of Hashem's word. The importance of feeling and showing gratitude told Moshe that Hashem could not have meant that he himself should be the one to lead the war against Midian.

Moshe had learned the lesson of gratitude while still in Egypt. All of the Ten Plagues against the Egyptians were brought about through Moshe, with the exception of the plagues of blood, frogs and lice. Moshe could not bring about the plagues of blood and frogs, which both came from the water, because as an infant he had been saved when his mother placed his basket into the water. He could not cause the plague of lice, which came from the earth, because he had been saved by the earth when he used it to hide the body of the Egyptian whom he had killed.[1] Though water and earth are inanimate, the attribute of gratitude did not allow Moshe to bring a plague upon them. From this, Moshe understood that no command of Hashem would ever indicate a denial of *hakaras hatov.*

❧ ❧ ❧

R' Shalom Eisen was a revered *dayan* (rabbinical judge) in Jerusalem for some fifty years. Toward the end of his life, he was stricken with a debilitating illness. He traveled to America for life-saving treatments and then returned to *Eretz Yisrael,* his condition deteriorating steadily.

On the night of *Taanis Esther,* 5746 (1986), the renowned *posek* of the generation, R' Moshe Feinstein, passed away. The funeral was held in New York that afternoon and then the deceased was taken to *Eretz Yisrael* where another funeral was held in Jerusalem, on the day of *Shushan Purim.*

R' Shalom, terribly weak and in agonizing pain, wanted very much to attend the funeral, in which a quarter of a million people would participate, but his son convinced him that his poor state of health surely exempted him from this *mitzvah.* However, he later asked his son to assemble a *minyan* of men to go to R' Moshe's grave on *Har HaMenuchos* and beg forgiveness in his name. R' Shalom's son did not understand. If he had been exempt from this *mitzvah,* then why was there a need to ask forgiveness?

R' Shalom explained: "As far as the *mitzvah* of honoring a great Torah personage is concerned, I am certainly exempt. But there is another factor which gave me cause to honor R' Moshe — *hakaras hatov.* When I was hospitalized in New York to undergo treatments, R' Moshe, who himself was not in the best

---

1. See *Rashi* to *Shemos* 7:19 and 8:12.

of health, took the time and effort to visit me. I am not certain that my ill health is sufficient reason to have freed me from the obligation to show gratitude."

R' Shalom was a *talmid* of R' Isser Zalman Meltzer, one of the leading Torah personalities of his day. R' Shalom had seen first-hand to what extent R' Isser Zalman would go to show gratitude.

It happened on a Shabbos, when R' Shalom was celebrating the bar mitzvah of his son. Following *Mussaf,* R' Shalom held a *kiddush* in his fourth-floor apartment. He had sent R' Isser Zalman an invitation out of respect, but never imagined that the aged and weak scholar would exert himself to attend the celebration. How shocked was he, and everyone else, when R' Isser Zalman appeared!

When R' Shalom told R' Isser Zalman that he had never expected him to come, the latter replied, "I came to express my appreciation to you. You see, when I received your invitation, I said to myself, 'R' Shalom is already celebrating the bar mitzvah of his son? Why, it seems as if R' Shalom's wedding was only yesterday!'

"This musing caused to me to focus on how quickly life goes by, which led me to ponder thoughts of *teshuvah* (repentance). And all this was a result of your invitation! Therefore, as a sign of *hakaras hatov,* I simply *had* to participate in your celebration!" (*Yalkut Lekach Tov*).

פרשת מסעי
Parashas Masei

The Right Surroundings

וְאֵת הֶעָרִים אֲשֶׁר תִּתְּנוּ לַלְוִיִּם אֵת שֵׁשׁ עָרֵי הַמִּקְלָט
אֲשֶׁר תִּתְּנוּ לָנֻס שָׁמָּה הָרֹצֵחַ.

*The cities that you shall give to the Levites: the six cities of refuge
that you shall provide for a murderer to flee there (Bamidbar 35:6).*

The Torah mandates that one who murders unintention-
ally must flee to one of the עָרֵי מִקְלָט, *cities of refuge,* where
he is to remain until the death of the *Kohen Gadol* (High
Priest).[1] It is not coincidental that these were Levite cities.

Though the murderer did not act willfully, his crime could
have been prevented had he exercised proper caution. As the
Talmud makes clear[2], his act requires atonement and that is
the purpose of his exile.

The Levites were teachers of their people and served in the
Beis HaMikdash. Their cities were permeated with an atmo-

---

1. See *Makkos* 11b.
2. Ibid. 2b.

sphere of Torah and heightened spirituality. Such a place would surely make an impact upon the murderer so that he would eventually leave as a better, more refined individual[1] (based on *Oznaim L'Torah*).

❦   ❦   ❦

A distinguished *talmid chacham* once presented the following question to R' Yitzchak Zev Soloveitchik, the Brisker *Rav*, during his years in Jerusalem:

He was a member of a small Torah community in an Israeli city, whose girls attended a Bais Yaakov school in a neighboring city which had a much larger religious population. There was no pressing need to open a Bais Yaakov school in his area, since all the observant girls had a school nearby and the secular population had no interest in a Bais Yaakov. On the other hand, if this community were to open their own Bais Yaakov, perhaps a few secular families would also enroll their daughters there.

The Brisker *Rav* responded with a story:

In Brisk, the Bais Yaakov school was situated in a predominantly secular neighborhood. Near the school lived a secular couple who enrolled their daughter there merely as a matter of convenience. The girl was profoundly influenced by her Bais Yaakov experience.

It happened that her father and mother had to go away for the weekend. They left their daughter in charge of their hardware store and warned her that the store was to be open on Shabbos as usual. The girl was afraid to totally disobey her parents but she was determined to do everything possible to avoid engaging in any transaction on Shabbos.

Shabbos day, a gentile entered the store, pointed to a small decorative item in the store window and asked its price. "One hundred *zlotes*!" the girl replied confidently. The gentile stormed out of the store in fury, for he knew that the item was worth only one half-*zlota*.

---

1. See *Sefer HaChinuch* for another explanation of why the Levite cities served as places of refuge.

A short while later, the gentile returned. "I really shouldn't offer you another *zlota*," he said, "but I'm willing to raise my offer to five *zlotes*." "I'm sorry," the girl replied firmly, "one hundred *zlotes* and not a *zlota* less."

Throughout the day, the gentile returned time and again, each time raising his offer a bit more, and each time he left empty-handed as the girl stood her ground. After Shabbos had ended, the gentile returned again. "Okay," he said grudgingly, "I'm willing to pay your price." He placed one hundred *zlotes* on the table. "Let me explain why I'm doing this: I recently redecorated my entire home. Everything looks beautiful, but I need one small item to make it complete. When I passed by your store and saw this item in the window, I knew that this was the item I needed. I know that I'm overpaying by a lot, but it's worth it to me to be able to have this item displayed in my dining room."

When the girl's parents returned home, she told them the entire story. So impressed were they by their daughter's steadfastness and by the result of her refusal to desecrate Shabbos, that they began to show interest in Jewish tradition and eventually became fully observant.

"And so," concluded the Brisker *Rav*, "it is obvious that having a Bais Yaakov in one's city can have a very positive effect!" (*Peninei HaGriz*).

פרשת דברים
Parashas Devarim

With Love and Respect

אֵלֶּה הַדְּבָרִים אֲשֶׁר דִּבֶּר מֹשֶׁה אֶל כָּל יִשְׂרָאֵל בְּעֵבֶר הַיַּרְדֵּן,
בַּמִּדְבָּר בָּעֲרָבָה מוֹל סוּף בֵּין פָּארָן וּבֵין תֹּפֶל וְלָבָן וַחֲצֵרוֹת וְדִי זָהָב.
These are the words that Moshe spoke to all Israel,
on the other side of the Jordan, in the Wilderness, in Aravah,
opposite the Sea of Reeds, between Paran and Tophel and Lavan
and Chatzeiros and Di Zahav (Devarim 1:1).

The words in the above verse, beginning with the word בַּמִּדְבָּר, *in the Wilderness,* hint to different sins committed by the Jews during their forty years in the Wilderness. Moshe wished to rebuke his people before he departed this world, but he wanted to do it with respect, without causing them hurt or ill will. Therefore, he began by only alluding to their misdeeds.

The Chofetz Chaim cautioned his students that when they would enter the rabbinate, they should be careful not to rebuke their congregants with harsh words, which leave no lasting impression upon one's listeners. They should rather explain to the people what Hashem expects of them and the seriousness of the matter at hand.[1]

When rebuke is offered with true love and respect, it will very likely leave its mark.

---

1. See footnote to *Chofetz Chaim al HaTorah, Parashas Ki Sisa.*

❧ ❧ ❧

Rabbi Avraham Yehoshua Heschel, the *Rebbe* of Kapish-nitz,[1] was a man of boundless kindness and *ahavas Yisrael* (love of his fellow Jew). These two qualities were primary factors in the *Rebbe's* success in bringing many people back to the Torah path.

One summer, the *Rebbe* was feeling ill and was advised to make use of the natural baths in Sharon Springs, New York, to help ease his pain. His place of lodging was a kosher hotel which was frequented by many Orthodox Jews. Though the *Rebbe* ate only food prepared by his family and on weekdays ate in his room, he still managed to get to know the other hotel guests and befriend them.

One guest was an elderly man who had suffered through the horrors of the Second World War and had subsequently forsaken the observance of *mitzvos.* The *Rebbe* engaged the man in friendly conversation on a number of occasions and the man, not surprisingly, was impressed with his wisdom and touched by his sincerity and warmth. One day, the *Rebbe* asked the man his age. "Eighty-three," he replied. "Well," the *Rebbe* responded, "seventy years is a generation,[2] and you are now thirteen years past that — you have reached 'bar mitzvah' a second time! I'll tell you what: you put on *tefillin* in honor of your 'bar mitzvah' and I will invite everyone to a festive *kiddush* in honor of the occasion!" The man was visibly moved by this offer. After a moment's thought he replied, "If the *Rebbe* will get me *tefillin,* I will wear them."

Soon after, the *Rebbe* left the hotel for a short trip. He returned with a new pair of *tefillin,* and with bags of cake, *kugel* and drinks for the *kiddush* which he had promised to serve.

The next morning, the man joined the *Shacharis minyan* and wore his new *tefillin.* After *Shacharis,* a *kiddush* was held in

---

1. See chapters to *Parshios Tetzaveh* and *Naso.*
2. See *Tehillim* 90:8.

honor of the man's "bar mitzvah." The man continued to wear the *tefillin* every weekday, and he was also inspired to cease from doing forbidden labor on Shabbos.

Walking down a street one Shabbos, the *Rebbe* passed two young men, both of whom were smoking. Knowing that they were Jewish, the *Rebbe* said, "My sons, perhaps we don't know each other personally, but I know that as Jews, both of you have caring hearts. If you knew how much pain it is causing me to see you smoke on the holy day of Shabbos, I have no doubt that you would drop your cigarettes immediately."

One of the men immediately dropped his cigarette. The other, however, took a different attitude. "Rabbi," he said, "America is a free country; each man can do as he pleases. I don't interfere in your affairs and I don't think that you should interfere in mine."

The *Rebbe* was not daunted by this retort. Smiling warmly, he replied, "You have raised a very good point. I will respond with a question. Suppose someone had collapsed in the street and was in need of emergency medical attention — how would you react? Would you say that in America each man is free to do as he chooses, and therefore you are under no obligation to help the man? Or would you see it as your moral obligation to try to save the person's life? Well, when I see a Jew desecrating the Shabbos, I see before me a precious *neshamah* (soul) whose spiritual lifeblood is ebbing away before my eyes. Dare I remain silent?"

The *Rebbe's* sincere words had a profound impact on both young men. They drew close to him and eventually returned to the path of Torah.

פרשת ואתחנן
Parashas Va'eschanan

An Act of Faith

אַתָּה הָרְאֵתָ לָדַעַת כִּי ה׳ הוּא הָאֱלֹקִים אֵין עוֹד מִלְּבַדּוּ.
You have been shown in order to know that Hashem,
He is the G-d — there is none besides Him (Devarim 4:35).

R' Yaakov Yitzchak Ruderman, late *Rosh Yeshivah* of Yeshivas Ner Israel in Baltimore, once met a Russian Jew who had risked his life to teach Torah during the Stalin era. The man told R' Ruderman the following:

It happened once that a teacher of Torah was caught in the act by the secret police. The police did their usual "friendly interrogation" and then issued the following ultimatum: The teacher was to stand before his students and declare loudly, for all to hear, that, Heaven forfend, there is no G-d. If he refused to do this, he would be sentenced to Siberia.

A deathly silence filled the room as the teacher slowly made his way to the front of the room to face his students. Standing before them, he shouted with all his might: "ה׳ הוּא הָאֱלֹקִים, ה׳ הוּא הָאֱלֹקִים, *Hashem — He is the only G-d, Hashem — He is the only G-d!*"

The teacher was immediately hustled away, and for years languished in Siberia. But with the help of Hashem, he was eventually released and managed to emigrate from the giant prison called Russia to *Eretz Yisrael,* where he could declare ה׳ הוּא הָאֱלֹקִים! without repercussion.

R' Ruderman had studied the man's face as he had related his story and had noted his emotions. He now said to the man, "And *you* were the teacher in the story."

The man nodded in agreement.

Saved by the Shabbos

שָׁמוֹר אֶת יוֹם הַשַּׁבָּת לְקַדְּשׁוֹ.
Safeguard the Shabbos day to sanctify it (Devarim 5:12).
כִּי אֶשְׁמְרָה שַׁבָּת קֵל יִשְׁמְרֵנִי.
If I safeguard the Shabbos, G-d will safeguard me (Shabbos zemiros).

When the Second World War ended, R' Moshe Neu-schloss overcame his personal losses to help other survivors rebuild their lives upon the ashes of destruction. He returned to the Slovakian town of Serdihely and started a yeshivah for teenaged yeshivah students who had been orphaned during the war. He put his vast knowledge of *halachah* to use in guiding survivors in matters of Shabbos observance, family life, the building of *mikvaos* and other crucial areas.

Two years after the war, with the Communist presence in Serdihely becoming ever more pronounced, R' Neuschloss decided to emigrate, along with his yeshivah, to America. He arranged for his students to make the journey by boat. However, this means of travel was not available to R' Neuschloss himself, for his wife was with child and therefore could not undertake the long sea journey. The two therefore made reservations on a flight departing from Prague to New York.

The plane took off on schedule, but problems developed in mid-flight, forcing the pilot to make an emergency landing in

Ireland. When the problems were corrected and the plane was ready for the next leg of the journey, the passengers were informed that the flight was due to arrive in New York on Saturday.

R' Neuschloss, who was known throughout his life for his great piety and awe of Heaven, informed the airline personnel that he was a Sabbath observer and would not embark on such a journey.[1]

Air travel in those days was not what it is today. Reservations had to be booked well in advance. R' Neuschloss was informed that if he and his wife did not board that flight, then there was no telling how long it might be before they could make reservations on another one. R' Neuschloss was not daunted by this warning. He and his wife would not be on that flight.

The frustrated airline personnel booked a room in a hotel for the Neuschlosses and provided them with ample food for the weekend. Rabbi and Mrs. Neuschloss returned all the non-kosher food and kept only the fruit. The language barrier made it difficult for them to explain why they would not eat the food, and the airline personnel misinterpreted their strange behavior as some sort of a hunger strike to protest what they considered to be mistreatment. The airline management, concerned that these war survivors not create a scene, contacted the American consulate. It was decided that the Neuschlosses would be sent to New York on the next available flight. And so, on *Motza'ei Shabbos,* R' and Mrs. Neuschloss were happily surprised when informed that they would be leaving for New York that very night.

The flight was uneventful. Upon their arrival in New York, R' and Mrs. Neuschloss contacted their hosts by phone. When R' Neuschloss identified himself, his host was incredulous. It was then that the Neuschlosses learned the shocking news: the plane which had departed before Shabbos had crashed into the sea, leaving no survivors. The Neuschlosses had erroneously been listed among the passengers.

---

1. See *Shulchan Aruch, Orach Chaim* ch. 248.

פרשת עקב
Parashas Eikev

To Go in His Ways

וְעַתָּה יִשְׂרָאֵל מָה ה׳ אֱלֹקֶיךָ שֹׁאֵל מֵעִמָּךְ,
כִּי אִם לְיִרְאָה אֶת ה׳ אֱלֹקֶיךָ לָלֶכֶת בְּכָל דְּרָכָיו
וּלְאַהֲבָה אֹתוֹ וְלַעֲבֹד אֶת ה׳ אֱלֹקֶיךָ בְּכָל לְבָבְךָ וּבְכָל נַפְשֶׁךָ.

Now, O Israel, what does Hashem, your G-d, ask of you? Only to fear
Hashem, your G-d, to go in all His ways and to love Him, and to serve
Hashem, your G-d, with all your heart and with all your soul
(Devarim 10:12).

In connection with the above verse, the Chofetz Chaim[1]
cites *Sifri*: "These are the ways of Hashem [in which a Jew is
commanded to go], as it is written, 'Hashem, Hashem, G-d,
Compassionate and Gracious . . .'[2] Just as the Omnipresent is
called Compassionate and Gracious, so too, should you be
compassionate and gracious, doing favors for all without any
thought of renumeration . . .

"All this is for our own benefit, as the next verse concludes,
'[To observe the commandments of Hashem . . .] for your
benefit.'[3] To the degree with which one utilizes the attributes of
goodness and kindness throughout his life, to that degree will

---

1. Introduction to *Sefer Ahavas Chesed*.
2. *Shemos* 34:6.
3. *Devarim* 10:13.

he merit a flow of goodness and abundant kindness from the Holy One, Blessed is He, all his life."

❧ ❧ ❧

It was just not fair. He was sure that he had made it across the intersection before the light turned red. Of course, the police officer disagreed. That's why he was now busy writing out a ticket. Well, Yitzchak[1] told himself, he was going to fight this one and he might even win.

He called the Motor Vehicles Bureau to arrange for a hearing. Not wanting to miss work, Yitzchak made sure to get the earliest appointment possible, at eight-forty in the morning.

He arrived at the hearing room early, and was happy to find the room empty. Hearings were held on a first-come-first-served basis, so Yitzchak assumed that he would be heading for work by nine o'clock. Just to make sure that the judge noticed him, he took a seat in the front row.

Eight-forty arrived and the judge, an elderly black gentleman, looked around the filled room and began the proceedings. Yitzchak recognized the officer who had ticketed him. It seemed that everyone in the room had come to contend tickets which had been served by this officer.

The judge called out someone's name — but it was not Yitzchak's, and he looked on in consternation as someone else came forward. He grew more upset as the judge proceeded to call a number of others ahead of him. The judge seemed to be quite unforgiving; virtually everyone was found guilty after the officer stated his side of the story. *"What is going on here?"* Yitzchak thought. *"Is this guy an anti-Semite that he's making me wait for last? Judging by what I've been seeing, he's sure to find me guilty. I'll be late to work and all I got for it was aggravation!"*

By nine-forty, there was no one left but Yitzchak. His name was called and he came forward. He stated his case: he had crossed the intersection when the light had changed from green to yellow. The judge motioned to the officer and, as

---

1. Not his real name.

if prearranged, he left the room without a word. The judge then shut the microphone and tape recorder. There was no one left in the room besides the judge and Yitzchak, who was thoroughly confused and a bit nervous. The judge leaned forward and said, "I'll take your word for it, because a person like yourself has it coming to him." Yitzchak did not understand. "You don't recognize me?" asked the judge. Yitzchak replied in the negative. The judge then reached into his pocket and withdrew a subway-and-bus token which he handed to Yitzchak. "I've been waiting four years to return this to you," he said.

Then, Yitzchak remembered . . .

       ❦ ❦ ❦

It was close to eleven o'clock on a wet, wintry night and Yitzchak and his wife were driving home after a long day. As precipitation took the form of snow showers which made the driving even more difficult, the couple noticed an elderly black gentleman struggling to push his stalled car off the road.

Yitzchak pulled over to the side of the road, got out of his car and offered his services to the very appreciative man. Together, they pushed the car into a legal parking space. Yitzchak turned to the man and asked where he had been heading. The man had been on his way home. Without a car, he was best off taking a city bus, which stopped a few blocks from where they now stood. Yitzchak invited the man into his car and they headed for the bus stop. As they neared it, they could see the bus a few blocks ahead of them. Undaunted, Yitzchak sped up just a bit as he attempted to overtake the bus. At that point, the gentleman mentioned that he did not have the exact change needed for the bus fare. Yitzchak handed the man a subway-and-bus token. The man looked at Yitzchak in amazement at the extent of his kindness toward him. They overtook the bus and the man expressed his thanks before alighting from the car.

       ❦ ❦ ❦

"I was waiting for the day when I would meet my Jewish

friend with the *yarmulka*," the judge now said, "and that day has finally come. I will never forget the kindness that you showed me."

פרשת ראה
Parashas Re'eh

Friends of the Poor

כִּי יִהְיֶה בְךָ אֶבְיוֹן מֵאַחַד אַחֶיךָ בְּאַחַד שְׁעָרֶיךָ בְּאַרְצְךָ אֲשֶׁר ה' אֱלֹקֶיךָ נֹתֵן לָךְ, לֹא תְאַמֵּץ אֶת לְבָבְךָ וְלֹא תִקְפֹּץ אֶת יָדְךָ מֵאָחִיךָ הָאֶבְיוֹן. כִּי פָתֹחַ תִּפְתַּח אֶת יָדְךָ לוֹ . . .

If there shall be a destitute person among you, any of your brethren
in any of your cities, in the Land that Hashem, your G-d,
gives you, you shall not harden your heart or close your hand
against your destitute brother. Rather, you shall open your hand
to him . . . (Devarim 15:7).

I t was a clear night in Jerusalem, and R' Avraham Elimelech of Karlin, along with his *chassidim,* had completed the recital of *Kiddush Levanah.* Yet R' Avraham Elimelech remained rooted in his place, seemingly lost in thought. Finally, someone asked him if something was wrong. The *Rebbe* smiled and pointed to the *Beis Yaakov shul.* From its windows, the sweet voice of a teenaged boy at study filtered towards them. "How can one tear himself away from such a beautiful *kol Torah* (voice of Torah study)?" the *Rebbe* asked.

The boy's name was Yosef Binyamin Rubin, known to all as "Yosse'le *Masmid*" (the Diligent One). He would study for eighteen hours a day, with a love for learning that was plainly apparent. His friends of that period still recall with admiration the incredible energy with which Yosef Binyamin studied Torah. After his passing, ledgers spanning a twelve-year period were found in which he recorded how many hours he had spent learning each day, and how much time he categorized as *bitul Torah* (time wasted from learning). The time learned ranged, day after day, from between fourteen to nineteen hours, while the time which he considered *'bitul Torah'* was very minimal.

He received *semichah* (rabbinical ordination) at a young age from the *Rav* of Teplik, one of the holy city's renowned *rabbanim.* He had a special love for R' Yosef Binyamin and reckoned with his opinions in matters of *halachah.*

Not surprisingly, as R' Yosef Binyamin's attachment to Torah grew, so did his feelings for the plight of his fellow Jew. As our Sages teach, one of the forty-eight qualities through which Torah is acquired is נוֹשֵׂא בְּעוֹל עִם חֲבֵרוֹ, *sharing a friend's burden*[1]. R' Yosef Binyamin felt someone else's pain like his very own and could not rest until he had done his best to ease that person's plight.

Sometimes, his family would hear him moaning as he walked up the steps to their apartment. When they would open the door anxiously and ask what was wrong, he would reply, "If you had heard the news that I have just heard, you would also be in pain."

A turning point in his life came at age eighteen. On his way home from *shul* on a Friday night, R' Yosef Binyamin decided to stop at the home of a married friend to wish him a *"Gut*

---

1. *Avos* 6:6.

Shabbos." Entering his friend's cramped apartment, he was met by a shocking sight. The young couple and their small children were sitting around the table partaking of their Shabbos meal — bread and yogurt. R' Yosef Binyamin could not rest until he had done something for this impoverished family. After Shabbos, he made the rounds of the city's *shuls,* collecting for the poor. It was a practice which he was to continue, day after day, until his passing some forty years later. Even during the festive week of *sheva berachos* following his own wedding, R' Yosef Binyamin stood on a street corner collecting for the poor. "Must the poor suffer because I got married?" he explained.

After his passing, ledgers spanning those forty years were found among his possessions, detailing how much he had collected each day and to whom the money had been distributed. Every cent was accounted for. There was something else remarkable about those ledgers. Throughout his decades as a *gabbai* (treasurer) of *tzedakah,* R' Yosef Binyamin distinguished himself for the way in which he distributed monies to the poor. As much as he wanted to help the poor materially, he wanted to do it in a way that allowed them to maintain their self-respect. In his ledgers, names of the poor were not mentioned, out of concern that someone entering his room might see an open ledger and discover the identities of his recipients. One recipient was identified as עָנִי הָגוּן, *an upright poor man,* while another was listed as אַלְמָנָה וּבָנֶיהָ, a widow and her children.

Our Sages tell of Mar Ukva and his wife, who would provide assistance to a poor man by slipping money through the man's front door.[1] This was done so that the man would not know the identity of his benefactor, which might cause him discomfort when they would meet. R' Yosef Binyamin went about his *tzedakah* distribution in a similar way. Often, he would slip money under a person's door. Other times, he would approach an employer and say, "Your worker, Baruch,

1. *Kesubos* 67b.

Baruch, is having a difficult time making ends meet. Please give him a 'raise' of fifty dollars per week — which I will provide."

After R' Yosef Binyamin's passing, an appreciation appeared in an Orthodox newspaper:

> In the areas of *tzedakah* and *chesed,* R' Yosef Binyamin was one in a generation. With unequalled self-sacrifice, he would hurry from *shul* to *shul* collecting for the poor of Jerusalem. In the torrid days of summer, in the pouring rains of winter, he would beam with happiness after having succeeded in his efforts. There were widows, orphans and others whom he supported with monthly assistance; scores of poor brides and grooms whom he helped generously; and hundreds of families who relied on him for their *yom tov* needs. He helped the poor discreetly, in a manner which always preserved their dignity. And he found ways to help those who refused to accept help from anyone.

His love and concern for every Jew caused him to notice what others did not. One hot summer day, he saw a little boy sitting alone on a stoop, a downcast expression on his thin face. Down the street stood a group of children, chattering happily as they licked their ices. R' Yosef Binyamin knew that the boy's parents were impoverished and could not afford a "luxury" such as ices. A few minutes later, the young boy was the happiest child on the block as he joined his friends and partook of his treat.

R' Yosef Binyamin's legendary efforts for the poor did not detract from his diligent Torah study. He served as *Rosh Kollel* at Yeshivah Chayei Olam. From the time that he accepted upon himself to care for the poor, he adopted a new study schedule. He would arise soon after midnight and study until dawn, and then pray *Shacharis* at the *Kosel Maaravi* (Western Wall) with the *minyan vasikin,* which begins the *Shemoneh Esrei* at sunrise, the most preferred time. Immediately after

Shacharis, he would begin his collections. Often, he would hail a taxi in order to be at each *shul* at the time most opportune for collecting *tzedakah* — paying for the fare with his own money. Following his collections, he would eat a quick breakfast — except on Mondays and Thursdays, when he fasted.

His powerful faith was plainly apparent. Regulars at the *Kosel minyan* testify that each time that R' Yosef Binyamin stood before the *Kosel,* it was with the emotion of one who stands at that holy site for the very first time.

The Beis Yisrael neighborhood where he lived is not far from the pre-1967 border with Jordan. As the Jews of Beis Yisrael sat huddled in bomb shelters during the Six Day War, the sounds of explosions could often be heard. While others trembled from fright, R' Yosef Binyamin would cry out, "The bombs are falling on our enemies! We are one step closer to [recapturing] the *Kosel!*"

Each year on Tishah B'Av, he would weep inconsolably, as if the Destruction was then occurring. On that day, he would encircle the outer wall of the Old City in fulfillment of the verse, "Walk about Zion and encircle her, count her towers" (*Tehillim* 48:13).

❧ ❧ ❧

Purim of 5737 (1977) in Jerusalem was unusual for two reasons. It was *Purim Meshulash,* the Three-Day Purim, when the fourteenth of Adar falls on Friday and the *mitzvos* of Purim are celebrated in Jerusalem over a three-day period, from Friday to Sunday. And it was a Purim when Jerusalem was blanketed by a deep snow, making vehicular travel impossible and traveling on foot extremely difficult. Yet this did not deter R' Yosef Binyamin from making his rounds to collect *matanos l'evyonim,* gifts for the poor, one of the precious *mitzvos* of the day. It was no secret that R' Yosef Binyamin had been feeling ill and someone who met him on his rounds expressed surprise that he would venture outdoors in such weather. "And why are you outside?" R' Yosef Binyamin countered. "Why, to hear the reading of the *megillah,*" came the reply. "And is not *matanos* l'evyonim a mitzvah as well?" R' Yosef Binyamin retorted. And he continued on his way, going from shul to shul, his familiar cry of "Yidden, gibt tzedakah, Jews, give tzedakah!" announcing his presence.

Soon after Purim, he suffered a stroke and was hospitalized. Even then, his concern for the poor did not wane. With his family at his side, he suddenly burst into tears, sobbing, "What will be with the poor who depend on me for tzedakah? Who will provide them with their Pesach needs?"

As the days passed, R' Yosef Binyamin slipped into a coma. His family stood at his bedside and spoke to him, in the hope that this would rouse him to consciousness, but to no avail. Then, his son-in-law bent down and whispered into his ear, "Tatte (Father), the tzedakah will be distributed to the poor before Pesach like every year." R' Yosef Binyamin opened his eyes and tears streamed down his cheeks. Shortly thereafter, on the sixth of Nissan, he passed away.

On his tombstone was inscribed, גַּבַּאי צְדָקָה שֶׁלֹּא עַל מְנָת לְקַבֵּל פְּרָס, a treasurer of tzedakah without pay. His family resolved to continue his great work and founded the renowned charity organization Od Yosef Chai,[1] which bears his name.

❧   ❧   ❧

The Kapishnitzer Rebbe, R' Avraham Yehoshua Heschel, lived in a very modest apartment on the Lower East Side. The furniture was plain and the floorings were worn. He and his rebbetzin had no need for more.

One day, the Rebbe's daughter asked her father, "Tatte (Father), the linoleum in the dining room is old and torn. Could we perhaps replace it?" The Rebbe responded that they had no money at the present for anything but necessities.

A few minutes later, the doorbell rang. A solicitor of a worthy tzedakah organization stood in the doorway. The Rebbe

---

1. *Yosef still lives;* from *Bereishis* 45:26.
2. A pidyon (redemption) is customarily given by a chassid to a Rebbe when seeking his blessing. Some understand its purpose as being similar to the

greeted the man warmly and handed him a generous donation. The *Rebbe's* daughter, who observed the scene, did not understand. Respectfully, she asked her father how he was able to give the man so much money when he had said only minutes before that there was no money for anything but necessities.

With warmth and understanding, the *Rebbe* explained, "My child, this money was given to me as a *pidyon* [2] by a man who sought a blessing on behalf of a sick relative. In *Shacharis* we say of Hashem: זוֹרֵעַ צְדָקוֹת מַצְמִיחַ יְשׁוּעוֹת, *He sows tzedakos, makes salvations flourish.* From using that man's *pidyon* for *tzedakah,* a salvation may flourish, but can one expect a salvation to flourish from buying linoleum?!"

---

food which Yaakov presented to Yitzchak prior to receiving his blessing (*Bereishis* ch. 27), which has been interpreted as a means of drawing the souls of Yitzchak and his son closer so that the blessing would be more efficacious.

פרשת שופטים
Parashas Shoftim

Faith in Our Leaders

וּבָאתָ אֶל הַכֹּהֲנִים הַלְוִיִּם וְאֶל הַשֹּׁפֵט אֲשֶׁר יִהְיֶה בַּיָּמִים הָהֵם.

*You shall come to the Kohanim, the Levites,
and to the judge who will be in those days (Devarim 17:9).*

The Torah leaders of each generation are Divinely selected as being particularly suited for their generation[1]. אֱמוּנַת חֲכָמִים, faith in the guidance of the generation's sages, is crucial for the proper transmission of Torah and tradition and is also vital to the lives and development of individuals and their families. A Jew who has a *rav*, a *rebbi*, a Torah authority to whom he can turn with important questions and issues, can rest assured that his important steps in life will be rooted in Torah and will be accompanied by *siyata DiShmaya* (Divine assistance).

❧ ❧ ❧

To the casual observer, R' Moshe Hilsenrath and his wife Shaindel were just an ordinary couple. R' Moshe was a clean-shaven, hard-working accountant for the Austrian railroad system. Shaindel was a housewife caring for their children. But those who knew this couple well understood that

---

1. See *Sichos Mussar* where R' Chaim Shmulevitz discusses this topic at length.

they were far from ordinary. Their *emunah* (faith) in Hashem and His leaders was of a level that stamped them as great people. Their lives revolved around the *tzaddik* to whom they had chosen to attach themselves.

R' Moshe was a *chassid* of the Skolye *Rebbe,* R' David Yitzchak Isaac Rabinowitz, who, after the First World War, resided in Vienna. One merely had to gaze upon the *Rebbe's* radiant features to realize that he was a G-dly individual. His every waking moment was devoted to Hashem's service. Every day and night, men and women would come to seek the *Rebbe's* counsel and blessings. His heart had room for everyone's sufferings and he showed an amazing understanding of people and their various difficulties. His days and nights were dedicated primarily to intensive Torah study and it was from Torah alone that he acquired such incredible practical wisdom.

The Hilsenraths, like many others, perceived on numerous occasions that the *Rebbe* possessed a degree of *Ruach HaKodesh* (Divine Inspiration). He could advise with a confidence about the future which made clear that he knew more than meets the eye. And those who followed his guidance without wavering never went wrong. R' Moshe and Shaindel Hilsenrath were such people.

When the Nazis marched into Austria in 1938, the Austrian masses welcomed them with open arms, while the Jews trembled. Almost immediately, the Nazis began implementing the wicked anti-Semitic decrees which had become the way of life in Germany. Jewish homes were raided, Jewish stores looted, and many Jews were randomly picked off the street, never to be heard from again.

One night, Gestapo trucks pulled up in front of the apartment building where the Hilsenraths lived. The pounding on the Hilsenraths' door was answered by Mrs. Hilsenrath, who, with trembling hands, handed the officer her husband's work papers, identifying him as a government employee. The officer perused the papers, handed them back to Mrs. Hilsenrath and said, "Fine, but get that off your doorpost," and pointed to the *mezuzah.* When the beast turned and left, the Hilsenraths breathed a collective sigh of relief, and offered a silent prayer of thanks to the One Who had watched over them — and they left the *mezuzah* in place. It remained on the doorpost until they left Vienna.

They continued to hide a *sefer Torah* in their home and to have a *shochet* come secretly for the ritual slaughtering of chickens, a serious crime under the Germans.

As in every land which they occupied, the Germans made the *rabbanim,* who they knew were the inspirational force of their people, prime targets. It was obvious that the Skolye *Rebbe* was in grave danger. He was forced to abandon his home and, together with his *rebbetzin* and children, take up residence with a relative. Each morning and evening, R' Moshe Hilsenrath and his sons would come to the *Rebbe's* secret residence to complete his *minyan.* Despite the apparent danger, R' Moshe felt certain that the merit of his helping this *tzaddik* to pray with a *minyan* would shield him from all harm.

At that time, it was still possible to obtain a visa to emigrate to America. Every day, hundreds of Jews would stand on line at the American consulate hoping to receive an application for a visa. Once an application was completed and returned, it was assigned a number, and one had to hope and pray that his application would be approved and that his number would be called.

But there were no guarantees. There was not even any assurance that standing on line for hours on end would result in receiving an application. And standing on line involved great risk, for it happened more than once that Nazi soldiers would suddenly appear, grab people from the line and take them away.

The *Rebbe,* for whom the Nazis were searching, could not allow either himself or his sons to stand on line. When R' Moshe Hilsenrath obtained an application, he gave it to the *Rebbe* without hesitation, confident that, with Hashem's help, he would be able to receive a second application for his family. Indeed, this is what happened.

The *Rebbe's* application was processed ahead of R' Moshe's and he was to depart Austria by plane, ahead of his own family and the Hilsenraths. R' Moshe decided to accompany the *Rebbe* to the airport. He owned a cap and a leather coat, similar in style to those worn by Nazis. It was this outfit which he had worn when escorting the *Rebbe* to the *mikveh* under the Nazi regime. With his hand grasping the *Rebbe's* arm, it had appeared as if the "officer" was leading the Rabbi away. Now, when escorting the *Rebbe* to the airport, R' Moshe donned the same outfit.

The trip to the airport passed uneventfully. Before they parted, the *Rebbe* told his beloved *chassid,* "We will see each other in America." R' Moshe had no doubt that this would come to pass.

R' Moshe watched from a distance as the *Rebbe* passed through customs. Suddenly, an officer came over, opened the *Rebbe's* suitcases and threw the contents on the floor, sure that this would cause him to miss the plane. The *Rebbe* scooped up his belongings as quickly as he could and dashed breathlessly to the plane. He arrived there past the scheduled time for takeoff, but, miraculously, the plane had not departed.

In America, the *Rebbe* and the Hilsenraths settled in Brooklyn's Williamsburg neighborhood, where R' Moshe and his wife remained bound to the *Rebbe* with heart and soul. Whenever the *Rebbe* would conduct a *seudah* for his *chassidim,* it was Mrs. Hilsenrath who would cook the meal. She worked in a factory during the day, and would prepare the *seudah* at night.

One day, R' Moshe awakened to find that he had lost his voice. Subsequent visits to doctors were not encouraging. Finally, one doctor told him that he would never regain his voice.

The Hilsenraths poured their hearts out in *tefillah* and, as always, came before the Skolye *Rebbe* to share their troubles with him. After listening to the latest developments, the *Rebbe* said to R' Moshe, "I seem to recall that back in Vienna, you once had this very same problem." R' Moshe nodded affirmatively, and added that in Vienna he had been cured by the renowned ear, nose and throat specialist, Dr. Eugene Grabscheid.

"*Nu,*" replied the *Rebbe,* "go seek out Dr. Grabscheid and he will help you again."

Seek out Dr. Grabscheid? But this was America, not Vienna! Dr. Grabscheid was a Jew. Who knew if he had survived the war, and if he did survive, who knew where he was residing at that time?

These questions did not perturb the Hilsenraths. They had already learned from experience that the Skolye *Rebbe* was a *tzaddik* whose words were never to be taken lightly. If the *Rebbe* said to seek out Dr. Grabscheid, then that is what had to be done.

They looked in the Manhattan phone book and found a Dr. Eugene Grabscheid listed. A phone call confirmed that this was the very same doctor and that he was still practicing as a throat specialist. The doctor, upon examining R' Moshe, declared that the condition was curable and prescribed that R' Moshe not speak for the next six weeks. With time, he regained full use of his voice.

The close relationship between the Skolye *Rebbe* and R' Moshe Hilsenrath continued until R' Moshe's passing on 26 Tammuz, 5726 (1966). When paying a *shivah* call to the family, the *Rebbe* told R' Moshe's sons, "You have lost a father; I have lost my best friend."

Extra Protection

וְעָנוּ וְאָמְרוּ יָדֵינוּ לֹא שָׁפְכוּ אֶת הַדָּם הַזֶּה.

They shall speak up and say, "Our hands have not spilled this blood"
(Devarim 21:7).

I f the corpse of an unwitnessed murder is found lying in the open, the Torah requires the elders of the town nearest to the corpse to perform a public ritual in which they declare that they were not guilty by way of neglect or indifference.

Regarding their declaration, "Our hands have not spilled this blood," the Talmud[1] asks, "Did anyone suspect the elders of murder?" Answers the Talmud, the elders were saying that they did not know of the traveler and had no part in allowing him to go on his lonely way without food or לְוָיָה, *escort.* *Maharal* notes that this implies that the murder might not have happened had the traveler been escorted even part of the way! He explains that when a host takes the trouble to escort his guest part of the way, he shows that he feels solidarity with his fellow Jew, and when Jews have such feelings towards one another, Hashem responds by providing them with an extra measure of protection.

❧ ❧ ❧

Once, someone came from Brooklyn to Monsey to discuss an important matter with R' Yaakov Kamenetsky. When their discussion ended, the person thanked R' Yaakov and left, and soon after R' Yaakov entered a car to attend a scheduled appointment.

R' Yaakov instructed the driver, "Before heading to our destination, please take me for a brief stop to the bus stop, on the corner of Maple and Main."

---

1. *Sotah* 45b cited by *Rashi.*

Waiting at the bus stop was R' Yaakov's visitor. R' Yaakov alighted from the car, spoke with the person briefly and then returned to the car. He explained to the driver, "That person left my house only a short while ago. After he left, I realized that he was setting out for Brooklyn and I had not fulfilled the *mitzvah* of escorting him out the door. I knew that he had not come by car, so I assumed that he would be waiting here at the bus stop. Thankfully, he was here and I was able to wish him well and that he should have a safe trip."[1]

---

1. The following is quoted in the name of R' Chaim Volozhiner:

The house of a wealthy Jew, known for his charity and hospitality, was consumed by fire.

He came to the Vilna *Gaon* and asked why this misfortune had befallen him. The *Gaon* told him: The Torah refers to the inn which Avraham had built for wayfarers as an אֵשֶׁל (*Bereishis* 21:33). The word אֵשֶׁל is an acronym for אֲכִילָה, *eating,* שְׁתִיָּה, *drinking* and לְוָיָה, *escorting.* The man had failed to escort the travelers out the door when they took leave of his home. Thus, all that remained were the first two letters of the word אֵשֶׁל, which form the word אֵשׁ, *fire (Peninim Mishulchan HaGra).*

פרשת כי תצא
Parashas Ki Seitzei

Two Sides of a Coin

לֹא תִרְאֶה אֶת שׁוֹר אָחִיךָ אוֹ אֶת שֵׂיוֹ נִדָּחִים
וְהִתְעַלַּמְתָּ מֵהֶם הָשֵׁב תְּשִׁיבֵם לְאָחִיךָ.

You shall not see the ox of your brother or his sheep cast off,
and hide yourself from them; you shall surely return them
to your brother (Devarim 22:1).

In Jerusalem a generation ago, there lived a man known to all as R' Bezalel *Milchiger,* the Milkman. R' Bezalel was known not so much for the bottles of milk which he sold from his wagon each day, but for the wine of Torah which flowed from his lips almost incessantly. He was a *tzaddik* and Torah scholar of rare repute.

Old Jerusalemites still vividly recall the sight of R' Bezalel stopping his wagon on one of the narrow streets in the city's Shaarei Chesed neighborhood and dashing into a *beis midrash* to snatch a few minutes of learning in the middle of a hard day's work ... A few hours later, R' Bezalel's wagon was still parked in the same spot, while he sat immersed in his studies oblivious to the passage of time.

Others still see before them the sight of R' Bezalel calmly steering his horse-drawn vehicle down the street when suddenly, a gleam shone in his eyes . . . As soon as he caught sight of a scholar, R' Bezalel jumped off his wagon. "R' . . .! Please, could you spare a minute? I have arrived at a solution to *Rambam's* question regarding . . ."[1]

Once, a Jerusalemite met R' Bezalel as he was carrying a sack and mumbling to himself. Upon being asked if something was amiss, R' Bezalel replied, "Yes, I've found this sack full of coins and I am now occupied with the great *mitzvah* of *hashavas aveidah* (returning a lost object). Now, I was thinking to myself, with how many *mitzvos* am I involving myself? Is each coin a separate *mitzvah* for itself, or is it all one *mitzvah* since the coins are collected together in a single sack?!"

The other man peered inside the sack and realized that it held thousands of dollars worth of coins. "R' Bezalel," the man said, "who says that you are obligated to find the owner and return this money? It seems to me that this sack and its coins have no *siman* (identifying characteristic) by which the owner can prove his claim! Perhaps you are entitled to keep this fortune?"

R' Bezalel became so distressed that he began to tremble. "What are you saying? Do you think that I would consider even for a moment keeping any of this money? Can you imagine the pain of the person who has lost it? Do you think that I would enjoy such money knowing that its original owner is suffering in misery?

"I will find the owner and return the money in any case. And you are trying to tell me that according to *halachah*, I am not obligated to return it and when I do, I will not have fulfilled the *mitzvah* of *hashavas aveidah*? And if, indeed, each coin is a separate *mitzvah*, I will not have fulfilled hundreds of *mitzvos* of *hashavas aveidah*?"

"I only had your best interests in mind, R' Bezalel," the other man replied. "Let's face it; you are a very poor man. Perhaps

1. The above was drawn from *Sippurim Yerushalmiyim* by Nun ben Avraham.

Hashem has sent this sack your way so that you will be able to live in a better apartment with more food on your table?"

"I am poor?" R' Bezalel retorted, still quite agitated. "What makes me poor? I have a roof over my head, don't I? And I have bread, thank G-d. So what am I lacking, a few delicacies? Do not our Sages teach, 'Before one prays that words of Torah enter his innards, he should pray that delicacies *not* enter his innards'?[1]

"And as I told you, what pleasure will I have from another Jew's pain?"

Now, the other man was acutely aware that the only thing he could do was try to calm down R' Bezalel. "Well, let's see now, R' Bezalel," he said, "perhaps this sack *does* have some indentifying features . . ."[2]

---

1. *Tana D'Vei Eliyahu Rabbah* ch. 21. Overindulgence in physical pleasures dulls a person's spiritual sensitivities and weakens his ability to "taste" the sweetness of Torah learning.

2. From *She'al Avicha Veyagedcha* (collected stories told by R' Shalom Schwadron) vol. III.

פרשת כי תבוא
Parashas Ki Savo

The Source of Plague

וְרָאוּ כָּל עַמֵּי הָאָרֶץ כִּי שֵׁם ה' נִקְרָא עָלֶיךָ וְיָרְאוּ מִמֶּךָּ.

*Then all the peoples of the earth will see that the Name of Hashem
is proclaimed over you, and they will revere you (Devarim 28:10).*

Many years ago in the city of Ostrow, Poland, a plague
struck which claimed many lives. Nothing physicians
could offer had any effect in stemming the plague's deadly tide.

The city's *rav,* along with his rabbinical court, declared a day
of communal fasting and prayer. A proclamation was issued
calling on everyone to examine his ways and to increase his
Torah study and *chesed.* Everyone was also asked to take note
of the wayward behavior of others and to respectfully reprove
one another or bring the matter before the court.

Two of Ostrow's citizens, while discussing the proclamation,
suddenly realized that for a very long time, R' Nachum, a
long-time resident of Ostrow, had not been attending *minyan.*
In fact, they did not recall having seen him set foot into the
city's *shul* all that time. They now began to wonder: With what
could R' Nachum be so precoccupied that made *minyan*
attendance impossible?! And if he was being woefully neglect-

ful of so important an obligation as praying with a *minyan*, then surely his entire lifestyle must have taken a turn in the wrong direction!

The two men decided to conceal themselves during evening hours near R' Nachum's home and observe him. Perhaps they would gain some clue as to what was occupying him.

The following night, they watched as R' Nachum emerged from his house near midnight, carrying a small sack. They followed him at a distance until they saw him entering a forest. The men were afraid to follow him any further. Why would he be entering a forest in the middle of the night? Perhaps he belonged to a gang of thieves, which would explain why he no longer came to *shul*?!

The next day, the two visited the *rav* and related their discovery. The *rav* refused to pass judgment on R' Nachum without definitive proof. He instructed the men to monitor R' Nachum's movements on the following night and to inform him as soon as they spotted the man leaving his house.

The following night, shortly before midnight, the *rav* was summoned. He joined the two men in stealthily following R' Nachum to the forest. This time, when he entered the forest, the others entered as well, making sure to maintain a safe distance behind him.

They watched as R' Nachum sat himself down under a tree and withdrew a *siddur* from his sack. Then, to their amazement, he began to shed bitter tears as he proceeded to recite *Tikun Chatzos*, the midnight prayers mourning the Destruction of the *Beis HaMikdash*. The *rav*, however, was most taken aback by something else. He saw only R' Nachum sitting there, but he was sure that he heard *two* voices reciting the prayers in unison.

The trio waited until R' Nachum had finished praying and then followed him back into the town. As R' Nachum neared his house, the *rav* caught up to him and told him that he had just been followed. The *rav* begged R' Nachum forgiveness for having suspected him of wrongdoing and asked who was with him in the forest. R' Nachum remained silent, not wanting to respond, until the *rav* said, "As *rav* of this city, I decree that you *must* tell me who was with you tonight."

R' Nachum responded, "It seems that Heaven is pleased with my midnight prayers. As a reward, I have been granted the privilege of being joined each night by the *neshamah* (soul) of the prophet Yirmiyahu, who foretold the Destruction and authored the Book of *Eichah* (Lamentations). Together, we plead for Hashem's mercy and ask that He rebuild His Sanctuary through the coming of *Mashiach.*"

The *rav,* shaken by this revelation, asked, "If you are so great, then surely you can tell us why this terrible plague has befallen us. And also, can you please tell me why you have refrained from joining our minyan for so long?"

R' Nachum replied, "Tomorrow morning I will come to your *shul* and both questions will be answered."

The two men who had accompanied the *rav* spread word through the town that a hidden *tzaddik* was living in their midst. The next morning when R' Nachum entered, wrapped in his *tallis* and *tefillin,* the *shul* was already filled to capacity. As R' Nachum made his way toward the front of the *shul,* those whom he passed were awestruck by his shining countenance. This was not the R' Nachum whom they knew as an ordinary fellow. This man's face radiated holiness; he was obviously a *tzaddik*!

The *rav,* too, was awed by R' Nachum's appearance, and as soon as *Shacharis* had ended, he said to him, "Rather than answer my two questions of last night, you have given me cause to ask a third question. How is it that this morning you appear so radiant?"

R' Nachum replied, "The answer to this question holds the key to your questions of last night. The Torah states, 'Then all the peoples of the earth will see that the Name of Hashem is proclaimed over you and they will revere you,' to which the Talmud states, 'R' Eliezer said: ". . . the name of Hashem will be proclaimed over you" — this refers to the *tefillin* of the head'.[1]

---

1. *Berachos* 6a.

"Since my youth, I have always treated my *tefillin* with utmost reverence. I speak nothing but words of Torah and *tefillah* while I wear them; not for a moment do I forget that I bear these sacred articles on my head and arm. Therefore, I merit the fulfillment of this verse, that my appearance evokes awe whenever I wear *tefillin*.

"In your congregation, unfortunately, there is no regard for the sanctity of *tefillin* — just as there is no regard for the sanctity of this *beis haknesses*. When I would walk in here in days past, I would find the people wearing *tefillin* and engaged in the most mundane conversations! — a disgrace to the *tefillin* and a disgrace to the sanctity of the *beis haknesses*. [2]

"This is the source of the plague that has attacked our city and this is also the reason why I have refrained from joining this *minyan*."

That same day, the entire community assembled in the *shul* to hear the *rav* relate what he had been told by R' Nachum. The entire assemblage burst into sobs. The people accepted upon themselves to refrain from conversation both in *shul* and whenever they wore *tefillin*. That very day, the plague came to an end (cited by the author of *Sefer Yemei HaBacharus* in the name of R' Shmuel Hominer).

---

2. The Chofetz Chaim (*Mishnah Berurah* 151:1 citing *Semak*) writes that the sin of speaking mundane talk in the synagogue transforms it into "a place of idol worship." He further notes that the *Zohar* speaks of this sin in most severe terms.

Worse yet, writes the Chofetz Chaim, is when one sits in a *shul* or *beis midrash* while speaking *lashon hara* or other forms of forbidden speech, ". . . for in doing so, one shows lack of regard for the *Shechinah*; [furthermore,] there is no comparison between one who sins in private and one who sins in the palace of the King, in the King's Presence. This evil is compounded when one causes others to join in his sin . . . so that from a few individuals come many groups which engage in strife with one another — until the synagogue becomes like one huge torch . . . And who is the cause of this, if not the one with whom it all started? Surely that person will be 'rewarded' for all that he caused.

"Therefore, one who is truly G-d-fearing should always be vigilant that he not engage in any mundane talk in the synagogue or in the study hall. Rather, these places will be used by him strictly for Torah study and prayer" (*Mishnah Berurah* 151:2).

פרשת נצבים
Parashas Nitzavim

Reunion

הַנִּסְתָּרוֹת לה׳ אֱלֹקֵינוּ וְהַנִּגְלוֹת לָנוּ וּלְבָנֵינוּ עַד עוֹלָם.
The hidden are for Hashem, our G-d,
but the revealed are for us and our children (Devarim 29:28).
אִם יִהְיֶה נִדַּחֲךָ בִּקְצֵה הַשָּׁמָיִם מִשָּׁם יְקַבֶּצְךָ ה׳ אֱלֹקֶיךָ וּמִשָּׁם יִקָּחֶךָ.
If your dispersed will be at the ends of heaven, from there Hashem,
your G-d, will gather you in and from there He will take you
(ibid. 30:4).

Ramban writes that the promise of the second verse
quoted above has not yet been fulfilled; it will come to
pass at the End of Days, in the Messianic era. At that time,
Hashem will bring His beloved people back to their Land from
all corners of the earth.

The phrase "the ends of heaven" has been interpreted in a
spiritual sense. No matter how distant a Jew has strayed, no
matter how entrenched he might be in his secular way of life,
Hashem's guiding hand can bring him back to the path and
traditions of his ancestors.

Rashi, in his commentary on *Tehillim,* [1] understands the first verse which we have quoted in this vein. "The hidden ones" refers to those Jews who have become so assimilated among the gentile nations that their Jewish origins have become forgotten. When the final redemption comes, these *hidden ones,* known only to Hashem, will be reunited with their people.

Our generation, which finds itself in the period known as *Ikvesa D'Meshicha,* the prelude to the Messianic era[2], has witnessed the reunion of thousands of *baalei teshuvah* with the way of life of their ancestors. More often than not, their stories of return are a chain of hidden miracles in which the guiding hand of Hashem is clearly evident.

The following real-life story tells of a different kind of reunion. It can serve as a parable to illustrate how Hashem has infinite ways of bring back that which seems lost forever.

❧ ❧ ❧

R' Yaakov Eisner,[3] a highly regarded *maggid shiur* (Talmudic lecturer) at an East Coast yeshivah high school, arrived in America in the early 1950's as a young boy. At the outbreak of World War II, his parents had fled Poland ahead of the advancing German armies and made their way deep inside Russia to Uzbekistan. A few days after Yaakov was born, his father was taken away by the Communists and never heard from again. After war's end, he and his mother were transferred from one Displaced Persons Camp to another, the last one in Fohrenwald, Germany.

Fohrenwald had a large number of religious Jews, including a number of children. A *cheder* (elementary school) was organized and a young *melamed,* R' Meilech, was assigned to teach a class whose students ranged in age from eight to

---

1. *Tehillim* 87:6.
2. The Chofetz Chaim, who passed away in 5693 (1933), said that this period had already begun in his day.
3. Not his real name.

fourteen. Yaakov Eisner was among the youngest in the group and he will never forget the love and devotion which R' Meilech showered upon his young charges.

When Yaakov needed to have his tonsils removed, his mother was told to take him to a Catholic hospital in a nearby city. They were told that the boy would have to be hospitalized for a few days following the procedure, but Yaakov's mother was not able to stay with him during that time. R' Meilech, therefore, sat at his *talmid's* bedside for three consecutive days, sleeping on a chair.

Five days each week, the boys were under R' Meilech's watchful eye from early morning until dark. Friday they learned only in the morning. R' Meilech became aware that on Friday afternoons, the boys were engaging in extracurricular activities which, to his mind, would distract them from their learning. He spoke to the boys about this, explaining that any activity should be avoided if it would be on their minds when they sat in front of their *gemara* delving into "the words of Abaye and Rava." However, R' Meilech understood that the boys needed something to do in their free time, and he offered a suggestion. A man named Yaakov Friedman was operating a printing press in the camp for the publication of *sefarim*. On Friday afternoons, the boys could go to the press and watch Mr. Friedman and his men at work. The boys were quite happy with this suggestion.

This activity turned into an unusual hobby for the boys as they became "page collectors." Mr. Friedman allowed the boys to keep the overruns which would not be bound. The boys would collect pages of *Tehillim, Mesilas Yesharim, Shaagas Aryeh* and other classic works and trade them with one another until they had a complete *sefer.* Then the boys would take the pages to the binder and, in exchange for a can of sardines, he would bind it for them.

During his stay at Fohrenwald, Yaakov collected a few such *sefarim.* When he and his mother left for America, his *Sefer Mateh Ephraim* somehow got left behind.

Some thirty years later, on a summer day in the 1980s, R' Yaakov Eisner was sitting in the dining room at a summer camp when a *talmid* came and told him, *"Rebbi,* a publishing company has just brought a truckload of old *sefarim* for burial.[1] I was examining the *sefarim* lying in the pit which had been dug, and I came across a *Mateh Ephraim* with your name in it. You probably don't want it since it looks very old, but I thought I would tell you . . ."

R' Eisner hurried to the pit with his *talmid* and found the *sefer*. It was the precious *Mateh Ephraim* that had been left behind in Fohrenwald. To this day, the *sefer* occupies an honored place among R' Eisner's personal *sefarim*.

In the winter of 1996, R' Eisner's son came to tell him that a stranger was at the door. R' Eisner did not recognize this elderly man with a flowing white beard. "Yaakov, is it really you?" the stranger asked. "I am R' Meilech . . ."

The two embraced and then spent a long time reminiscing about their days at Fohrenwald. R' Eisner told his *rebbi* how in more than three decades as a teacher of Torah, he has inspired his own *talmidim* with numerous stories of R' Meilech's love, devotion and wisdom in guiding his post-war *talmidim,* who had experienced great tribulations and had been living under difficult conditions. R' Meilech listened as his *talmid* related story after story, and he wept with great emotion.

---

1. *Sefarim* (Torah works) which have fallen into disuse are buried. See *Shulchan Aruch, Yoreh De'ah* ch. 282.

Choose Life

וְהַחַיִּים וְהַמָּוֶת נָתַתִּי לְפָנֶיךָ הַבְּרָכָה וְהַקְּלָלָה, וּבָחַרְתָּ בַּחַיִּים . . .
. . . I have placed life and death before you, blessing and curse;
and you shall choose life. . . (Devarim 30:19).

L ife, says *Mesilas Yesharim,* is an endless series of tests. The Torah exhorts us to "choose life," that is, to make the Torah's teachings our barometer in deciding what our priorities should be. Those who make spiritual pursuits their primary purpose in life are blessed both in this world and the next.

R' Yisrael Zev Gustman related to his *talmidim* the tragic circumstances where he saw first hand the futility of pursuing material wealth in this world.

❊   ❊   ❊

It was the year 1940, after Germany had taken control of all of Poland and Lithuania, including Vilna where R' Gustman served as a *rav.* One day, the Germans announced that all Jews were to line up in front of the city's Great Synagogue. As R' Gustman waited on line, the man in front of him, a wealthy gem merchant, turned around to face him, looking frantic.

"*Rebbi,*" he whispered, "what shall I do? The people in front of me just informed me that the Nazis are searching everyone for valuables. There are diamonds in the lining of my coat! They will surely find them! What shall I do?"

R' Gustman replied, "Open a small amount of stitching in the lining, take the diamonds out and give them to me."

The man wasted no time in following these instructions. It had rained the previous day, and the ground was very muddy. R' Gustman dropped the diamonds into the mud, one by one, and with his foot covered them with a thick layer of mud.

The merchant was searched without incident, but his precious diamonds were lost forever.

As related above,[1] R' Gustman himself spent almost five years hiding in the suburbs of Vilna, enduring daily terror and deprivation. All those years, he did not have a single *sefer* from which to study. Yet the Torah which had been absorbed into his mind and soul remained intact. Only weeks after leaving the Displaced Persons camp after the war, he was delivering *shiurim* (Torah lectures).

His were diamonds that could not be taken away.

פרשת וילך
Parashas Vayeilich

Model Lesson

הַקְהֵל אֶת הָעָם הָאֲנָשִׁים וְהַנָּשִׁים וְהַטַּף . . .
*Gather together the people — the men, the women,
and the small children . . . (Devarim 31:12).*

Once every seven years, the Jewish people would assemble in the courtyard of the *Beis HaMikdash* and hear the king read from the Book of *Devarim*. The Talmud asks,

---

1. See chapter to *Parashas Bamidbar.*

"Why were the young children present? To give reward to those who bring them" (*Chagigah* 3a cited by *Rashi*). It is clear that the Sages understood the term עַף in this verse as referring to infants. *Ramban,* however, understands the term as referring to children who have reached the age of understanding. The plain reading of the verse seems to support this, "Gather together . . . the children . . . so that they will hear and so that they will learn . . ." In *Ramban's* words, "They will listen and ask, and their fathers will teach them and train them . . ."

❀ ❀ ❀

It was a *Chol HaMoed* practice of R' Moshe Neuschloss[1] to call on great Torah personalities with whom he enjoyed a close relationship. Among those whom he would visit was the leading halachic authority of his time, R' Moshe Feinstein.

One year on *Chol HaMoed Succos,* R' Neuschloss visited R' Moshe in his *succah* and brought along his son, who was then a child of about seven. The boy was bright and astute; as he entered the *succah,* he looked up at the *s'chach* (covering), pointed to it and exclaimed, "*Tatte! A passe'le succah!* (Father! An invalid *succah*!)" The *succah's* covering was made of thin slats of wood; in the neighborhood where the Neuschlosses lived at the time, all *succahs* were covered by either evergreens or bamboo.

Before R' Neuschloss could say anything, R' Moshe, seemingly amused by the child's outburst, said, "*Mein kind* (My child), what is your name?"

"Yidde'le."[2]

"Come, Yidde'le, sit on my lap." R' Moshe helped the child onto his lap and made sure that he was comfortable and unafraid.

"Now, Yidde'le, we are going to learn some *Mishnayos* together."

R' Moshe reached for a volume lying on the table. He turned

---

1. See chapters to *Parshiyos Noach, Va'eira* and *Va'eschanan.*
2. An affectionate variation of "Yehudah."

to a *mishnah* in the first chapter of *Masechta Succah* which discusses the maximum width of a valid piece of *s'chach*. A proper study of the *mishnah* makes it obvious that thin slats of wood *are* valid as *s'chach*.

R' Moshe, the world-renowned *rosh yeshivah* and *posek*, whose intricate Talmudic lectures were not easily grasped by accomplished scholars, now taught the child the *mishnah* with the skill of an expert pedagogue. After explaining its concepts in lucid terms, R' Moshe quizzed his young student to make sure that he fully understood. Satisfied that the boy did understand, R' Moshe said, "So now, Yidde'le, look up at the *s'chach* and tell me — is it *kasher* (valid)?"

"Yes, *Rebbe!* It is *kasher!*"

"Good!" replied R' Moshe. He and R' Neuschloss smiled at one another with delight and then entered into a Torah discussion, while little Yidde'le observed in respectful silence. It was an experience that neither he, nor his illustrious father, would ever forget.

פרשת האזינו
Parashas Ha'azinu

Fulfilling the Promise

וַיָּבֹא מֹשֶׁה וַיְדַבֵּר אֶת כָּל דִּבְרֵי הַשִּׁירָה הַזֹּאת בְּאָזְנֵי הָעָם.

*Moshe came and spoke all the words of this Song
in the ears of the people (Devarim 32:44).*

Ramban writes that the word כָּל, *all,* in the above verse alludes to the fact that the Song, which constitutes most of *Parashas Ha'azinu,* encompasses the entire sweep of Jewish history, including all that will come to pass at the End of Days.

The song begins with the boundless favors Hashem bestowed upon His people, and how the Jewish people would eventually stray from the proper path. Israel's disloyalty, the Song continues, would bring it famine, cruel attackers and, ultimately, exile and dispersion. All these predictions have been fulfilled.

The song concludes, "O nations — sing the praises of His people, for He will avenge the blood of His servants; He will bring retribution upon His foes, and He will appease His Land and His people" (v. 43). Without a doubt, states *Ramban,* this refers to the Final Redemption. When the Jews returned to their Land from Babylon to rebuild the *Beis HaMikdash,* they did not earn the praise of the gentile nations or see their spilled blood avenged. Just as all previous predictions mentioned in the Song have come to pass, so too, will this final prediction come true as well.

> "[This song . . .] is a document of testimony . . . that Hashem, Blessed is He, . . . will not let us be destroyed; He will relent, and punish our enemies with His great, mighty, destructive sword, and He will forgive our sins for the sake of His Name. This Song is a clear promise of our ultimate redemption" (*Ramban*).

The previous *parashah* states that this Song contains yet another promise: "It shall be that when many evils and distresses come upon it, then this Song shall speak up before it as a witness, for it shall not be forgotten from the mouth of its offspring" (*Devarim* 31:21). This is the comforting promise that though the Jewish people may suffer deprivation and persecution, the Torah will never be forgotten from its people (*Rashi*).

The truth of this promise is clearly evident in our day, when only half a century after the Holocaust, we are witness to a worldwide resurgence of Torah study that many never imagined would come to pass. Even while the flames of the Holocaust were consuming millions of our people, Providence was keeping alive a chosen few who would play a major role in the resurgence of Torah life during and after the War. Two such individuals were Rabbi Dovid Bender and his wife, Rebbetzin Basya.

❧ ❧ ❧

At the conclusion of Rosh Hashanah 5693 (1932), Dovid Bender approached his father, R' Avraham. "Papa, I had a *hergesh* (feeling) about something this Rosh Hashanah. I feel that the time has come for me to leave America to study Torah in one of the great European yeshivos."

"And I had that very same feeling about you," his father replied. "There is one problem: My fund-raising for the

Yeshivah often takes me abroad for weeks on end. You are our only child; I cannot ask your mother to part with you and be left here all alone. If you go to study in Europe, then your mother will have to come along."

After Succos, Dovid left by boat for the great yeshivah in Mir, Poland, accompanied by his mother. Mrs. Bender took up residence in Mir and her apartment became a "home away from home" for American students at the yeshivah.

Dovid Bender spent the next five years immersed in Torah study at the Mirrer Yeshivah. In 1938, he became engaged to Basya Epstein of Otvosk. Her family was distinguished for its dedication to Torah and *chesed.* During World War I, when the Epsteins had relocated to Minsk, they had as their guest the holy Chofetz Chaim, who had been forced to leave Radin ahead of the advancing German armies. For six weeks, the Chofetz Chaim slept in the bed which had belonged to little Basya, while she slept on the kitchen floor.

In Minsk, Mrs. Epstein would dress five-year-old Basya in her warmest winter clothing and entrust her with a chunk of butter to be delivered to a sick Torah scholar, *HaGaon* R' Refael Shapiro, *zt"l,* who also had taken refuge in the city.

On the night following the week of *sheva berachos* celebrating the marriage of R' Dovid and Basya Bender, R' Dovid's mother told her daughter-in-law, "You do not need your mother-in-law in such close proximity — I am returning to America."

The new couple settled in Mir where R' Dovid continued to pursue his studies. In the summer of 1939, they spent a few weeks at Neveyelnia, a resort city where R' Boruch Ber Lebovitz and other great Torah personalities vacationed. Rebbetzin Basya Bender would later say that it was the best summer of her life. She and her husband basked in the radiance of Torah and piety which emanated from R' Boruch Ber and his peers. And the atmosphere was one of tranquility; the Polish government was doing a good job of playing down the German threat. No one, at least in Neveyelnia, had any idea of what was to come.

On August 20th of that year, the Benders received two

telegrams from R' Dovid's parents, informing them that R' Dovid's mother had taken sick and that their presence was urgently needed. For the next seven days, two such telegrams arrived each day. On August 29th, *three* such telegrams arrived. R' Dovid understood what was happening; his parents wanted them home because there was now a real threat of war. The message about his mother being ill was intended either to convince him to return home, or to convince the authorities to grant them the necessary papers.

On August 30th, the couple headed for Otvosk to discuss the situation with Basya's parents, R' and Mrs. Yaakov Epstein. Mrs. Epstein withdrew from a hiding place five hundred *zlotes* which she had been saving for emergency purposes. "Go, save yourself!" she instructed her daughter as she handed her the money. "For us, money will no longer help," she added sadly.

There was no time to lose. Passage on a boat would have to be booked, but that was not the most difficult hurdle. As an American citizen, R' Dovid possessed all the necessary papers to leave the country; however, this was not the case with his wife, a Polish citizen from birth.

The next day, August 31st, they entered a consulate in Poland that was preparing to close as war rumblings grew ever louder. Entering the director's office, Rebbetzin Bender presented the telegrams sent by her in-laws and explained that although as a "loyal Polish citizen" it pained her to leave at such a time, her mother-in-law's poor health impelled her to travel to America. She then added, "However, being a loyal citizen, I wish to do whatever I can to help the Motherland's armies" — and she placed the five hundred *zlotes* on the table.

She knew very well that the money would never come near the army's treasuries. She had given the money with other intentions, and her plan worked. The official picked up the phone and dialed the number of a crony in a nearby government building. He spoke in Russian, unaware that the young woman standing before him was fluent in seven languages. "There's a young lady here who wants a passport to go to America so that she can visit her mother-in-law who's ill.

She put down five hundred *zlotes.* I'll take half and you'll take half. Can I send her over now?" Hanging up the phone, he informed her that though the other building was officially closed, they would admit her and process her papers.

With the papers in order, the Benders rushed breathlessly to the port to board the boat on which they had booked passage. They arrived moments too late — the boat had just left the dock. The next day, September 1, 1939, World War II erupted with Germany's invasion of Poland. On that day, the last passenger boat sailed out of Poland with the Benders on board. They later learned that the boat which they had missed had been sunk at sea. Their boat arrived safely in Switzerland, but on its return trip to Poland, it too was sunk.

On *erev Yom Kippur,* the Benders arrived in New York. R' Avraham Bender had a police car waiting at the dock to ensure that his children would arrive in Williamsburg in time for *yom tov.* But papers had to be processed, so R' Dovid remained behind while his wife entered the police car and arrived at her in-laws' home ten minutes before *yom tov.* R' Dovid walked home from Manhattan's West Side at dawn and arrived later on Yom Kippur.

On *Motza'ei Yom Kippur,* Rebbetzin Vichna Kaplan, who knew Rebbetzin Basya Bender from Europe, asked her to join America's first Bais Yaakov high school for girls. After Succos, Rebbetzin Bender began teaching her first class in America, consisting of eight girls. Thus began an illustrious career on these shores which saw her educate thousands of young women in the way of authentic Torah values, a career which lasted more than half a century until her passing in the spring of 5756 (1996).

R' Dovid Bender served first as a *rebbi* and later as *Menahel* of Yeshivah Torah Vodaath, where he had a profound impact upon scores of *talmidim* until his sudden passing in November 1965.

This unusual couple left behind thousands of students, and children of their own who perpetuate the Bender legacy of teaching the way of Torah to the youth of today, the leaders of tomorrow.

פרשת וזאת הברכה
Parashas Vezos HaBerachah

For One and All

תּוֹרָה צִוָּה לָנוּ מֹשֶׁה מוֹרָשָׁה קְהִלַּת יַעֲקֹב.
*The Torah that Moshe commanded us
is the heritage of the Congregation of Yaakov (Devarim 33:4).*

T he Torah is the heritage of every single Jew. Everyone,
rich and poor, young and old, deserves the opportunity to
study and attach himself to our holy Torah.

Hashem in His infinite wisdom finds ways to help even those
most distant to experience the beauty and truth of Torah study
and the life it represents.

⚘ ⚘ ⚘

On a typical spring afternoon, a teenaged yeshivah student
walked down a street in his Flatbush neighborhood. The boy, a
quiet, studious type, was unprepared when an obviously
non-observant woman walked up to him and said, "My son is
going to be bar mitzvah and I need to send him to a Jewish
heritage center for lessons. Can you give me the phone number
of one?"

The boy was rather flustered. A Jewish heritage center? He
certainly did not know of any. How should he respond? Only

one number came to mind. "Here, try this . . ." It was the number of a pay phone in Mesivta Rabbi Chaim Berlin, where he was a student.

A few minutes later, the pay phone rang in the lobby of the yeshivah. As Heaven willed it, Chaim Nosson Segal,[1] a student in his early twenties, answered the phone. "My name is Mrs. Stevens. Is this the heritage center?" the voice on the other end asked. "How can I help you?" the young man responded. "Well," she said, "my son is only eight years old, but I'd like him to start getting some Hebrew lessons so that he'll be ready for his bar mitzvah in five years."

Chaim Nosson replied that this could be arranged and he invited the woman to come that afternoon for an appointment.

She and her son, Jonathan, were met at the door of the yeshivah by another student, who escorted them to an office where Chaim Nosson was waiting. He greeted his visitors and got to know Jonathan a bit. Afterwards, he told Mrs. Stevens, "Your son has a lot of learning to do before he can begin bar mitzvah lessons. The first step is to teach him the Hebrew alphabet. I have some free time and I'd be happy to learn with him once a week — free of charge."

The faculty and students at the yeshivah became used to the sight of this slight, charming boy who wore a tee-shirt and shorts, and a *yarmulka* provided by Chaim Nosson. They befriended him and made him feel welcome. Meanwhile, Chaim Nosson was discovering how distant from his heritage Jonathan actually was.

As Pesach approached, Chaim Nosson asked Jonathan if he knew what a *"seder"* was. It took some prodding before the child responded, "Yes, I remember now. It's that meal where we have those big crackers." When told about how Moses took the Jews out of slavery, the boy interjected, "You mean Abraham."

"No," replied Chaim Nosson patiently. "Abraham was the first of our forefathers, but Moses was the one who took

_____
1. Today, R' Segal is Director of Community Development at Torah Umesorah.

our people out of slavery."

"That can't be!" Jonathan argued. "I learned in school that Abraham Lincoln freed the slaves!"

Jonathan planned to spend his summer at a nonsectarian camp. Shortly before his departure, Chaim Nosson brought him to the *Rosh Yeshivah* of Mesivta Rabbi Chaim Berlin, R' Aharon Schechter. Jonathan proudly read the letters of the *Aleph-Beis*, recited *Modeh Ani* and the opening verse of *Shema*, and received the *Rosh Yeshivah's* heartfelt blessings.

Upon returning from camp at summer's end, Jonathan told his teacher and friend, "Chaim Nosson, every day at camp, I put on my *kippah*, opened my Hebrew book and said *Modeh Ani* and *Shema.*"

Jonathan continued to progress in his studies, and as his knowledge grew so did his feeling for Torah and *mitzvos*. But the road to spiritual success was not to be an easy one for him, as he faced tests on many fronts. His home situation was unsettling; his brother was a drug addict. One night, his brother went on a rampage and Jonathan had to grab his *kippah* and run for his life. He spent most of that night in a police station.

While Jonathan was proud of his new-found connection to his heritage, he did not find it easy to completely break with his secular upbringing. When the family ate a tasty non-kosher supper, he found it difficult not to partake. Years later, he clearly recalled the night when he woke up from a dream and said to himself, "The choice is up to me; if I really choose to eat only kosher, I can do it." And he did.

The yeshivah "family" hosted a *seudas mitzvah* on the occasion of Jonathan's bar mitzvah, to which the boy's relatives were invited, and Chaim Nosson delivered an emotional address in which he explained why all those assembled should be proud and gratified that "Jonathan" had now become "Yonasan."

When Chaim Nosson's schedule no longer allowed for him to study with Yonasan, other students, under the constant direction of the *Rosh Yeshivah*, undertook responsibility for the boy's spiritual and material welfare. Yonasan was enrolled in

Yeshivah Rabbi Chaim Berlin. Not all of Yonasan's classmates were quick to accept this boy who was so obviously different from them. Their *rebbi* expended great effort to bridge the gap and showered Yonasan with love and concern. Eventually, he gained acceptance.

In later years, Yonasan moved in with a religious family and the yeshivah community provided him with financial support. When in seventh grade, however, he still lived at home and there was no money for even his basic needs. He desperately wanted a new pair of sneakers but was too ashamed to ask his *rebbi* or older friends for help. The yeshivah was offering one dollar per *blatt* (folio) for students who would recite their *gemara* studies by heart. Yonasan, driven by his need for sneakers, was the only student in his class to recite the entire first chapter of *Masechta Kiddushin* — *forty blatt* — by heart. As a result of his success, he was skipped to ninth grade at year's end, where he was finally with boys his own age.

One day, as he stood at a bus stop in Flatbush, Yonasan noticed two rough-looking youths whom he remembered well from his days at public school. They were staring at his *yarmulka* and Yonasan recalled that the two always enjoyed snatching *yarmulkas* off the heads of yeshivah children and throwing them away. Yonasan's trials and tribulations had left him with an inner toughness. No one was going to throw away *his yarmulka.* As the two hooligans closed in on him, Yonasan thrust his *yarmulka* into his pocket and slugged the youth in front of him. He paid for this with a beating that left him bruised and bleeding, but he succeeded in holding on to his *yarmulka.* Soon after his attackers left, Yonasan's *rebbi* drove by. Shocked by the sight of his battered *talmid,* the *rebbi* jumped out of the car, pulled Yonasan inside, and spent a long time comforting him.

As the years went by, Yonasan pursued his Torah studies at Chaim Berlin and other yeshivos on the East Coast and developed into an outstanding *ben Torah*. At age seventeen, he was possessed by a burning desire to study Torah at a yeshivah in *Eretz Yisrael.*

His mother, however, was not at all keen about the idea. Since the day that she had brought her son to the yeshivah, she had never prevented him from realizing his aspirations, and she would not stop him this time — but she would not help him, either. If he wanted to go to *Eretz Yisrael,* he would have to do it alone.

Yonasan conferred with his *rebbeim* and older friends, who were all of the same mind: There was really no choice. According to law, anyone under the age of eighteen required parental consent to be issued a passport. Yonasan would have to continue his studies in America for another year.

But Yonasan, who had worked so hard and with such determination for so long, would not let his dream fade so easily. He headed for New York's main passport office, taking with him three pieces of identification, none of which matched. His birth certificate bore his family name, which was later legally abbreviated. His Social Security card bore his English first name and abbreviated family name, while his driver's license bore his Hebrew first name.

Yonasan waited patiently on line until his turn finally came. With a self-assured air, he placed his application and mismatched identification on the counter. The passport clerk hardly looked at the material. Instead, she eyed the teenager carefully. Finally, she exclaimed, "Oh, I know you! You live on my block — near the synagogue, right? You're a fine young man." The two carried on a friendly conversation for a couple of minutes and then, still smiling and without examining the material, she quickly affixed her stamp to his application and wished him well. Later that night, Yonasan called one of his Chaim Berlin confidants and told him the incredible news. His friend could only marvel at what was clearly Divine intervention on Yonasan's behalf.

The next night, Yonasan departed for *Eretz Yisrael.* He devoted himself to the full-time study of Torah until his marriage a few years later. Today, Yonasan is a very successful disseminator of Torah, spreading the light of its teachings to young and old.

It's in Our Hands

W hile the verse quoted above speaks of the Torah as our *heritage,* a *Mishnah* in *Avos* states: "Apply yourself to Torah study, for it is not your inheritance" (*Avos* 2:17). This means that unlike a monetary inheritance, which is acquired effortlessly, Torah knowledge can be achieved only by those who actively seek it (*Rashi, Rav*).

❦ ❦ ❦

Yisrael Eliyahu Dubin arrived in America in 1913 at age sixteen. He had attended *cheder* (elementary school) in Europe as a young boy, but the difficult economic situation in Eastern Europe had forced him to go to work soon after his bar mitzvah. In America, he worked long, hard hours as an upholsterer. At work, he was surrounded by Jews who had strayed far from the way of Torah. Yet Yisrael remained unaffected by the ridicule of these unfortunate souls. Their comments made him even more determined to remain steadfastly attached to Hashem and His Torah.

The long factory hours left him with barely enough time to eat supper and fall into an exhausted sleep, so he made the trolley ride to and from work his primary learning time each day. He began with the Book of *Yeshayahu.* Each day, on the way to work he memorized one side of a page, and on the way home he memorized the other side. Over the course of time, R' Yisrael committed to memory the entire Books of *Yeshayahu, Iyov, Tehillim,* and more.

In 1929, R' Yisrael decided that it was time to leave Philadelphia, where he had lived since his arrival on these shores. His oldest son was turning six and there were no yeshivos in Philadelphia at that time. His friends and relatives tried to discourage him from going ahead with his planned move to New York. R' Yisrael had no relatives in New York and he certainly had no assurance of finding a job which did not require him to work on Shabbos. But nothing could deter him from realizing his dream.

As he wrote in his memoirs:

> I had no close relatives or friends in New York on whom I could rely — except for Hashem. From the moment I took my seat on the train to New York, I received the great gift of strength from Hashem. He greeted me in New York with kindness and accompanied me everywhere I went.

After spending a few weeks trying to find steady work and set up an apartment, R' Yisrael brought his family to New York and registered his oldest son, Ovadiah, in Yeshivah Rabbi Chaim Berlin. R' Yisrael wrote:

> If someone at that time had offered me a lot of money to return to Philadelphia, I would have laughed at him. Had I won the grand prize in the lottery, I would not have been one-hundredth as happy. The thought that my children would go on the correct way and would grow to become *talmidei chachamim* filled me with strength and happiness.

But trying to earn a living proved to be a difficult test, as R' Yisrael was unable to find steady work in his field of upholstering. One night, as he lay awake in bed, an idea came to him. His wife would bake potato knishes and he would walk the streets peddling them. R' Yisrael's wife agreed, and "Dubin's Knishes" was born.

The first day, R' Yisrael sold all fifty knishes in a short time. He then hired a tinsmith to construct a wagon which would have three shelves for knishes and a coal pan on the bottom to keep the knishes hot. The knishes were immensely popular, especially among Orthodox working people who were hard-pressed to find a snack during the day that was kosher, pareve and hot. Before long, R' Yisrael had a crew of twenty workers baking the knishes and a group of religious young men selling them on the streets using the wagons which R' Yisrael had invented.

However, financial success did not satisfy R' Yisrael. Even the success which his children were seeing in yeshivah did not cause him to rest on his laurels. He sought to draw close to great Torah personalities, to learn from their ways and to gain merit by tending to their needs.

One such personality was the renowned *posek* and *tzaddik,* R' Yosef Eliyahu Henkin, president of the *Ezras Torah* organization. R' Yisrael would drive R' Henkin to *shul* every morning and would take a break from his work to drive him home for lunch. At the end of R' Henkin's life, when he was blind, R' Yisrael would sit with him every Friday night and help him fulfill the *mitzvah* of reviewing the weekly *parashah,* reading each verse twice and the *Targum* once.[1] Once, R' Yisrael misread a word of *Targum* and R' Henkin corrected him.

One day, R' Yisrael bemoaned his standing as a student of Torah. He attended daily *gemara* classes and had already committed a number of books of Scripture to memory, but he was not satisfied. "I don't know enough," he told R' Henkin. R' Henkin suggested that he embark upon a study program in *Mishnayos.*

R' Yisrael wasted no time in purchasing a set of *Mishnayos* with *Yiddish* translation. Carefully, he undid the binding of one volume and separated the pages. Each day, he placed one page on his knish wagon and studied as he pushed his wares down the street. Over the years, he mastered much of this body of Oral Law, and committed at least two entire *sedarim* (orders) to memory. When his brother died, R' Yisrael was able to recite from memory a chain of *mishnayos* whose initial letters formed the deceased's name (ר׳ אשר זעליג בן ר׳ גרשום).

In 1968, one of R' Yisrael's sons visited him in Jerusalem, where he and his wife had settled a year or so earlier. At 4:00 A.M., R' Yisrael's son found him murmuring words to himself. His son thought that he was *davening,* and remarked that since

---

1. See *Shulchan Aruch, Orach Chaim* ch. 285.

it was not yet morning it was too early for *Shacharis.* R' Yisrael explained that he was reciting *Mishnayos* from memory. He added, "I worked so hard to memorize it — should I let myself forget it?"

When he died, he left behind packs of *mishnayos* pages and volumes of *mishnayos* which were worn from use. And he left behind more — generations of *talmidei chachamim* who are deeply committed to the study and teaching of Torah.